More Praise for *From Bud to Boss*

"*From Bud to Boss* will help new leaders gain insight into the challenges ahead, develop the tools to master those challenges, and embrace the next rung on the career ladder with confidence."

—Jen Wilson, SPHR, VP, Human Resources & Loss Control,
Great Lakes Energy

"There are few things in life as vital as making a healthy transition into a leadership role. Whether at home, work, or church, each of us will be called to a task that is beyond our intellect and ability. When backing away and cowering in fear is not an option, I recommend *From Bud to Boss*. Kevin and Guy have the rare gift of being comprehensive as well as conversational. They have produced a book that functions like a toolbox. You'll go back to it again and again as you face the complications and opportunities of daily leadership."

—Aaron Brockett, lead pastor, Traders Point Christian Church,
Indianapolis, IN

"*From Bud to Boss* is the single most comprehensive book you can find on making the challenging transition from doing the work yourself to getting the work done through others. It is an indispensible guide and gift for how to achieve immediate and ongoing success in the messy, complex world of leadership."

—Vicki Halscy, Ph.D., vice president of applied learning,
The Ken Blanchard Companies

"While other books might toss around words such as 'leadership' and 'potential,' this one actually brings them to life in a powerful and actionable way. As remarkable leaders in their own lives, Kevin and Guy show us all how to become more successfully engaged in our work and in our lives."

—Sally Hogshead, speaker, and author of *FASCINATE*

"Finally, a focus on the career transition that can make or break a new supervisor (and their entire team). Kevin and Guy offer practical how-to's for every worker who suddenly sees the Supervisor title on the door. I've already told my clients that this is on the way!"

—Steve Roesler, principal and founder,
Roesler Consulting Group

"If you just got promoted, you owe Kevin Eikenberry and Guy Harris a great big thank you! Going from Bud to Boss is one of life's toughest transitions. This encouraging but realistic book will tell you what to expect and help you survive the trials and seize the opportunities that will come your way. It's a must-read for new bosses."

—Wally Bock, author of *Performance Talk: The One-on-One Part of
Leadership*; writer of the Three Star Leadership Blog

"*From Bud to Boss* is a compassionate book that will help two kinds of people. Those who are about to transition to a leadership role can learn how to grow into leadership, and those who are already in a leadership role can help others grow into one. Bravo!"

—Rajesh Setty, entrepreneur, author,
and speaker—rajeshsetty.com/blog

"*From Bud to Boss* works for you like a wonderful coach. It is with you every step of your way to success, challenging you to think and take action, giving great advice when you need it, and most importantly, encouraging and supporting you to make sure you get there."

—Heli Jarvelin, solution-focused coach and entrepreneur

"*From Bud to Boss* is like a bible for new managers. This remarkable book is like an inoculation against the Peter Principle—absorb the powerful lessons in this book and you will never be promoted to a level of incompetence. I just wish the authors had written it thirty years ago so I could have had it when I began my management career."

—Joe Tye, CEO, Values Coach Inc.; author of
*All Hands on Deck: 8 Essential Lessons
for Building a Culture of Ownership*

"If you have become a boss or are thinking about becoming a boss, do yourself a huge favor and read this book. With its combination of practical advice and self-assessments, you will gain insights into your management style that will help you lead more effectively. I would also recommend this book to bosses who are grooming their successors. Don't wait until you promote, start the management development process now. *From Bud to Boss* can be a practical jump start to your step into management."

—John Baldoni, internationally recognized leadership
development consultant and coach;
author of *Lead by Example* and *Lead Your Boss*

"*From Bud to Boss* is a realistic and easy read. It felt like I was reading my autobiography and reviews from early in my career."

—Tom Butera, plant manager and senior business leader

"Just the sort of guide that anyone needs when making the transition to a leadership role. I wish I'd had it early in my career! The ideas, skills, and commitments you will find in this book are appropriate for anyone who is stepping into a leadership role, whether they are just starting or have been at it for many years. What you will learn here are life lessons more than job lessons."

—Jeff Evans, Ph.D., CEO of Envision Global Leadership

"I started reviewing *From Bud to Boss* at the same time I was reviewing student forum posts in which they were required to analyze a challenging leadership situation in their own lives. One student described *exactly* the situation this book addresses. I told her that a new book would be coming out soon that would be of tremendous value to her. Great stuff!"

—Kelly Trusty, director, Master of Science in Leadership Program,
Trine University

FROM BUD TO BOSS

Secrets to a Successful Transition to Remarkable Leadership

Kevin Eikenberry

Guy Harris

JOSSEY-BASS
A Wiley Imprint
www.josseybass.com

Published by Jossey-Bass
A Wiley Imprint
989 Market Street, San Francisco, CA 94103-1741—www.josseybass.com

Jossey-Bass books and products are available through most bookstores. To contact Jossey-Bass directly call our Customer Care Department within the U.S. at 800-956-7739, outside the U.S. at 317-572-3986, or fax 317-572-4002.

Jossey-Bass also publishes its books in a variety of electronic formats. Some content that appears in print may not be available in electronic books.

Library of Congress Cataloging-in-Publication Data

Eikenberry, Kevin, 1962-
  From bud to boss : secrets to a successful transition to remarkable leadership / Kevin Eikenberry, Guy Harris.
    p. cm.
  Includes bibliographical references and index.
  ISBN 978-0-470-89155-1 (cloth); 978-0-470-94389-2 (ebk); 978-0-470-94390-8 (ebk)
  1. Leadership. 2. Supervision. 3. Management. I. Harris, Guy, 1962- II. Title.
  HD57.7.E38 2011
  658.4'092—dc22

                                                                    2010042996

Printed in the United States of America
FIRST EDITION
HB Printing   10 9 8 7 6 5 4 3 2 1

CONTENTS

PART III
Communication

PART IV
Coaching

PART V
Collaboration

PART VI
Commitment to Success

Kevin—For Parker and Kelsey, who have taught me as much about leadership as anyone else.

Guy—For Mac Harris, who set a leadership example for me, and for Sandra, who helps me become a better leader every day.

FROM BUD TO BOSS

A NOTE FROM THE AUTHORS

Congratulations!

You are now the supervisor. The manager. The foreman. The boss.

Your role has changed and you are being asked to be a leader.

There is no better word to say than "Congratulations!"

You've probably heard it already. People have shaken your hand, patted you on the back, and told you "good luck." This book is about what comes after those predictable responses. But we are getting ahead of ourselves. . . .

First Things First

There is plenty of time for us to talk about your next steps; discuss how to get better; answer all your questions; allay all of your fears; reduce your anxiety; build your confidence; and generally help you make a successful transition to supervision, management, leadership. But first you need to take a deep breath . . .

Relax . . . and claim the congratulations!

Chances are you fall into one of several groups right now.

- The "I've been planning for (expecting) this for a long time" group
- The "I really didn't expect this" group
- The "I'm not really sure I wanted this" group
- The "I thought they'd give it to John" group

Whichever group you fall into, and whatever you are feeling now, you need to recognize that someone felt you could succeed in this new role. Quiet the voice of self-doubt that says things like, "They only picked me because no one else would take it," or similar thoughts. Your organization picked you because they believe you can succeed. They definitely want (and need) you to succeed.

Before we get into all of the specific principles, techniques, and ideas, we need to talk about *you and your belief in yourself.*

- ○ Someone (or many people) think you can succeed—or you would not have the new role.
- ○ Those who care most about you think you can succeed—and if you aren't sure, just ask them.
- ○ We believe you can succeed—because we believe that anyone can bring his or her unique strengths to the role and be successful.

Isn't it great that others believe in you?

Yes, it is.

But it is more important that *you* believe in your ability to succeed.

So when we say congratulations, we are saying: congratulations on the opportunity to use your skills and experience as a starting point on your path toward becoming a remarkable supervisor/manager /leader.

You are embarking on perhaps the toughest professional transition you will ever make. Going from being an individual contributor to being the leader, especially when those you are now leading are your former peers (and perhaps your friends) is tough. Although we hope you are excited by this challenge (and if you aren't you will be by the time you are done with this book), it isn't going to be easy.

And since it isn't going to be easy, it is extremely important that you bolster your belief in yourself.

However you feel about what is in front of you, remember that your confidence in your ability to succeed is important. We aren't talking about an outward "of-course-I'm-a-rock-star" bravado, but a quiet, modest belief that while you may not get it right the first time, or every time, over time you can and will become a very successful (we'd say remarkable) supervisor/manager/leader.

The two most important building blocks for your success in the transition from Bud to Boss are the *desire to succeed* and the *belief that you can succeed.*

If you are reading these words we assume that you have a desire.

Having a belief and a confidence that you can be successful is just as important. We promise to do everything we can both inside and outside the confines of this book to build your skills and your confidence, but in the end you must own this belief.

And you must start now.

If your confidence and belief are a bit weak now, relax. And if you feel good about your prospects and your confidence is higher, smile.

Either way, rest assured that if you engage with us in the pages that follow, you will make a successful transition, and you will be on a path toward being a remarkable leader.

So congratulations on what has gotten you here.

And congratulations in advance for where you are going.

We are glad to join you on your journey.

A ROADMAP FOR THIS BOOK

One of the many things we as authors have in common is a love and appreciation for roadmaps. Although both of us are pretty tech-savvy—we are aware of and owners of many of the latest gadgets—neither of us owns a GPS. Both of us have early memories of reading maps, and by the time we took geography in school we already knew what the various markings, codes, and symbols meant. From an early age, we have both liked maps and what we can learn from them.

This book is like a roadmap—a roadmap guiding you to your future as a remarkable leader. As such, like any good roadmap, it has some symbols and conventions that make it easier to read and that direct you to important and useful points of reference and destinations. The rest of this brief chapter is like the key to your roadmap.

Self-Assessment

At the start of each of the six parts of the book that follow we have included a brief self-assessment. Each assessment is meant to help you gauge your current skills to help you focus better on each individual chapter. We encourage you to invest the time in doing these assessments as you come to them. They will inform your reading, will aid your learning, and can serve as benchmarks for you to go back to later to see how much you have improved.

When you see this icon, we are pointing out a key principle for all of us as leaders. In many cases, these principles move beyond leadership to human nature and life in general. They are principles that support the text around them. When you think about and use them, they will serve as a guide to you in navigating the complex waters of leadership for the rest of your career.

Consider this icon as the little pot of gold on a treasure map. Although neither of us has ever owned a map with one of these symbols on it, now you do. Each time you see this icon in the book, we are offering you some treasure: a checklist, a tool, greater depth on a subject, and more. Consider these Bonus Bytes as additional resources to help you deepen your understanding and accelerate your growth and development as a leader. None will be academic or theoretical in nature. All will be practical and immediately useful.

You can get these Bonus Bytes at the free, online Bud to Boss Community. Go to www.BudToBossCommunity.com/join-now and complete the brief and easy form on that page to join the community. After you join, you can log in for access to all of the Bonus Bytes and many other leadership resources. Since it is a community site, you will be able to interact with us, other leadership experts, and other people like yourself who are also making the transition from Bud to Boss.

Once logged in, you can find the Bonus Bytes by clicking on the Bonus Bytes link in the navigation bar at the top of each page.

Note: The keywords we use throughout the book will be the names on the buttons on the Bonus Bytes page in the community, and they will be organized by the six parts of the book to make it easy for you to find them.

Your Now Steps

The material in this book, although we hope it is easy to read and at least mildly entertaining, is of no value until you *use it*. As trainers and facilitators of learning, as well as practicing leaders, we designed this book to help you take action on what you are learning. While we realize what actions you take (including continuing to read) are in your control, not ours (more on this in Chapter Nine), we know that we can influence them. Providing these practical steps at the end of nearly every chapter is our way of encouraging you, urging you, and, we hope, influencing you to use what is in this book. Each of these sets of steps includes things that you can apply immediately to improve your skills and results.

3

NOW WHAT?

Imagine entering a room that is familiar to you, but you are having trouble getting around in it because the lights are out. It is completely dark. If you have found yourself in that situation, chances are that you wished you had a flashlight to help you.

If you had that flashlight, it would make getting around the room easier, faster, safer, and more comfortable. Wouldn't it?

As a new supervisor, you are likely to find yourself in similar surroundings. Perhaps you are still coming to the same place and interacting with the same people as you had before your promotion. The room might be the same, but we bet it feels a bit like that dark room. It is a familiar place but dark and hard to navigate.

Consider this book to be your flashlight.

We will illuminate the most important things you need to make the transition. We will shine the light on important principles, actions, and outcomes that will make your work much clearer.

As you move through the book it is our goal that the room becomes lighter and stays that way! This illumination will allow you to move about the "room" of your new job more effectively.

By the end of the book, you will have more than just a narrow view from the flashlight, you will gain a clear and focused view of both your role and how to operate in this room. And, just like when walking around a well-lit room, your work will become safer, a little bit easier, and a whole lot more productive.

We close this chapter with the key things we recommend that you do during your first month as a leader (or the next month) to set you up for the best possible success in your new role. But before we get to those ideas, let us share some thoughts about three important words. By the time you read the few hundred words that follow, you will have a much better sense of who we are and what our beliefs are, and, perhaps most important, you will have a clearer view of you and your future in your new role.

The Three Important Words

Before we go any further we need to talk about three words that are important to this book—in fact, they are all in the title. It is important that you know why these words matter and why we have chosen them.

Boss

Although this word has a prominent place in the title of this book, we aren't big fans of it. Yes, it is what many of you are called. It is certainly how some will refer to you.

"Hi Boss."

"This is Sandy, she's my boss."

We recognize that it is common nomenclature, and that it makes for a lovely title for the book (alliteration is catchy and memorable). Yet we really don't like the word.

In fact, Kevin often finds himself going out of his way to correct people when they call him "the boss."

Why don't we like it, and why has Kevin avoided it? Because we believe the word carries baggage and suggests some incorrect assumptions about your role and the expectations others have of that role.

Dictionary.com defines *boss* in these ways:

Noun—

1. A person who employs or superintends workers; manager.
2. A politician who controls the party organization, as in a particular district.
3. A person who makes decisions, exercises authority, dominates, etc.: *My grandfather was the boss in his family.*

Verb (used with object)—

4. To be master of or over; manage; direct; control.
5. To order about, especially in an arrogant manner.

Verb (used without object)—

6. To be boss.

7. To be too domineering and authoritative.

Controls, dominates, exercises authority, orders about, arrogant, domineering, authoritative.

These are not the ideas we promote, teach, and illuminate in this book.

Perhaps in your organization you are called the boss, the superintendent, shift supervisor, office manager, manager, or lead. All of these are titles, and all of them, in our view, are ultimately about leadership. That is why we choose not to use the word *boss* in this book. We call you a *leader,* because that is what you can and will be if you are as successful in your role as you and your organization want you to be.

The title *From Bud to Boss* sounds great (we think), and it gets our point across. But it is the promise of the subtitle that has informed and guided the writing of this book: *Secrets to a Successful Transition to Remarkable Leadership.* This book is about those secrets and helping you become the leader you were born (and selected!) to be.

Remarkable

The second important word in this book is *remarkable.* This book builds on the concepts, principles, and competencies of Kevin's earlier book, *Remarkable Leadership: Unleashing Your Leadership Potential One Skill at a Time.* The word *remarkable,* again according to Dictionary.com:

Adjective—

1. Notably or conspicuously unusual; extraordinary: *a remarkable change.*

2. Worthy of notice or attention.

We believe that in your role you can be and should strive to become remarkable. Why wouldn't you want your results to be "worthy of notice or attention"? Why would you strive for less than extraordinary?

That is our goal for you, and *we believe that you can be remarkable.* You have it in your DNA to be a remarkable leader. It is our goal with this book to aid you in that lifelong journey.

Leader

The third word is *leader*. This is the root of the word in the book's title that we most love. To be consistent, let's look at the Dictionary.com definition of *leader*, too.

> Noun—
> 1. A person or thing that leads.
> 2. A guiding or directing head, as of an army, movement, or political group.

These definitions, while instructive, aren't as complete as we need for our purposes here. Instead, since we've told you we are going to call you, and think you are, a leader, let's talk about what leadership is and isn't.

What Leadership Is

Leadership is complex. In visiting with an experienced aerospace engineer (a.k.a. a rocket scientist), Kevin asked him which was more complex—rocket science or leadership. His response was swift and simple. He said:

> Leadership is much more complex. In my world we can come up with the right answer. We know the equations and formulas. If we put the right numbers into them and do the right things we will get guaranteed results. But as a leader you are dealing with *people*—and people are inherently more complex. And the issues, while perhaps not as dramatic as sending a rocket into orbit, are far more dynamic and contain tremendous amounts of gray area.

We couldn't have said it better. Leadership isn't easy or simple. And, like rocket science, it is something that requires lots of study and practice to become skilled.

Let's take this point a little further. Two professors who make the study of complexity their life's work, Brenda Zimmerman of York University and Sholom Glouberman of the University of Toronto, think all problems can be defined as one of three types: simple, complicated, and complex.

By their definition, a simple problem is baking a batch of Grandma's sugar cookies—there is a recipe. When you follow the recipe, you will get predictable results. Complicated problems are more like the problems our aerospace engineer faces. When you break the larger task down, it becomes a series of simple problems, but, still, success isn't likely to be achieved alone—coordination, collaboration, and many other factors are at play. And throughout the process of solving a complicated problem there will be unanticipated situations. As our friend at NASA says, though, once we do the right calculations and make the right decisions, we will achieve success. And by the way, once you have solved one complicated problem—such as launching a rocket—successfully, it gets easier to do the next one, and the next one, and so on.

Contrast the complicated with the complex. By Zimmerman and Glouberman's definitions, the complex problem is one with multiple interdependencies where the rules and guidelines of the simple and complicated aren't enough. With complex situations, experience is valuable but never sufficient. The researchers liken a complex problem to that of raising a child. Equally apt is being a leader. What works once doesn't guarantee success the next time.

Before you throw up your hands in futility, though, recognize that children are successfully raised and people are successfully led. Although the problem is complex, you can do it.

Leadership is an action. Leadership is a thing, and certainly leaders are people; in other words, "They are the leaders." Although from a dictionary perspective *leadership* and *leader* are nouns, we want you to think of them both as verbs (with apologies to Kevin's grandmother, who taught grammar in school).

Leadership is not really something that we have or possess; it is something that we *do*. When you think about leadership, think actions, think behaviors. It is with better actions and behaviors that we will gain better results. This book will help you think about leadership and take actions that help you lead.

Leadership is a responsibility. You've been placed in and accepted a formal role of leadership (regardless of your job title). By definition (and whether you know the extent of it or not) you have taken on a responsibility. It is easy to see that responsibility if you are a president, a CEO, or a business owner; as a reader of these words, you may not be in any of those roles. And still, the fact is every leadership role carries responsibility with it. People are looking to you. People are expecting things of you. If you are really leading, people are *following* you. You therefore have a responsibility for more than just yourself and your own results. Recognizing these responsibilities is one of the challenges of your new role. The sooner you recognize these responsibilities, the more quickly you will build comfort and confidence in your new role.

Leadership is an opportunity. Beyond your daily task responsibilities (and we realize you may be a working leader—with your own nonleadership tasks), you also, as a leader, have an opportunity to make a difference: for customers, for the organization, for those you lead, for the world at large. When you exhibit the behaviors of leadership, you are actively trying to create new results that will make a positive difference in the world. Few things in life hold greater opportunity than this.

Recognizing and accepting both the responsibilities and the opportunities leadership offers you is a significant step in your development as a leader.

What Leadership Isn't

We've talked about some of the things leadership is; now here are four things that leadership isn't. These are common misconceptions. As you move into your new role, it is important for you to think about these things, too.

Leadership isn't management. The skills of management are focused on things, processes, and procedures. The skills of leadership focus on people, vision, and development. Both are valuable skill sets, and in many cases we need to build both sets. But great leaders aren't necessarily great managers and vice versa.

There are leadership skills and there are management skills. The skill sets overlap, but they are not the same. When you realize the differences in the skill sets and focus on what your situation requires, you will be more successful. For the purposes of this book, we focus on the leadership skill set. Though, like Figure 3.1 suggests, some of what is included here helps with the management component of your job as well.

Leadership isn't a title or position. It is really this simple: you are a leader when people follow you. If they do you are, if they don't you aren't. Influencing the actions of others isn't guaranteed by your

Figure 3.1. Management Skills Versus Leadership Skills

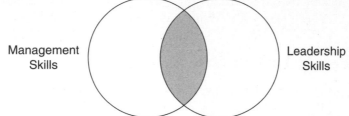

Management
Skills

Leadership
Skills

job title, the color of your desk, or the size of your office. A title that proclaims you a leader doesn't make you a leader any more than calling a lion a zebra creates black stripes. Too often, people in your situation assume that the title is enough to get other people to follow them. Don't make that same mistake. Always remember that leadership is about *what you do*, not the title on your business card.

Leadership isn't a power grab. Real leaders, though their actions may carry a great deal of influence and therefore a certain amount of power, are not driven by power alone. The opportunity to have power may be one of the things that led you to be interested in your new job (and if that isn't true for you it certainly is for many). But the behaviors that lead to others granting you "power" don't come from your wanting or expecting power. Your power or influence will come from a variety of factors based on your behaviors and values, not your position. While we will talk about this throughout the book, here is a principle to remember:

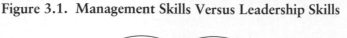 Focusing on others will give you more influence and power than focusing on yourself.

Leadership isn't a gift from birth. Leadership skills aren't doled out in the genetics of some while others are left wanting. All of us have a unique bundle of DNA that can allow us to become highly effective, even remarkable, leaders. Do some people have innate strengths that help them as leaders? Of course they do. And so do you—even if your strengths are different from the strengths of the people you thought about when we asked the question above.

None of that matters, though, if you don't *use those strengths* and do the things to *improve in areas that are harder for you*. Few things are sadder or more regrettable than unfulfilled potential. Leadership success is about learning and improving much more than genetics.

Five Keys to Your Successful Transition

Although the context we have just shared is critical, now it is time to get really practical. In order to be most successful in your new role, you must behave like, believe like, and build your skills like a leader. Though we wrote this book from the perspective that you are just joining the ranks of supervision and leadership, the advice that follows applies even if you are two years in and you feel like the transition isn't yet complete. Completing these steps will help you transition to your role most effectively, comfortably, and confidently.

Talk with Your Boss

Any successful transition will be most successful in partnership with your boss. You want to build a dialogue with her that gets her assistance in and commitment to your success. If she doesn't initiate it quickly, take responsibility for making that conversation happen. When you do this, several things happen:

- ○ *It shows your commitment.* When you take the initiative and the responsibility for your successful transition, your boss will see that you want to be successful and are committed to that success.
- ○ *It elicits her support.* Most any boss wants you to succeed, but some may not be thinking about how they can best help. Even if your boss has thought about how to help you, you are moving this issue up her priority list.
- ○ *It builds positive momentum.* By beginning proactively, rather than going to your boss after you are stuck, you change the relationship dynamic and expectations entirely. You truly have the chance to build a partnership in success.

Once you have created this dialogue, what do you talk about? Consider questions in these areas to get started:

- ○ *Determine her expectations.* Ask questions and get a complete understanding of her expectations. If something isn't written down, take responsibility for getting it written for clarity's sake.

○ *Get a common description of success.* How would she describe success? What does it look like to her? Again, having it written is important.

○ *Talk about your role.* Get a mutual agreement on paper that describes your role. A job description may be a jumping-off point for this discussion, but we rarely see job descriptions that outline roles completely in practical terms or clearly or personally enough to define success.

Getting roles, goals and expectations written down isn't about "documentation to cover your butt" (though it might do that); rather, it provides clarity and a common foundation.

○ *Ask about her experience.* Pick her brains for what she learned when she made the transition you are now making.

○ *Build a schedule for ongoing conversations.* You will want her assistance in your transition. Asking for it up front improves the chances that you will both make time to do it.

For more thoughts and a detailed checklist on how to engage with your boss during your transition, go to the Bonus Bytes page at BudToBossCommunity.com and click on the Talk with Boss button.

Talk with Your Team

When you start in your new role, your team has all kinds of questions (whether or not they say them or you hear them). If you are moving into a leadership role after having been a peer, this step is especially important even though it would be valuable in any circumstances. By having this talk, you are setting the stage for an ongoing conversation, and you have the chance to set the tone. Hall of Fame basketball coach John Wooden had a talk he shared with his teams at the start of every season. As outlined in *Wooden on Leadership,* he talked about several factors, including

○ Defining success

○ Setting goals

○ Defining control and influence

○ Focusing on those things under the players' control

Although his situation was somewhat different in context, and he wasn't transitioning into leadership like you are, his process and messages should be very instructive for you. Here are some additional messages you will want to share.

○ *Acknowledge the transition.* Let people know that things may seem a little weird to them—and tell people the change feels weird to you, too. (Be genuine here. Share how you are feeling and what you are thinking.)

○ *Talk about the changing relationships.* Acknowledge that there will be changes. Share your hope that the changes can be positive, and recognize that the nature of the changes will be different for different people.

○ *Talk about your role.* This should include your thoughts and your agreements with your boss. If you have the meeting with your team before the meeting with your boss, loop back to your team with a complete description of your role after speaking with your boss.

○ *Talk about your expectations of them.* This requires that you think about these ahead of time—be prepared to share those expectations.

○ *Ask them their expectations of you.* Ask, listen carefully to their responses, take notes, and clarify what they mean. Even if you might not be able to meet all of the expectations immediately, tell your team that you want to know all of them as a starting point. Save "negotiations" or adjustments to the list for a future conversation.

○ *Ask for their help and patience.* Remember that just because you are now the leader doesn't mean you suddenly have all the answers! If you thought you did, you wouldn't be reading this book, would you?

You might not be able to accomplish all of these points in one conversation, and you might not initially get the kinds of open responses you are looking and hoping for. Don't despair; be patient and persistent in having these conversations with the team as a whole and with specific individuals as appropriate. There will be many things to talk with your team about in the future. The important point is that you get started!

Talk to Yourself

Now that you have this job, you need to give yourself some slack. Recognize that

- Your world is changing and you must change with it.
- You won't get it right the first time (or every time).
- You need to be patient with yourself.
- You can succeed.

Personal clarity about the transition and your belief in your ultimate success are as important as anything else on this list or in this book.

 Your success in any endeavor begins with your belief that you can succeed.

Determine Your Strengths

Coming into your new role, you have some skills and talents that will aid you in your success. It is very possible, however, that right now you are overwhelmed with thinking about all the changes, what you need to do, the questions you have, and more.

All of these changes can lead to feelings of inadequacy, fear, and frustration. When people are in this mental place, they are typically more focused on what they lack than on what they have. Do yourself a favor. Recognize your weaknesses and understand your strengths, too. If you don't know what your strengths are, or feel too buried to find them, there are several ways to determine them:

- *Think about past successes.* What have been the keys to your successes?
- *Think about what others tell you.* What things do people tell you that you do well? (Even if you dismiss them as easy or trivial.)
- *Ask people what they think.* Asking people who know you well, and support your success, will give you clues to your strengths.

o *Consider a 360 assessment.* A 360 assessment allows you to get anonymous feedback from the people around you—most tools allow you to get feedback from your boss(es), peers, those who work for you, and others (hence 360 degrees of feedback). This process can be very powerful and provide you with feedback and perspective that would be hard to gain otherwise. This step may not be the first thing you want to do (especially if you are a brand new leader), but putting it on your list sooner rather than later is a great idea.

 For more details on how to use and select a 360 assessment process, go to the Bonus Bytes page at BudToBossCommunity.com and click on the 360 button.

o *Make a list of strengths.* As you gather feedback—however you do it—make a list of strengths.
o *Refer to this list often.* The list is only valuable when you remember its contents. Reviewing it regularly will boost your awareness and confidence.
o *Balance your efforts.* Spend at least as much time developing and using these strengths as you do trying to improve your weaknesses.

 The highest achievers in any endeavor recognize, use, and build their strengths. They know that the greatest leverage for improvement comes from their strengths.

Build a Plan

The first four steps give you lots of fodder to build a plan. Think about what you have learned from the other four steps, then build a plan of action to improve, build, and grow. Remember that if you want to succeed in your role as a leader, you must take action. No action, no growth. This book can be a part of your plan, but remember that reading alone isn't enough.

 For a checklist of steps to help you build this development plan, go to the Bonus Bytes page at BudToBossCommunity.com and click on the Your Plan button.

Your Now Steps

The best way to get going now, regardless of how long you have been in your leadership role, is to take care of the items from this chapter.

1. Spend some quiet time thinking about your new role, your strengths, and more. Spending time thinking and reflecting is a great habit to create.
2. Schedule a meeting with your boss to discuss your role, your plans, and how they can help you.
3. Schedule a meeting with your team to begin discussing any open or transitional issues that face you.
4. Read the rest of this book, and think about how you can apply what you are learning as you read it.

HOW TO GET THE MOST
FROM THIS BOOK

While we hope you enjoy the experience of reading this book, our main goal is to help you become a more confident, competent, and, ultimately, more successful leader. To reach that goal requires a partnership between what we have done and what you will do. Reading this book will give you some ideas, some inspiration, and, perhaps, some hope. But becoming a better leader requires you to *use* the ideas, tips, techniques, and concepts on these pages. To achieve success, you need to try and apply the ideas to make them a part of who you are as a leader.

We have done a number of things in this book to help make your job of applying these ideas easier. We've tried to write from a very practical perspective, always tying things back to what you can do. We have incorporated what we have learned from teaching new supervisors, including the questions they have asked us, into this book. And in the tradition of Kevin's book *Remarkable Leadership,* we have incorporated some specific learning tools throughout the book that we mentioned in Chapter Two, "A Roadmap for This Book."

Now, we offer some thoughts on how to get the most from everything you will find here....

Some Thoughts on How to Read This Book

Here are five strategies to consider that we think will make this book a more powerful part of your transition to leadership. The more of these ideas you apply to this book (and any other books you will read in your personal and professional development activities), the better.

Read with a Purpose

Any speed-reading or reading acceleration program will teach you to prescan a book before beginning it. Although the techniques may vary, the basic concept is to look over the book, read the table of contents, and scan the chapters, subheads, and sidebars before beginning to read. The strategy is to give you a sense of the book and its purpose, messages, and layout before you begin.

These strategies will help speed up your reading, and they also help you answer this most important question: What do I want to get from this book?

Spend a few minutes after your initial scan to think about your goals and fondest wishes for the book. If you have a journal (which we highly recommend), write down the key questions you want answers to or what you want to learn. Specifically write down the top three to five questions you have as a new leader. With this list in hand, you can focus your attention on the items that are of the most immediate concern to you as you read the book.

Books can surprise you with knowledge or ideas you didn't expect (and we hope that happens here), but having a clear purpose at the start, rather than just sitting back and waiting for the big "aha," will help you maximize what you can glean from a book.

Read with a Pen

In school you probably read with a highlighter to highlight key passages you thought might be on a test. While this advice may seem like a "back to school" comment, it really isn't. To get the most from your reading, you may want to highlight ideas that you can use. Highlight not for a test, as you did as a student, but to capture the things that will make a difference for you. Although a highlighter is great to focus on our words, we suggest that you use a pen or pencil to write personal notes as well. Lose the belief that you can't write in a book. Litter these margins with questions, thoughts, and connections. If you use a journal or a notepad, you can make your notes or expand on the ideas there.

Most important, remember that your notes should be about actions you can take in connection with your purpose for reading this book.

Read Through the Filter of Your Goals

Even with a great prescan, you don't know exactly what is in the book or what it will teach you. So as you read, keep thinking about questions such as

- How can I use this?
- How does this relate to my goals?
- What is the big message for me here?

Asking questions like this as you read allows you to synthesize what we are thinking for your purposes, rather than just accepting or letting our words bathe over your brain. When you read through the filter of your goals, you begin to actively use the book for your purposes.

Read to Translate

As you read, look for the action steps. We hope the Now Steps will help you with this activity. This is a very helpful component of the book, but it is still incomplete. We don't know your situation or goals perfectly, and so it is your responsibility to determine exactly what you can do with the ideas. Reading to translate is about determining what actions you will take as a result of what you have read.

These four ideas are important strategies, and although they will help you improve the value you get from this book, it is the final item that will make the real difference.

Transform Your Ideas into Action

This is the logical extension of the last point but with an important difference. If you want the book to make a difference, you aren't done when you read the last page. Your most important task has just begun!

Take the notes and ideas you wrote in the margins and rewrite them in a journal, notebook, or computer file. This rewriting and review process is important to help you lock in the knowledge you gained from the book. This step is about more than knowledge; it is about action. As you are taking your key learning points from the book and putting them down in your own words, also create the short list of actions you want to take.

Here is where the first step, "Read with a Purpose," is important. We hope you gain many great ideas from this book. Your job now, in terms of taking action, is to *prioritize the best, most important, and most valuable actions you can take to move you closer to accomplishing your goals.*

Yes, you may get many other cool suggestions, and perhaps one or more of them warrant your attention. But you must start in relation to your goals, because otherwise you will get overwhelmed by the number and quality of the ideas and do...nothing.

 This book can't change your life and make you a better leader. Only you can do that by applying what you learn.

If all of these ideas seem like work, it's because they are. The bottom line is that if you want to have a book be the impetus for change, *you must do more than read it.* You must use it as a tool to fuel your personal growth and development, and this means that you must engage in an active process of learning. Of course, maybe you "just want to read," and this is fine. Just don't expect that type of reading to lead to significant change, growth, or development.

The Reticular Activating System

There is an important brain function that we want to describe for you now. We will connect this powerful fact to the skills of coaching, mentoring, and conducting performance reviews, among other things. First, though, we will consider it from the perspective of how it impacts your learning from this book.

Our brains contain a collection of cells known as the reticular activating system (RAS). The RAS does a number of things in the brain related to consciousness, sleeping, waking, and so forth. Many researchers believe that one of its functions is to filter the stimuli we receive from the world so that our brains do not get overloaded with input.

The RAS in Action

You can see an example of how the RAS works when you purchase a new car.

Prior to starting the car-purchasing process, you might not have noticed the number of cars on the road that are just like your new one. But when you start to research or make the decision to purchase a particular car, you almost immediately notice all of the other cars just like it. We bet you have experienced this phenomenon.

Before you have that new car (or are looking at cars to make a purchase), many of the makes and models of cars on the road are just noisy input that the RAS filters out so that you can focus on more important things. When you start looking for cars or comparing cars, or when you actually make a purchase, specific makes and models become more relevant to you. As a result, the RAS lets that information through to your conscious mind.

In all likelihood, the number of cars like your new one did not change overnight. However, your conscious recognition of them changed significantly.

And what, you might ask, does this have to do with the topic of this book in general, or, more specifically, our suggestions about how to read this book?

The short answer is this: each of our suggestions helps to prime your RAS for learning. For example, writing down your three to five most important questions can program your RAS to let that information through rather than filter it out as noise. Writing things that you want to do, become, learn, or observe seems to condition you to recognize those things when you encounter them.

In general, we recommend that you read the book from cover to cover so that you see all of the connections between the various sections. Since we also understand that you might have immediate concerns that you want to address before reading everything, we want you to get those answers quickly.

When you

o Read with a purpose

o Read with a pen

o Read through the filter of your goals

o Read to translate, and

o Transform your ideas into action

you can focus your attention where you will get the most benefit as you read this book. You can avoid getting overwhelmed by a barrage of new information, and you are likely to get more from your efforts.

Information Overload

The issue of getting overwhelmed with new information is also worth considering because it affects how you get the most from this book and how you can understand your role as a leader more fully.

Trying to focus on too many things at one time can lead to frustration and failure. Chip and Dan Heath, in their book *Switch* (2010), discuss psychological research indicating that when we have to exercise self-control in one area of our lives, it causes us to have less self-control in other areas of our lives.

Since learning new skills and new ways of doing things requires you to exercise the self-control to *not* do things the old way, you can quickly "use up" your self-control. When you do this, you do at least two things that hurt your effectiveness as a leader. You limit your ability to

1. Apply the lessons you are learning
2. Control your responses to people and situations

In short, you learn less and you react negatively more. This is not a good combination of outcomes.

We come back later to the RAS and the issue of limited self-control as factors affecting your effectiveness as a leader.

Your Now Steps

Let's take all of the ideas from this chapter and make them practical ideas for using this book most effectively.

1. Write down a list of three to five main concerns or questions you have about leadership right now.
2. Look through the table of contents and scan the chapters to get a big-picture view of what is in the book.
3. Start reading the book in more detail. Read cover to cover or by immediately picking the spots that seem to address your questions first—it is your book, read the way that will best serve you.
4. Highlight and mark in the book as much as necessary while you read to help you remember key points.

5. Keep a learning journal or notebook with you so that you can capture key lessons and actions you want to take as a result of what you learn as you read this book.

6. When you have finished reading the book, go through it again and review your highlights and notes to reinforce the key points.

7. Teach what you have learned to someone else.

If you take these actions, you will get faster results, greater value, and more learning from the effort and time that you invest in reading this book.

Now it is time to *really* get started!

PART I

SUCCEEDING IN YOUR TRANSITION TO LEADERSHIP

For most people reading this book, your choice to accept the move to a leadership position put you into a time of transition. The transition from a role that mostly called for you to focus on your performance and results to a role that calls for you to focus on both your results and the results of other people. We have already offered some thoughts and encouragements for you as you make this transition. Now we move our focus to some of the specific issues you will need to consider and address in the transition process.

The first section of this book is mostly about mind-sets, attitudes, and ways of thinking about your new role and what it demands of you. Some of what we cover here might be new to you or phrased in a way that you have not thought about before now. That's perfectly normal and OK. All of us need to learn new ways of thinking and acting as we move into new roles.

Thinking about your new role in terms of all the new things you need to learn might get a little discouraging. So, we would like to offer you a word of encouragement before we dig into the specific topics we plan to address concerning your transition to leadership.

You probably already understand much of what we will address in the next few chapters. As we said before, someone probably saw some and maybe even all of these attitudes and mind-sets in your past work performance or they would not have offered you the opportunity to move into a leadership position. You are up for the challenge. You have what it takes to become a truly Remarkable Leader!

So that you get the most from the chapters in this section of the book, we recommend that you take a moment to consider your current thoughts, perspectives, and comfort with the concepts we discuss here.

Self-Assessment

Here is a quick assessment to help you think through some of the issues and concerns you might need to address as part of your transition to leadership. Use the following scale of 1 to 7 on each question:

1   Almost never
2   Rarely or seldom
3   Occasionally
4   Sometimes
5   Usually
6   Frequently
7   Almost always

I stay focused on what I need to do to become a remarkable leader.   _____

(Chapters 5, 6)

I apply my energy to the most significant changes I face in my transition to leadership.   _____

(Chapter 7)

I see the impact I am making as a leader.   _____

(Chapter 8)

I control what I can control. I influence what I can influence. I ignore everything else.   _____

(Chapter 9)

I apply the power of expectations in my role as a leader.   _____

(Chapter 10)

Based on your self-assessment, you now have an initial glimpse into your strengths and weaknesses, concerns, and worries in these areas. Use those insights as you read the pages that follow. Yes, you will want to read carefully in the areas in which you are weaker, *and* resist the urge to skim the other areas, for the nugget we share (or you extrapolate) may be the single insight or idea that takes you to even higher levels of skill and achievement.

Thoughts About This Transition (and Transitions in General)—From Others and Us

Adults don't need to be taught so much as they need to be reminded.

—Unknown

We recognize that you might have already thought about some of the concepts to come in the next few chapters. If these ideas were already part of the understanding and skill set you had that led to your promotion, we offer them as either a new way of considering the concepts so that you can view them from a broader perspective or as a reminder for you to keep them in the forefront of your thinking as you move into a leadership role. If you have not seen them before, we hope that they give you greater insight and perspective in preparation for the parts of the book that follow.

Not in his goals but in his transitions is man great.

—Ralph Waldo Emerson, writer and philosopher

Moments of transition require us to wrestle with the frustrations of learning new ways of thinking and new skill sets. In the process of learning, we will, by definition, make mistakes. Mistakes, failures, and frustrations are a normal part of the learning process. None of us knows how to do something we have never done before until we try to do it. And then we cannot learn how to do it well until we make a few mistakes.

The good news is that the greatest accomplishments and victories go to those people willing to take the risk and to experience the temporary discomfort of trying new things. You took the challenge. Good for you! You must be a person who is willing to attempt new things. It is your victory in this transition that will give you great satisfaction and joy when you "get to the other side of it." (Do we ever really "get to the other side of it"? We don't think we have yet. We continue to learn and grow right along with you.)

The real art of conducting consists in transitions.

—Gustav Mahler, Austrian composer

Guy's daughter, Lydia, really enjoys studying and playing music. One day she explained to him how an individual conductor's interpretation of a piece of music can affect the sound and feel of it. The composer uses standard musical terminology and rules for writing the music. The conductor then manages the interpretation of what the composer wrote. He adds his interpretation as he leads the beat, suggests how to move between different parts of the piece, and signals when each part of the orchestra should start or stop. Through the conductor's interpretation, he creates the overall feel of the performance.

The conductor understands the rules, the terminology, and the principles of music composition that the composer used to convey musical ideas. The art of conducting lies in how the conductor applies those rules, terminology, and principles with the orchestra that *he* leads.

Many conductors are also performers. They usually learn their craft as they perform in an orchestra, and each eventually gets the chance to lead it as the conductor. They know their instruments, their parts, very well. As they become conductors, leaders, they have to learn how all of the parts come together to create beautiful music.

Like a composer writing music for the conductor, we can share rules, terminology, and principles of effective leadership with you. You have that all in your hands as you read. As you make the transition from individual contributor to leader and experiment with how to apply these principles to your situation and with your team, your interpretation of what we have written comes to life. The art of leadership lies in how you make the transition and how you apply the principles with your team.

5

COMMON CONCERNS ABOUT THE TRANSITION TO LEADERSHIP

As we lead workshops and consult with our clients, we often get the opportunity to ask new leaders about their concerns, struggles, and frustrations. Through these conversations, we have learned that many people making the transition from Bud to Boss have similar concerns.

By expressing those concerns as questions, we get a list that looks like this:

○ How do I make discipline stick with my "friends"?

○ How do I get "lazy" people to work?

○ What is the best way for me to communicate with my peer leaders?

○ How do I get a better understanding of my new role/responsibility?

○ Who communicates my new role to others?

○ How do I communicate with new peers that have been at this longer than me?

○ How do I work with groups led by people with leadership styles different from mine?

○ How do I work with distant or virtual teams?

○ What can I do to deal with the grapevine?

○ How do I deal with multiple bosses?

○ What can I do to deal with problem employees?

○ How can I best delegate to my former peers?

○ How can I change the culture on my team?

- What am I supposed to say to an employee who says: "Your job should have been mine"?
- How do I gain respect, trust, and credibility in my new role?
- What is the best way to communicate about difficult issues?
- How do I manage professionals?
- How do I gain influence with my boss?
- What do I do to build a high-performing work team?
- How do I separate my personal relationship with my team from my professional relationship with them?
- What if people perceive that I am showing favoritism toward my friends?
- How can I resolve conflicts between employees?
- How can I communicate with and motivate people who are different from me?
- What should I be doing to conduct better performance evaluations?
- How do I get employees to buy in to my new role?
- What do I do to help people deal with change, and how do I communicate about changes to minimize resistance?
- How can I better understand other people's needs?

While this isn't a complete list, you get the idea!

Although we think that all of the answers to these questions are addressed in either the book itself or in other Bonus Bytes, you might want to get a quick glance at the answers we have for these questions. We don't think this Bonus Byte substitutes for reading the book, but it might make quick reference easier for you. To get our answers to these questions, go to the Bonus Bytes page at BudToBossCommunity.com and click on the Starting Concerns button.

In the transition from friend and coworker (Bud) to leader (Boss), you probably share many of the concerns on this list. You might not have all of them, but we are guessing that you can identify with many of them. You might even see some concerns that you had not considered before you began to read this book, but they look very real to you now that you have seen the list.

As you read this book and look for answers to your specific questions, remember that leadership is a complex skill set. It includes communication skills, persuasion skills, change management skills, team skills, conflict resolution skills, coaching skills, and many others. Since it is a complex skill set, there are very few simple answers to leadership challenges.

There are, though, a few foundational principles that will help you in nearly every situation. When you get a good handle on those core principles, the techniques, approaches, and specific skills needed for a given situation will become clear to you.

Complex problems such as the ones you will face as a leader often have multiple "right" answers. As a result, we cannot tell you the absolute "right way" to address every situation you will encounter. We can equip you with the concepts and principles you can apply to figure out the "most right" answer for *your* situation.

> Remarkable Principle
>
> **Complex problems like the ones you will face as a leader often have multiple "right" answers.**

Leadership problems are like the problems that a craftsman—a cabinet maker for example—might face as she practices her craft. A cabinet maker usually has multiple chisels, saws, planes, and hammers. Each tool works well in a particular situation. Cabinet makers do not have one chisel, one saw, one plane, and one hammer. They have multiples of each so that they can chose the best chisel, saw, plane, or hammer for a given situation. To be effective in their craft, cabinet makers create a large cabinet maker toolbox.

We encourage you to do the same thing as a leader. Developing your ability to solve complex leadership problems such as those that you will face as a leader demands that you have a large "leadership toolbox." We suggest that you learn multiple change management, communication, persuasion, coaching, team-building, conflict resolution, and goal-setting skills and techniques and that you practice applying them in different situations so that you can learn to identify the best approach to use in your environment. (Good news, you will learn about all of these areas in the pages that follow.)

In *The Psychology of Science,* Abraham Maslow, a sociologist and organizational behavior researcher, said: "I suppose it is tempting, if the only tool you have is a hammer, to treat everything as if it were a nail." In this statement, Maslow points to a common challenge we face when we approach complex problems: we tend to limit our view of the problems to make them fit neatly within the limits of the tools we have. So that you do not exemplify the thought behind this quote, keep building your leadership toolbox. Make it big and full.

Remarkable leaders learn to use a wide range of communication, conflict resolution, and team-building approaches and techniques so that they know the best tool to use for a given situation.

As we answer the common questions we listed above, we offer tips, techniques, and insights that you can put to use right away to make your life as a leader easier. If you see a technique that does not fit your specific situation, look beyond the surface explanation for the principle behind the technique so that you can find a way to modify or adjust the technique to make it work for you.

Through the course of this book, we address the main concerns and frustrations that we listed above and some others. By the time you reach the end of the book, you should be able to find at least one answer to each of the main concerns that new leaders face.

Your Now Step

1. If you have not already done so, get your learning journal and write the three to five biggest concerns you have related to your transition to leadership.

IMPROVING YOUR RESULTS BY UNDERSTANDING SOME CRITICAL COMPONENTS OF YOUR LEADERSHIP ROLE

In your transition from Bud to Boss, you will have to confront many new issues that were not part of your responsibilities before you became a leader. Suddenly you are the leader and all of these issues land squarely in your lap. To be successful, you have to find a way to deal with them—you cannot just ignore the problems that come your way. And the sooner you learn to deal with them the better. We know you can handle the challenges, and we have some perspective to share with you that we think makes the list a little less daunting.

In the last chapter, we discussed many of the common concerns of new leaders. As we said, the list of common concerns comes from what we have heard new leaders say to us in our workshops and consulting work. In another exercise, we ask people to list what they see as the critical components of the leadership role. Since everyone doesn't see leadership the same way, everyone doesn't see the components of leadership the same way. From these conversations, we have collected a list of frequently mentioned components and combined them into what we call the critical components of your leadership role.

Some Critical Components of Your Leadership Role

1. Helping people decide to change/make changes
2. Coaching team members
3. Delegating tasks

4. Getting things done/creating results

5. Inspiring people to action

6. Setting goals

7. Communicating up, down, and across the organization

8. Developing others

9. Building a team

10. Resolving conflicts

11. Holding people accountable

We realize that other people might combine some of these items or add others to the list. And we are okay with that. We are not trying to develop an all-encompassing list. We are trying to break the complex skill set of leadership into more manageable pieces to make it easier for you to learn these skills.

In an effort to simplify things even more, we further divide the critical components of your leadership role into two *very* broad categories:

1. Components that are mostly about task accomplishment

2. Components that are mostly about interacting with people

Using these two categories, we would list the components this way:

Mostly About Task Accomplishment	Mostly About Interacting with People
o Getting things done/creating results o Setting goals	o Helping people decide to change o Coaching team members o Delegating tasks o Inspiring people to action o Communicating up, down, and across the organization o Developing others o Building a team o Resolving conflicts o Holding people accountable

We do not believe that the way we have these components listed is the absolute and final word on how to categorize them. As examples, some people say that setting goals and getting things done have a great deal of Interacting with People skills in them. Other people say that holding people accountable has a strong Task Accomplishment piece. We can see arguments that validate both of these perspectives.

How you see these issues is probably related to your personal bias or focus toward accomplishing tasks or building relationships as your highest priority. As a result of these personal biases, you might break the list down a little differently than we did.

We will discuss the challenges of personal bias more in later chapters. For our purposes now, we listed the components like most people in our workshops respond to the exercise of assigning a task or a relationship perspective to each of them.

Discussing where each individual component lies on the list is not the main point we want to observe from this exercise. Mainly, we suggest that you look at the overall breakdown and note that most of what you have to do to succeed in a leadership role has more to do with a focus on people than on tasks. Regardless of how you would personally divide the list, we'd guess that you also came to the conclusion that most of the components fit on the Interacting with People side of the table.

> Remarkable Principle
>
> **The skills of interacting with people are a bigger portion of your leadership responsibility than is your personal ability to accomplish tasks.**

If you are like many leaders, you became a leader because you are good at getting things done. You are probably willing to work hard for long hours in the interest of making things happen. Now, your focus has to shift to getting things done through and with other people rather than doing it yourself. This change in focus is a common struggle and a point of frustration for many new leaders.

Since you already know how to get things done on your own, you might get frustrated with people who do not get things done as quickly or to the same quality that you could do them.

You might feel the pressure to take over a task so that you can "just get it done". Rather than coach someone else on how to do it properly. Maybe you hold onto tasks that you enjoy doing rather than giving them to someone else. Or, you might feel stressed by the constant interactions, communications, and work necessary to get things done through others. You might simply feel better when you do it yourself.

Resist the urge to hold onto tasks or to take them away from the people on your team. Instead, focus on developing your skills at connecting with, inspiring, and coaching others. Because we recognize this part of the transition can be difficult for many people, we have concentrated our efforts in those areas as we developed the suggestions that come in later chapters.

Your Now Steps

1. Go back to the list of the components of your leadership role and rate your current skill level in each component on a 1–10 scale. (A score of 1 means, "I really need some help with this one" and a score of 10 means, "I have got this component figured out.")
2. Add any areas with a rating of less than 5 to the list of your top concerns that you developed in the previous chapter.

7

CONFRONTING IMPORTANT CHANGES YOU FACE AS A NEW LEADER

As you grow into your new role, there are some common and predictable changes you will face. Understanding some of the changes and how you can approach them as they come can help you through the transition stage.

Role Changes

When you moved from an individual contributor position to a leadership position, the entire focus of your role within the organization changed. As we have already said, you have gone from being responsible for yourself and your work output to being responsible for the work output of a team. This dual responsibility means

○ You represent the organization to your team.
○ You represent your team to the organization.

As the organization's representative to your team, you are responsible for communicating and representing its mission, vision, and values to your team. You can only successfully fulfill this role to the extent that you understand and accept the organization's mission, vision, and values.

We start with the assumption that you buy in to the overall direction and mission of your organization even if you have concerns about some details or specifics on a few issues. As Kevin often says, "You probably don't want to be a vegetarian working as a server at a steak house." If you cannot accept the overall mission and vision of your organization, you will experience a constant struggle in your role as leader.

In those situations in which you encounter difficulty understanding or accepting a specific decision, task assignment, or rule change, we recommend that you adopt this policy for your communications up and down your organizational structure: *disagree in private and agree in public.*

At some point, every leader in an organization will face a situation of needing to communicate a decision that he or she does not fully understand or that challenges his or her personal perspective. When that time comes, engage in private dialogue and discussion with your leader as much as necessary to understand and accept the direction or decision before you say anything in public to your team.

We do not suggest that you blindly go along with illegal, unethical, or otherwise immoral decisions just to present a good face to your team. Nor do we recommend that you take a "yes person" stance with leaders above you and agree to everything without discussion. If you have information that might keep your leader from making a mistake, you certainly should share the information. Tell them what you know and what you think. Don't just stand by and watch the mistake happen. And once you have voiced your thoughts, accept that the final decision is his or hers to make.

On this point, we are referring to decisions that are mostly a matter of judgment or perspective—and much of what you will encounter as a leader falls into this category. Many of the situations you will face in your new role do not have simple black-and-white, right-or-wrong answers. You will often be involved in discussions or have to deliver communications about decisions that have no clear-cut and single right answer. Policy, rule, direction, or task-assignment decisions frequently call for balancing multiple variables that leave lots of room for subjective rather than objective decision criteria. When you do not immediately see or understand your leader's or your organization's decision, voice your concerns to your leader in private. Work hard to understand the decision so that you can "sell" it to others.

Sometimes you can make great progress, organizationally and in your relationships, by agreeing to disagree.

Recognizing the dual nature of your role as a leader, you need to do the work in advance with your boss before you speak with your team to make sure that you understand the changes or directions that you need to communicate, and that you can deliver the communication with authority and conviction.

Relationship Changes

The role changes you confront and work through often lead to major changes in several professional relationships.

With Your Former Peers—The Team You Lead

We know. This is the one you are thinking about the most. You were part of the team, now you aren't.

One of Guy's friends noticed this upon his promotion to plant manager. After the promotion his former peers stopped calling.

No dinner party invitations.

No BBQs.

No ball games.

Here's another example of drastic change. Two brothers in one of our workshops were promoted to leadership positions in a growing company with a long history in their small hometown (the same company their dad has worked for his whole career). Some of their former peers have *known them their whole life.* Just a little change here, don't you think?

Although your experience might not be this drastic, there is no denying that the change can be difficult (and if your experience is not this drastic, congratulations, it could be more challenging than what you are experiencing). You may have "grown up" in the organization. Perhaps some of your peers are older than you, and that changes the dynamic. Perhaps you've always gone out on Friday night after work for a beer. Maybe one of your former peers is your best friend. All of these things are possible, and all of them have an impact on you personally and professionally.

As you begin this transition into your role as a leader, you might experience some tension and friction in your relationships with the people you now lead and once worked with as peers. The good news is this: you can manage this transition successfully. Some will expect special favors or treatment. Some might resent your promotion. On average, though, most people will accept your new position well—especially if you apply the lessons in this book.

As you apply the techniques and concepts we share throughout this book, you must constantly be aware of the impact and the magnitude of this change on and in these relationships. This issue is so important that we talk about it in many ways throughout this book. At this point, we just want you to remember (as if you could forget) that this relational change plays a role in everything you do as a new supervisor-leader—especially until you get these relationships stabilized in a new comfort zone for both of you.

One temptation for many new leaders is to work to be friends with the people they lead. We recommend that you be on guard for this temptation.

> Remarkable Principle > **Be *friendly* with your former peers. Do not focus on creating new *friends*.**

In other words, work to create a positive, supportive, and friendly environment. Be willing to spend time talking with and listening to people. Show an interest in them and their families. And know where to draw the line between your personal and professional relationships.

You can, and should, attend parties, picnics, and special events that include most or all of your work team. You can host social gatherings for your team. Carefully consider whether or not it is wise to spend purely social time with specific individuals on your team.

As with any technique, suggestion, or rule for working with people, there are exceptions to this guideline. If you have a very mature and stable relationship, you might be able to continue being close friends. In most situations, though, trying to be friends can create more challenges for you. For example, you might set yourself up for accusations of favoritism and bias. In other cases, being seen on the friend level might interfere with your efforts to create accountability. You might find yourself having difficulty with maintaining objectivity in work assignments and conflict resolution discussions. And the list goes on.

We are not suggesting that you immediately end your friendships. We are suggesting that you carefully and seriously consider the long-term implications of making workplace decisions when your friendship with an individual might be the primary factor that determines the outcome of your decisions and interactions with the people that you lead.

Depending on the individual relationships you have with former peers, we strongly recommend that you have specific conversations with each individual about this change in your relationship.

 To download a specific coaching and planning tool for these conversations, go to the Bonus Bytes page at BudToBossCommunity.com and click on the Friend Talk button.

With Your New Peers—Other Leaders

The situation with your new peers could be quite different—you may not have known each other at all before your change in role. Depending on your organizational culture, this could be a relatively easy transition, with your new peers welcoming you to the group, or it could be more challenging. Since we don't know exactly what you will find or have found in this situation, it is hard for us to give you super-specific advice. Whatever the environment, though, make building these relationships a priority. Your peers can become your new trusted advisors, help you learn your role more effectively, and become a great support system.

You certainly provide value to them as well, but no one will benefit if these relationships are not actively nurtured. If you make the effort, you will be glad you invested the time to build or strengthen these relationships.

When you accepted the promotion to leader, you may have become a member of many teams. You have a different role on each team, and each team should have a different place on your priority list. You are the leader of your work team. You are a member of the leadership management team with your peers. You might even have responsibilities on cross-functional teams within your organization. Each of these teams and responsibilities can create some interesting relationship dynamics for you to sort through.

In his best-selling book *The Five Dysfunctions of a Team*, Patrick Lencioni introduces the concept of your first team. Your first team is the team to which you owe your first priority and commitment. Lencioni says that the leadership team you are on should be your first team, and we agree with his assessment.

As a leader, the team of first priority is the leadership team—the team of your peers.

If there are strained relationships, turf wars, lack of communication, or other struggles between members of the leadership team, those struggles will magnify and expand in the teams that those leaders lead. The dysfunction caused by poor teamwork at the leadership level only gets worse as it trickles down in an organization.

In your role as a leader, you now have an obligation to consider the larger interests of your business or organization beyond the direct concerns of the people that you lead. Yes, you are responsible for protecting the interests of the people you lead. And you have a higher level of accountability and responsibility to the team of leaders that you work with because of the impact of dysfunction at the leadership level on the overall organization.

 You have a higher level of accountability and responsibility to the team of leaders that you work with because of the impact of dysfunction at the leadership level on the overall organization.

With Your Former Boss

Again, your situation may vary—your former boss may now be a peer, or you may now be in a different location or part of the organization. Use your best judgment as to what the next steps should be for you. Overall your goal should be to continue your relationship with your former boss, using this change of situation as a chance to talk with him and further build that relationship.

With Your Leader

You are likely to have a new boss, and this presents a great opportunity for you!

You should invest some time in nurturing this relationship. It is important professionally, and the effort can be mutually rewarding over the long term. When you take active steps to connect and build a relationship with this person, you will be setting yourself up to make this a great relationship (and probably set you apart from most anyone else she has ever supervised).

At one time, she might have been two or three levels higher than you in the leadership structure of your organization. You might not have needed to frequently interact with her before you received your promotion. Now you probably speak or interact with her in some other way on a daily, maybe hourly basis.

When we begin our discussion of communication techniques and strategies in the chapters to come, we primarily focus on how those communication skills impact your effectiveness in working with the people that you lead. As you interact with your new boss, remember that she is also a person! The same communication strategies that will improve your effectiveness at assigning tasks to people on your team can help you better understand your leader's communication style and preferences and how you can connect with her on a highly productive level.

> **Remarkable Principle** — **Effective communication strategies work with all people. They work down with the people you lead, across the organization with your peers, and with your leader.**

Part of the challenge in making the move from Bud to Boss lies in the number of changes you face in a short time. Understanding, thinking through, and developing an action plan for handling these changes can smooth out the bumps in your transition.

Your Now Steps

1. Make a list of the relationships in which you are experiencing the greatest tension due to the change in your role.
2. Pick one of the relationships listed above and take action today to build or strengthen it. Schedule a time to speak with him or her about the change in your relationship: new expectations, new ways of communicating, and so forth.
3. Repeat step 2 until you have spoken with everyone on your list.

8

YOUR UNSEEN IMPACT AS A LEADER AND WHY YOU SHOULD UNDERSTAND IT

As we said once before, you are probably good at getting things done—on your own. In fact, your ability to get things done probably figured heavily in your promotion to leadership. And now you find yourself needing a whole different set of skills—the skills of getting things done through other people. How you accomplish these tasks determines the mark you leave as a leader.

In *Integrity: The Courage to Meet the Demands of Reality*, Dr. Henry Cloud writes about a concept that he calls "the wake" with regard to how leaders impact their organizations. In his description of the wake, he compares leaders in organizations to boats moving through the water. Because of Guy's background and experience, this particular analogy struck him with both its simplicity and its elegance. So we share the general concept with you here in the hope that it gives you a powerful mental picture to guide you in your transition to leadership.

Guy has spent lots of time with and on boats. As a teenager, he spent most summer weekends on a freshwater lake water skiing with his family. After college, he entered the U.S. Navy Submarine fleet and qualified as a Submarine Watch officer. He has seen lots of boat wakes from boats of all kinds and sizes.

From this experience, he noticed that every type of boat leaves a different wake. If you study a boat's wake, you can learn a great deal about the boat. You can guess its speed, its size, its weight, its direction, and many other things. Some of these things you can guess because of the significant differences between boats. For example, a sailboat and a power boat will have major differences between their wakes. And despite the differences, all boat wakes have one thing in common: they have two sides.

You can tell a great deal about a boat by looking at its impact on the water as revealed by its wake, and some of the most telling differences between boats are revealed by comparing the things they have in common—the two sides of the wake.

Getting back to the analogy, we see that just as a boat leaves a two-sided wake in the water, a leader leaves a two-sided wake in an organization. And like a boat, you can tell a great deal about leaders, even if you have never met them, by looking at their wakes—their impact on the organization.

The two sides of a leader's wake are

1. The tasks or results he or she accomplishes
2. The people or relationships he or she impacts

It was this observation about a leader's leaving a two-sided wake that first grabbed Guy's attention, and we hope it makes sense to you as well. You see, Guy is pretty focused on tasks. He likes structure, order, and logic. He prefers to work alone and to take care of his own work without having to interact with people too much. Because he is so focused on tasks, he is more comfortable with the leadership components of getting results and setting goals. The components that call for working with people are a little less comfortable. So by nature he relies on task-focused leadership strategies. Although these strategies work great in many individual contributor roles, they are not so effective when it comes to working with people like you do (and he has done) in a leadership role.

Let's go back to the boat analogy again.

A boat that is heavily loaded to one side will lean toward the heavily loaded side. As it leans to one side, it will turn in that direction unless the driver compensates for the off-balance load. A boat that gradually turns to one direction for a long-enough period of time will eventually make a circle in the water.

Leaders can do the same thing.

Like a boat, failing to compensate for these tendencies can cause leaders to "circle" in their organization. Boats that circle keep covering the same water. Leaders who circle keep experiencing the same problems.

Leaders who lean to a focus on tasks might focus on making things happen at the expense of building relationships with and within their team. If they fail to compensate for this tendency, they will keep having people problems.

Leaders who lean to the people side might focus on making people happy at the expense of getting results. If they fail to compensate for this tendency, they will keep having problems with task and goal accomplishment.

In your leadership style, you probably have a natural "lean" that is a little more toward getting things done or toward people and relationships. One major key to leadership success lies in learning to compensate for the way that you lean so that you stay balanced between getting things done and building relationships.

Learn to balance your focus between getting results and building relationships.

Although finding this balance may be difficult, it is possible. We both know many people who have successfully learned to compensate for their natural tendencies, and if you think about it, you probably have too. We believe that you, too, can find this balance.

Sometimes, people hear a contradiction in what we are saying here. We first make the point that most of the components of the leader's role call for skills related to interacting with people, and then we say that you should seek balance between a focus on tasks and a focus on relationships. The way that we align these thoughts is to say that even though more of the individual components relate to interacting with people, the full situation you face as a leader is a *both-and* scenario rather than an *either-or* scenario. In other words, for long-term success, you cannot choose between getting tasks done *or* building relationships. Like a boat that needs to travel straight through the water, you need to find ways to compensate for your natural tendencies and preferences so that you get things done *and* preserve relationships.

You cannot choose between getting tasks done *or* building relationships. Find ways to get things done *and* preserve relationships.

We have already talked about the difficulty of making the shift in focus from getting things done on your own to getting things done through others. The boat wake analogy adds another dimension to understanding the struggles of this transition. Not only do you face adjustments demanded by your change in role but also you have to address challenges caused by the internal tensions and pressures you feel as a result of your personal comfort, perspective, and natural tendencies.

Later, in Part Three, we share a model for better understanding both yourself and others so that you can develop deeper insights into ways that you can achieve this balance. For now, we keep our focus on understanding the concept of balancing the task and relationship components of your leadership role.

 For specific tips you can use to gain better balance between the task and people sides of the leadership role, go to the Bonus Bytes page at BudToBossCommunity.com and click on the Balance button.

As you work to grow your skills in this area, we have two encouragements to offer you:

1. You are not alone.
2. It can be done.

Your Now Steps

1. Growth in this area starts with self-awareness. Reflect on your natural tendencies by thinking about a recent leadership decision you made.

   a. Did you focus on getting things done and then think about how it affected people? (Task focus) or

   b. Did you worry about how people might feel and then think about how to get the task accomplished? (People focus)

2. The next time you face a leadership decision (that shouldn't be too far in the future), remember your natural focus and think how it might look from the other perspective before you make the decision or offer your input.

9

WHY YOU MUST GIVE UP
CONTROL TO GAIN INFLUENCE

What is the difference between control and influence? How do the differences between these two words affect the way you empower the people that you lead? And does the difference really matter in your life as a leader?

To answer these questions, let's start by taking a closer look at the definitions of *control* and *influence*. According to Dictionary.com, the primary definition of each word is

- *Control*—to exercise restraint or direction over; dominate; command.
- *Influence*—the capacity or power of persons or things to be a compelling force on or produce effects on the actions, behavior, opinions, etc., of others.

Notice that control is direct—you can control the things that you can make happen without the cooperation of others.

Influence, on the other hand, is more indirect. It begins with you and your behaviors, and then it extends to other people. Once other people are involved, you need their cooperation. In other words, you cannot directly "produce effects on the actions, behavior, opinions, etc., of others." Their actions, behavior, and opinions are their choice.

To expand this idea, consider a concept that comes from *The Seven Habits of Highly Effective People* by Stephen R. Covey. In this classic self-improvement text, Covey writes about what he calls the Circle of Concern and the Circle of Influence. For our purposes, we will modify the description slightly to speak specifically to people who work as leaders.

In a very broad sense, everything in your role as a leader fits into three categories (Figure 9.1). There are things that you can

1. Control (your personal circle of control)
2. Influence (your personal circle of influence)
3. Neither influence nor control (everything else)

Figure 9.1. Control, Influence, and Everything Else

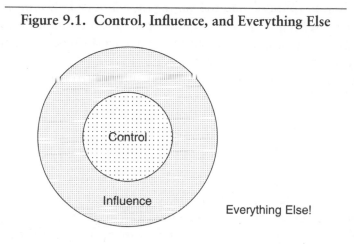

The things that fall within your circle of control are those things that you can make happen without the cooperation of others. Your circle of control includes your own words and actions. There might also be some work rules and other procedural items that you can control, and that's it.

Your circle of influence includes things outside of your direct control that you can cause to happen through the help and cooperation of others. This list includes their words, actions, motivations, and desires. Everything about other people is outside your circle of control.

> **Remarkable Principle** You can influence other people. You cannot control them.

As a leader, the difference between control and influence is a critical concept to grasp. You will be responsible for the results of your team.

You will be responsible for influencing their behaviors to get tasks accomplished. And you cannot control them.

We often get questions like

- "How do I get my team to _____?" or
- "How do I make my team members do _____?"

The intent behind these questions often stems from the leader's desire to get results and to make things happen. We see no problem with the desired goal in asking the questions. We do see a problem with how they are phrased and the assumptions implied. The problem is that they are control questions rather than influence questions. By the way the questions are asked, the person asking them is asking how he or she can control another person.

We suggest rephrasing the questions above to something like this:

- "How do I change my words and behaviors so that I communicate with my team more effectively?" or
- "What can I do to create an environment where my team members want to do _____?"

Rephrasing the questions in this way shifts the focus *away from controlling others toward controlling your own words and actions so that you can gain greater influence* with them. This shift in focus helps you concentrate your energy and efforts where they have the greatest impact.

Attempting to control something that is outside your circle of control is usually frustrating, tiring, and ineffective. When you realize that something lies in your circle of influence rather than in your circle of control, you will begin to look for different, more effective strategies and tactics. You will waste less time and energy on activities that simply do not matter and will not have a positive impact on your results.

> "You must give up something you have never had to gain something you have always wanted."
>
> —Dr. Robert Rohm
>
> Or, you might say:
>
> "You must give up control over others to gain influence with them."

Likewise, realizing that an issue lies outside your circle of influence, in the "Everything Else" category, frees you to not worry about it or to waste energy on attempting to change it.

For example, most company policies and procedures lie outside the circle of influence for front-line leaders. If you are a front-line leader and you invest time, effort, and energy into discussing these issues beyond casual conversation, you are wasting your time, effort, and energy. Rather than worry about, complain about, or discuss these items, focus that energy on what you can control (your words and actions) and where you can have influence (the people with whom you have a direct relationship). To demonstrate the importance of this concept, let's look at a real organizational example.

Guy once worked with two people we will call Sam and Joe (not their real names). Senior technical leaders in the same organization, Sam and Joe had markedly different approaches to their leadership responsibilities and different impacts on their organization.

Sam was a senior engineer who was incredibly skilled and knowledgeable. He would do what was asked of him, and he would do it well. Sam knew how to solve incredibly complicated technical problems. He also spent several hours every week complaining about decisions and actions of people in other departments and organizational rules established far beyond his circle of influence. In some cases, he would invest lots of time and great effort trying to persuade people to change their minds about decisions that had already been reached and implemented. As a result, he had a negative impact on the people who worked with him and frequently heard his complaints.

Sam consistently complained that he felt powerless to make a difference and that no one listened to him. Eventually, even those close to him began to ignore him. In many cases, people stopped acting on his suggestions even when they were valuable. He gradually became more and more isolated from virtually all of the decision-making processes in that part of the organization.

Joe, like Sam, was a senior technical person who did what was asked of him and did it well. He also had strong opinions, and he would occasionally comment, in private conversation, on what he believed to be unwise decisions. As a general rule, Joe did not invest his time and efforts into trying to change decisions that were already in place or the minds of people with whom he had no relationship. He rarely made any type of negative comment about overall organizational strategy, rules, or processes if they were beyond what he could change. Joe stayed almost exclusively focused on doing a good job in his personal area of responsibility and on working with the people close to him to get things done. He spent virtually no time or energy on the things outside his circle of influence.

On several occasions, Joe's positive influence on the people who worked directly with him created a ripple effect that also had a positive influence on people two or three relationships removed from him. People outside the department often came to him because of his proven ability to identify problems and to propose viable solutions and alternative ways of looking at issues. He consistently voiced his opinion in a way that did not alienate, demean, or criticize others. His circle of influence continued to grow larger and larger over time.

Sam failed to understand that applying his energy to issues beyond his circle of control or influence diluted his efforts and minimized his effectiveness. As his overall influence diminished, he became more directive in his communication style, and he tried harder to control everything about the people on his team. Others began to view him as a complainer and a negative influence, an energy drain. Many people actively avoided interacting with him. Sam's circle of influence diminished over time.

There were many differences between Sam and Joe. The biggest difference was not in their level of expertise, level within the company, ability to solve problems, strength of their personal opinions, or ability to effectively communicate their perspective. The biggest difference was in their focus. Sam worried about things beyond his control, and he diminished his influence. Joe focused inside his circle of control, and he increased his influence.

Beyond their personal influence, both people also affected the level to which their team members felt empowered to act and to take responsibility.

Sam's growing disconnection from the larger organization was obvious to everyone around him. He felt powerless. He communicated in negative ways. As a result, his team felt disconnected, isolated, and powerless. They often complained about things beyond their control. Sam's bad behaviors were replicated in the people he led. Even when they attempted to participate in cross-functional teams to get new experiences, Sam would discourage their efforts by telling them how pointless it was to get involved. They began to work at a bare minimum performance level as they eventually did just enough work to stay employed.

Joe's growing circle of influence gave him opportunities to interact with people far beyond his immediate work group. He learned of opportunities, ideas, and approaches to solving problems long before they became general knowledge throughout the organization. As a result, his team learned of new approaches and new projects early. They often volunteered for cross-functional teams with Joe's encouragement. He saw the value of staying connected throughout the organization and of working with others to solve problems together. Joe's people acted as (and felt like) engaged and empowered members of both his team and the larger organization. They worked hard, they volunteered for extra assignments, and they got things done.

 Control *what* you can. Influence *who* you can.

When you approach your job using this remarkable principle, you will get positive results like Joe did.

Empowerment and Delegation

You can see two practical applications of the concepts of control and influence when you attempt to empower others to act by delegating tasks or responsibilities to them. We offer more insights and specific tips related to this topic in Parts Four and Six.

As we have done on other points already, let's start the discussion by looking at some definitions.

Dictionary.com defines the words this way:

> *Empower*
>
> Verb (used with object)—
>
> 1. To give power or authority to; authorize, esp. by legal or official means: *I empowered my agent to make the deal for me. The local ordinance empowers the board of health to close unsanitary restaurants.*
> 2. To enable or permit: *Wealth empowered him to live a comfortable life.*

Delegate

Verb (used with object)—

1. To send or appoint (a person) as deputy or representative.
2. To commit (powers, functions, and so on) to another as agent or deputy.

When you look closely at these words, you see that they are closely related. When you *delegate* a task to a member of your team, you *empower* that person to do the task. Like so many concepts discussed in the context of working with people, it sounds easy in concept and it is difficult to do. We like to say that the concept may be simple but the application is not easy.

The act of empowering another person looks like a simple act of giving that person authority and assigning the task. Although you can tell another person that he or she is empowered, that person will not act empowered until he or she feels that way. That point is where the concepts of control, influence, delegation, and empowerment meet.

 You can't tell another person that he or she is empowered. That person will not act empowered until he or she feels that way.

You can control *how* you communicate when you delegate a task to another person. How you communicate affects how you influence that person. You hope that the way that you delegate the task influences the other person to feel empowered so that he will take action on the delegation. In reality, you cannot empower someone else, because his feelings of empowerment are outside your circle of control.

The art of delegating so that the other person feels empowered combines many concepts that we discuss through this book. Specifically, pay close attention to Part Three: Communication, Part Four: Coaching, and Part Six: Commitment to Success. You will also find some insights in Chapter Forty, where we discuss assertive communication.

 Many new supervisors struggle with delegation when they have to delegate or assign tasks to their friends. For more specific insights on this situation, go to the Bonus Bytes page at BudToBossCommunity.com and click on the Friend Delegation button.

Your Now Steps

1. Watch *Star Wars Episode Six: Return of the Jedi.* Focus on the scene where the emperor is trying to get Luke Skywalker to turn to the dark side. Look for the lessons about control and influence this scene demonstrates.

2. Reflect on your most recent conversation when you were delegating a task or responsibility to someone on your team, and then answer this question in your learning journal. Based on what we have discussed in this chapter, were you trying to *make* this person feel empowered or to *influence* him or her to feel empowered?

HOW TO USE THE POWER OF EXPECTATIONS FOR GREATER RESULTS

Expectations are often hard to clearly see. They are inside a person. They lie in the world of what people think and feel rather than in the physical, tangible world of workplace behaviors and results. Still, understanding the power of expectations—both yours and those of the people you lead—can give you insights you can use to become a truly remarkable leader.

Although we have highlighted the importance of discussing and understanding the expectations of roles and tasks, this conversation will take us further, and deeper. There are two sides to understanding expectations. To get maximum value from understanding them, you need to see and understand the impact of

1. Your expectations of others (the Pygmalion Effect)
2. Their expectations of themselves (the Galatea Effect)

In Chapter One, we said that one of the two most important building blocks for your success in the transition from Bud to Boss was the belief that you can succeed. That belief in your own success lies in the realm of your expectations. Let's explore this concept and how it impacts performance more thoroughly.

The Pygmalion Effect: Why Your Expectations of Others Matter

First, let's take a closer look at the power of your expectations of others.

Your word choice, tone, and body language communicate elements of your expectations to others. Parts of your communication are clear-cut and obvious statements about your expectations. Other parts of your communication come through in more subtle, and possibly unconscious, ways. (Remember this point when we get to Part Three: Communication.)

In a famous educational study reported on in 1966 by Robert Rosenthal and Lenore Jacobson, known as the Rosenthal-Jacobson Experiment, the researchers found that student performance tracked with teacher expectations. When teachers had high expectations of students, student performance went up more than for students for whom teachers did not have high expectations.

Likewise, in case studies reported by a professor of business administration at Harvard Business School, J. Sterling Livingston, leaders who had high expectations of employees got consistently better performance from their teams than leaders who had low or average expectations of their employees.

> Remarkable Principle
>
> **In general, people tend to live up (or down) to your expectations of them.**

When you speak with or write to people about task assignments, goal setting, performance issues, changes to organizational procedures or practices, and the inevitable interpersonal conflicts that develop, you are expressing and communicating your expectations to them. Some of your communications are overt—people can see and hear them. Some of your communications are subconscious—people merely "sense" what you mean by your words and actions.

> "The difference between employees who perform well and those who perform poorly is not how they are paid but how they are treated."
> —J. Sterling Livingston

To put the Pygmalion Effect to work for you, check your thoughts about and intentions toward other people. Remember our brief discussion about the reticular activating system? In this context, you are likely to find what you are looking for—either good or bad—and your expectations might hinge on what you see. The next time you have a challenge with a person, we recommend that you ask yourself this question about your expectation of him or her: Do I expect great things from this person or do I expect this person to be a trouble maker?

 Whatever you expect, you are likely to get.

The Galatea Effect: Why People's Expectations of Themselves Matter

Now, let's consider the other side of the expectation equation: what people expect of themselves.

Here's the simple explanation of what many researchers call the Galatea Effect: *people with positive expectations of themselves tend to perform better than people who have negative expectations.*

This point is important enough that you might want to read it again and let it sink in before you continue reading. . . .

Notice that this phenomenon lies outside your circle of control and within your circle of influence. This observation means that although you cannot control another person's expectation of him- or herself, there are things you can do to influence it.

The Galatea Effect works in conjunction with the Pygmalion Effect because they represent two sides of an interaction between people. As a result, most of what you do on one side of the expectation equation impacts what happens on the other side as well.

With that idea in mind, here are some things you can consider doing in your efforts to trigger the benefits of positive expectations with the members of your team:

○ *Assign progressively more challenging task assignments.* This action shows your confidence in them, and it gives them confidence in their own abilities. Be careful as you apply this concept. Research (Livingston) indicates that when people view tasks or goals as a "sure thing," the task or goal creates very little positive motivational influence. Likewise, when people perceive a task or goal as too hard, the task or goal can become a negative motivational influence. As a leader, you want to work closely with people to define task and goal assignments that are both believable and slightly challenging so that you create positive expectations and a desire to achieve. You will see an application of this concept in Part Six when we talk about the *bigness balance*.

o *Do one-on-one coaching focused on what they do well.* Many people default to commenting on what went wrong without noticing what went well. During your one-on-one coaching discussions, comment on the positive as well as the negative parts of the employee's performance and results. We share specific insights on how to coach more effectively in Part Four.

o *Catch people doing the right things.* Consistent, informal affirmation of good performance (when actually justified by performance) can inspire continued and increasing high-level performance. We share more suggestions for doing this effectively in Part Four.

o *Have experienced employees mentor and train junior employees.* This task assignment shows your confidence and trust in the senior employee, and it sets a positive example for the junior employee. In making this assignment, you grow your senior employee's leadership abilities, free yourself for other tasks, and build cooperative relationships within your team.

Your Now Steps

1. Watch the movie *My Fair Lady* and look for the leadership implications (this movie is all about the Pygmalion Effect).

2. Consider the members of your team individually. As you think of them, consider what your expectations of them are. If you have positive expectations, that's great. If you find that you have negative expectations, look for something in their performance that you can celebrate. (If you can find nothing to celebrate about them, you might consider whether they should be on the team or not.)

3. Look for an opportunity to work toward creating a positive expectation in others. Within the next 48 hours, tell each of your team members what you appreciate about them in terms of specific behaviors, actions, or accomplishments.

PART II

CHANGE

We've set the stage in many ways, and while we've already given you a number of things to think about and to do, now it's time to roll up your sleeves and really get started. In this section we get practical and pragmatic, and we deal with some of the most important parts of your new role. Some of these parts you may not have thought about much in the past; that's fine since your perspective in your previous job may not have required it. But now the world is different, and your perspective must, necessarily, change.

This topic is important to everyone personally. If you have just been promoted, you may be extra interested in this topic for yourself and your organization. Think about it this way. As a leader, you are responsible for leading people someplace—by definition, taking them to a destination. If you move people physically or in any other way, there is change involved.

Let's be more direct. You can't lead without change being involved.

So in order to be a successful leader, you must understand the nature of change for both individuals and organizations and how to influence and help people make the choice to change, whether in small, incremental ways or in big, challenging ones.

Before we go too far, let's open with a short self-assessment, like we did before and will do for each of the parts that follow. This assessment will help you focus and will improve your ability to apply what you learn in the pages to come.

Self-Assessment

Here is a quick assessment to help you think about change and your comfort with it in your new role. Use the following scale of 1 to 7 on each question:

1   Almost never
2   Rarely or seldom
3   Occasionally
4   Sometimes
5   Usually
6   Frequently
7   Almost always

I am comfortable with change personally. _____

(Chapter 11)

I understand how change happens and what contributes to it. _____

(Chapter 12)

I am able to successfully influence others to make changes and try new things. _____

(Chapter 13)

I know what to do when change is forced upon me. _____

(Chapter 14)

I am comfortable with my role in communicating change. _____

(Chapter 15)

I am able to recognize and overcome resistance in a productive way. _____

(Chapter 16)

Based on your self-assessment, you have an initial glimpse into your strengths and weaknesses in these areas. Use those insights as you read the pages that follow. Yes, you will want to read carefully in the areas in which you are weaker, *and* resist the urge to skim the other areas, for the nugget we share (or you extrapolate) may be the single insight or idea that takes you to even higher levels of skill and achievement.

Thoughts About Change—From Others and Us

Life belongs to the living, and he who
lives must be prepared for changes.

—Johann von Goethe, writer

Goethe died in 1832, so don't think this change stuff is new or even somehow more relevant now than in the past. Change is expected today in business and organizations. More to the point, change is life. We must learn to accept and understand it. And to be most effective, successful, and happy as leaders, we must embrace it. This idea leads us to the next thought . . .

Embrace change. It's going to happen
whether you like it or not.

—Odette Pollar, speaker and author

At some level you've done that by accepting the promotion that led you to read this book. Throughout your life you have experienced changes of all sorts, and certainly you have had many experiences with change in an organizational setting. But now, as a leader, your world related to change is, well, . . . changed! Now you will find yourself initiating, promoting, and being asked to institute change. It comes with the territory. After all, if everything were perfect in your organization, no change would be required (and no leaders needed, either). Change requires leadership because someone must move the group toward an improved (changed) future. Congratulations. That is your job. We suggest you embrace it!

Since changes are going on anyway, the great thing is to learn enough
about them so that we will be able to lay hold of them and turn them
in the direction of our desires.

—John Dewey, psychologist and educational reformer

In this section, we give you tools to better understand an individual change (like the one you are facing with your transition to leadership or anything else that is going on organizationally as you read this). More important, we give you tools to dissect and understand change and the process of change so that you can lead it more successfully.

BEFORE WE GO TOO FAR, OR THE NATURE OF CHANGE

As a way to get started on the topic of change, let's do an exercise. First write down three situations in which you have experienced change. These can be organizational or personal; recent or distant in the past; big or small. While your transition to leadership may be an obvious one to think about, you can pick anything. There are no wrong answers. Write them down here as you think about them.

1. _____

2. _____

3. _____

Next, write down a list of words or phrases that you think about when you think about these particular events. Write down whatever comes to your mind. Do this quickly—the goal is to get something down, not to create the perfect or exhaustive list. Again, there are no wrong answers.

Obviously we don't know exactly what you wrote down. But from our experiences in talking and working with people on change events and situations, we are very confident that the following are true:

1. *You have emotional words on your list.* Not everything we think about in a change situation is logical and fact based. You are likely to have words such as *painful, fear, scared,* and *exciting* on your list.

2. *You have a mixed list of words.* Although some of the words on your list may be neutral, most likely some of your words are positive in your mind while others are not so. And chances are you have more than a couple of positive, and more than a couple of negative.

Even if we missed our guess and one of these statements isn't true for you, rest assured they are for most people. And since in your new role how others experience change is as important as how you experience it, let's talk about the implications of this brief personal exercise.

 As a leader, how others experience change is as important as how you experience it.

Your relationship to how others view and act in regard to change probably isn't something you needed to think much about in the past, except perhaps in a family setting. We wrote Part Two because of this shift in your perspective and your need to succeed in this critical area of leadership. So let's look at two important concepts to understand about how people respond to change.

Change Is Emotional

First, let's think about your experience. Again, we are confident that at least some (if not a majority) of your words were about emotions.

○ Change can be associated with loss:
"When I got promoted, I felt like I lost the friendships of my peers." The loss may or may not be factually so, but the feeling of loss can have an impact on our thinking and actions.

○ Change can be associated with the unknown:
"When I got promoted, I was scared—I wasn't sure what was next." Change events may be fact based, but our response is often about our emotions. If we are scared or anxious, it will change how and what we think and do.

○ Change can also be associated with excitement and anticipation:
"When I got promoted, I was excited! I have been looking forward to a new challenge. I don't know exactly what it all means, but I am excited." There really isn't a question that excitement will affect our behavior and thinking. Is there?

So our emotions in a change situation are real. *And they are real for everyone else, too.*

 There is an emotional component to change. If we deny or ignore it, change will be drastically slowed, or it won't happen at all.

Change Is Situational

We are also sure that your list had some words that you consider positive, some negative (and perhaps some neutral). This is natural. Not everything about change is great—or awful. This variation in emotion is why people will sometimes seem like a Jekyll and Hyde when it comes to a change—sometimes reluctant and other times ready to go.

Perhaps an even more important point: what we think and how we feel about change (and therefore how we will behave in the face of it) depends both on the context and our recent personal experiences with change.

Context matters. Some people are more comfortable with changes in certain situations (like at work)—even if they are less so in other situations (like at home). The opposite is also true.

If someone has recently gone through, or is in the midst of, a difficult change situation in one part of his or her life, that person will be more cautious and hesitant with other changes at the same time or soon after. Alternatively, people who are feeling good about things that are changing in their lives will generally look more favorably on other changes at that same time and soon thereafter.

The Leadership Implications

All of what we have just described is true for everyone. But not everyone has the same recent experiences, and not everyone has the same thoughts and emotions about a given change. This difference between personal perspectives explains why change for an individual is one thing, and why crafting a change across a group, whether of three or three hundred, is much more challenging. Each individual within the group is in a different place mentally and emotionally about the change.

So think about this: as a new leader, you need to manage, lead, and somehow get everyone on board to make a change really happen. . . .

Welcome to leadership.

The good news is that there are tools, strategies, and actions you can take that will make all of this complexity less confusing and more doable. At the same time, this complexity is real and must be noted. That simplification is the goal of the rest of Part Two: Change—to help you understand and navigate changes both for yourself and as a leader of others.

Your Now Steps

In order to lead change successfully, you must first understand its nature. In the coming chapters we outline a process that will help, but it all starts with how you feel about change. These Now Steps are designed to help you think about those emotions. Capture your thoughts and reflections in your learning journal:

1. If you didn't do the exercise at the start of this chapter, do it now. The self-awareness that comes to you about how you feel about change is valuable.

2. If you didn't include your promotion as one of your changes, make sure to list the words you think and feel about this change, too (perhaps making it a separate list for the sake of comparison).

3. Buy a cup of coffee for your new boss or someone else you know who has been in a leadership role for a while and talk with this person about her experience and the lessons she learned when she transitioned to leadership.

12

IF CHANGE IS A CHOICE, HOW DO WE DECIDE?

You may be thinking... Change is a choice? Where did that come from?

Let's start with this assertion: people don't resist change, they resist being changed.

We have talked about change being challenging, and our experience says it can be. We also know that we have all made changes, and we *chose to make the changes.* (If your mind is filled with a bunch of "yes, buts" hold them until Chapter Fourteen, "Why All Change Isn't Created Equal, but the Principles Still Apply.")

We change all the time. We go to new places on vacation. We go to new restaurants. We watch new television shows. We use new work processes. We buy new products. Although we certainly don't change everything at once (routines and habits are among the most powerful forces on earth), we all do change. And the resistance that we sometimes experience with change is reduced or eliminated when we *choose* the change. We talk about resistance in a later chapter, but for now let's talk specifically about how we make the choice to change.

 Change is a choice. People don't resist change, they resist *being changed.*

As new leaders, this concept is critical to understand. Not only do you, as a new leader, represent a change, you will also be leading and supporting changes of all sorts in the future. If you want to reduce resistance to and build acceptance for the changes you represent and will support, understanding what we are about to talk about is critical to your success.

In one way or another, the content of the rest of this book relates to change. When you understand and can apply the ideas in this chapter, you will be more successful with everything in this book and in your role overall.

Reasons People Give for Not Changing

If people make the choice to change, the opposite is also true. People choose not to change. In fact, consciously or not, until they choose to change, they are choosing not to change. So if you as a leader need to promote a change, you might best start by understanding why people aren't changing yet.

To do that, let's do an important thinking exercise. Think about all of the change conversations you've had in the lunch room, on break, at the coffee shop or bar, and at home. Think, too, about the conversations you have had with yourself when it comes to a change situation. Make a list of the things you hear people say (or you have thought or said to someone else) to explain why they don't want to change or don't agree with a change. Try to come up with at least ten explanations before you continue reading.

Obviously, we can't see your list. But again, because of our experience in working with change efforts and observing change conversations, we have put together a partial list of the things we hear. Consider this list a hit parade of reasons, rationalizations, justifications, and excuses for why people choose not to change.

- Things are pretty good already.
- When something is good, why must we change?
- There's no reason to rock the boat.
- I'm almost to retirement (you can begin hearing this when people are in their mid-forties).
- I don't think that change will be an improvement.
- Change is too hard.
- I'd rather put up with the problems I know about than trade them for the unknown.
- Things are already working!
- I don't think we can make that change happen.
- I don't know what people are trying to accomplish.
- There are problems now, but they are no big deal.
- That may help the organization, but I don't see how it will make my life/job any better.
- No one can tell me how we will get to the change.
- How do we get started?
- What is the plan? or There isn't a plan to get there.
- It will cost too much.
- There is too much risk involved.
- I don't think we need to be the first ones (to make this change).
- I agree with the need to change, but I want to see someone do it successfully first.
- This won't be worth the effort.
- This will be too much work.

Now compare our list to the one you made above. Then put a star by any items on your list that weren't mentioned on our list—we'll come back to those in a few minutes. In the meantime, let's look at the reasons we listed and see if we can categorize them a bit.

The Four Categories: The Components of a Choice to Change

Let's look at the big list above and try to categorize it into some key areas. Once we have them categorized, we'll explore and discuss each of the categories.

Satisfaction with the Status Quo

Here are the items from our list that fit in this category:

- Things are pretty good already.
- When something is good, why must we change?
- There's no reason to rock the boat.
- I'm almost to retirement (I only have ten more years!).
- There are problems now, but they are no big deal.
- _____
- _____
- _____

Vision for the Future

Here are the items from our list that fit in this category:

- I don't think that change will be an improvement.
- I'd rather put up with the problems I know about than trade them for the unknown.
- I don't know what people are trying to accomplish.
- That may help the organization, but I don't see how it will make my life/job any better.
- _____
- _____
- _____

The First Steps (or the Plan)

Here are the items from our list that fit in this category:

- I don't think we can make that change happen.
- No one can tell me how we will get to the change.
- How do we get started?
- What is the plan? or There isn't a plan to get there.
- _____
- _____
- _____

The Costs and Risks Associated with the Change

Here are the items from our list that fit in this category:

- Change is too hard.
- It will cost too much.
- There is too much risk involved.
- I don't think we need to be the first ones (to make this change).
- I agree with the need to change, but I want to see someone do it successfully first.
- This won't be worth the effort.
- This will be too much work.
- _____
- _____
- _____

Now, if you starred any other ideas on your list, decide where they fit within these categories. If you still don't see where your item fits, hold on to it. After we explain a bit more about these four components, we bet you will see where they belong.

The reason we were so confident that most, if not all, of your ideas would fall into one of these four categories is that these four categories represent the components of the change choice. When we look at any change opportunity (personal, organizational, or cultural) through the lenses of these four components, we can understand why the change is moving forward or not, and if not, what is needed to help people make a choice in support of the change.

If this exercise was useful to you personally, you might want to facilitate a version of it with others—your team, a project team, or any other group. For help in facilitating the exercise and conversation, go to the Bonus Bytes page at BudToBossCommunity.com and click on the Change Exercise button.

Before we can use these components as diagnostic tools, we must understand them a bit more.

Exploring the Four Components of Change

So that you can develop greater insights into the four components of change, we explore each of them in a little more detail. These four components are critical to your understanding of the change choices we all make.

Satisfaction with the Status Quo

How likely are you to want to or choose to change anything if you are happy with the way things are? Not likely.

One of the reasons people don't choose to change is that they are in their comfort zone. When we are in our comfort zone, we have no dissatisfaction (by definition), and therefore the status quo looks just fine, thank you very much!

The obvious, but too often overlooked implication of this fact is that if people are comfortable with the status quo, they won't change. Zero dissatisfaction = zero choice to change.

And it makes total sense.

> If you are doing something you enjoy, why would you do something else?
>
> If you love your Mac, why would you buy a PC?

If you live in Buffalo and love the snow, why would you move?

If you are pleased with your current job, why would you look for a new one?

If you like and are comfortable with your work routine, why would you want to adopt a different work process?

Even though we wrote these in second person, these questions aren't just about you—they are about everyone you lead who would be involved in or impacted by a change you are leading.

> **Remarkable Principle** No change will occur if people are happy with the way things are now.

Creating dissatisfaction with the status quo is one way to influence people to choose to change. If you realize someone's dissatisfaction is nil or very low and you want to help him choose to change, you can help him become more aware of his dissatisfaction or help create that dissatisfaction. This approach is often called creating a "burning platform."

THE BURNING PLATFORM

The term "burning platform" is often used in the business world as a reference to situations that cause people or organizations to make a sudden decision to change. The term comes from a story that goes something like this:

A man working on an oil platform in the North Sea wakes up to the sound of an explosion in the middle of the night. As he climbs out of his bed, he is immediately in a chaotic situation. He works his way up ladders, to the deck, and eventually to the edge of the platform. Standing on the edge, he has a rapidly spreading fire behind him and the frigid North Sea waters below him. Looking at the water, he also sees that it is covered in debris and flaming patches of oil.

He is confronted with a choice:

1. Stay on the burning platform and certainly die from fire, or

2. Jump 150 feet into 40°F water and probably die from either the fall or exposure to cold.

He chooses to jump.

Fortunately, he survives his jump into the water, and he is rescued. When his rescuers ask him why he jumped, he says, "Better *probable* death than *certain* death."

The point of the story is that the "burning platform" created so much dissatisfaction that he was willing to take a risk, and he changed his behavior.

We do not know if this story actually happened or if it is just a good story to make the point, and it doesn't really matter. The story does make a good point about the choice to change.

A burning platform creates an obvious case of dissatisfaction with the current state!

You can create a "burning platform" for the people you lead so that they make a choice to change. And that might be exactly the right thing for you to do. However, without a well-defined safety escape plan, without a vision of what success looks like (and a way to make that happen), you run the risk that people will panic rather than change. They might freeze rather than act (not everyone would make the same choice as the man on the oil rig).

The burning platform approach can create the desire for change, and it can create some problems—unless you give people a great option to ease or erase the discomfort/dissatisfaction, you may create chaos. So as powerful as dissatisfaction is, and as necessary as it is to create a choice for change, trying to use it alone is inviting disaster both for your change efforts and productivity overall.

The good news is that the next two components can reduce, and possibly remove, the risk of panic and chaos. The bad news is that too many leaders figure that if they can create enough dissatisfaction with the way things are now, they have solved the change equation by creating a felt need for change.

 To help you (and others) better understand the role dissatisfaction plays in any change, download the Five Reasons Why Dissatisfaction Is Important—and How to Use It to Your Advantage. Go to the Bonus Bytes page at BudToBossCommunity.com and click on the Dissatisfaction button.

Since the dissatisfaction caused by the burning platform alone isn't enough, let's look at the next component, vision.

Vision for the Future

As we have just suggested, you can't create successful long-term change for yourself or a group without a clear picture of where you want to go. You must know what the result, or at least the likely result, of the change is before people will choose to change.

In its most basic form, vision is a goal or a mental picture of a desired future state or situation. Although that is a good shorthand definition, you, as a leader, must understand this concept much more completely. For your vision to be most powerful and effective in stimulating and maintaining change, it must include these five attributes:

- The vision must be *positive*. If the vision of the future doesn't seem better than the status quo, why would anyone want to change? First and foremost as a leader helping people choose to change, realize that people must see the change as creating something better than what exists now.

- The vision must be *personal*. If people don't see how they will benefit after the change, why would they choose to change? Too often organizations and their leaders talk only about the organizational benefits. As a leader, you can change that. Always help others translate organizational change into personal terms.

- The vision must be *possible*. People might be very inspired by a picture of the future, but if they think they are not capable, the organization is not committed, or that the goal is too big, the vision becomes less compelling. Confidence, past experience, and trust in organizational commitment are just a few of the barriers here. As a leader, you must help people see that the changed world is possible.

- The vision must be *visual*. Although some of us are more visually oriented than others, it is hard for any of us to believe what we cannot see. As you have learned so far, there is more to a vision than just a picture, but a picture is worth a thousand (or a million) words. So leaders must help people truly *see* the future. Help them get a clear picture of the changed state.

- The vision must be *vivid*. Our minds can't tell the difference between something real and something vividly imagined. If you have ever been moved to laugh, cry, or get a knot in your stomach at a movie, you know what we mean. In reality, you were merely hearing sound and watching light images on a screen, but you felt as if you were in the scene. What created your visceral and emotional reaction was how vivid the image was to you. When you make those mental images of the changed state more vivid (using more emotions and more senses), you will make the vision more attractive, lasting, and powerful.

 For a tool to help you create and communicate a vision that includes all of these attributes, go to the Bonus Bytes page at BudToBossCommunity.com and click on the Vision button.

Think about the last few organizational changes that affected you. How much of each of these attributes existed in the way the vision was communicated? The more of each attribute that was present, the more likely it was that you had a successful change effort. When some or all of these attributes are weak, the overall vision for the change is weakened. If the vision is too weak (especially if the dissatisfaction level is low and the plan is weak or nonexistent), few people will choose to change.

Before we leave the vision component, there is something more to remember.

Have you ever had a product you really loved, or a restaurant that was your all-time favorite? In the moments of thinking about that product or restaurant, were you dissatisfied?

Of course not.

However, if you suddenly became aware of a new model, or if a new type of restaurant came to your town and you heard great things about it, would you be interested in trying the new model or restaurant? Most likely, yes. If and when we become interested in or attracted to the new option, it doesn't mean we have become dissatisfied with the existing option, *except in comparison to the new situation*. In terms relating to our conversation that means...

 A strong, compelling vision will create dissatisfaction with the current situation by comparison.

So as a leader one of the ways you can create dissatisfaction with the current situation is to build a stronger and more compelling picture of the future once the change is made. The best and most effective way to overcome the apathy, complacency, and comfort of the status quo is to create a picture of something better—a vision of the future that is better enough to overcome inertia (and the comfort zone).

The First Steps (or the Plan)

You can be very uncomfortable with how things are, and you can know exactly how you would like things to be different. But if you don't know how to get from where you are to where you want to be, you won't move at all.

In order for anyone to choose to change, one must know how to get there or, at least, how to get started.

We have words for situations in which people don't have a plan or know how to get started. We say people are stuck, immobilized, or frozen. The situation here isn't that people don't want to move, it is that they can't—because, at least to them, they don't know how to get started.

Diets and diet books exist because of this component of the change choice. People want to lose weight—they have some amount of dissatisfaction and some vision of the future, but they are stuck until they have a set of steps, a guideline, or a plan. It is worth noting that the most popular diets all provide a "Getting Started diet." When you analyze these getting-started plans, you will find a couple of commonalities: they are about two weeks long and they are very detailed.

Why are they built this way?

1. People need a set of first steps, and two weeks, in the case of a diet, is a reasonable length of time. It is long enough to get started and to see some results. If, however, the diet author or editor provided a full year-long plan, people wouldn't believe that they could stick to it. So they probably wouldn't try. As a leader, the lesson is twofold: when introducing change or influencing people to a change, you must give them some clear first steps, but you don't need to give them the full plan toward implementation (if the change is of any size). People will be skeptical of the accuracy of the longer plan, and paradoxically, like with the diet, feel like it is too hard if all the steps are laid out too far in advance too early. Like with the diet, the goal of first steps is to get people moving.

2. People need a detailed start so they know exactly what to do. Behaving through a change is tough (remember our comments about information overload in Chapter Four?). It is especially

tough when you are trying to overcome deeply ingrained habits and routines. By providing very detailed steps with your plan at the start, you are doing two important things:

- First, you are helping people have initial success, which reinforces the validity and the value of the change.

- Second, when people have success, they build their trust in you as their change leader. Their logic goes like this: "It is working so far. I guess if we stay on this path we will keep making progress."

 For tips on how to craft initial change plans when you are initiating or leading change, go to the Bonus Bytes page at BudToBossCommunity.com and click on the Change Plan button.

The Costs and Risks Associated with the Change

If you want to influence a choice to change, the first three components are all things you want more of—more dissatisfaction, a greater or stronger vision, and at least some first steps. Put another way: if there is none of any of the first three, there will be no choice to change.

The fourth component is different in that you want less of it. The costs or risks of the change are the counterbalance to the other three. You can have massive dissatisfaction or discomfort, a very strong vision, and a clear plan, and yet if the costs are too high, the choice to change won't happen.

What are these costs?

The costs associated with the change can be real or perceived.

For example, Kevin's mother has a lifelong hobby of sewing. Over the years she has bought many sewing machines, continually upgrading along the way. She is knowledgeable about the features and benefits of the new models of her chosen brand, and she knows when new models will be coming out. Over the past decade, within a short time of each successive model's being introduced, she owned one... until the last model was introduced. She hasn't yet, at the time of this writing, upgraded again.

Let's look at our change components to understand her choice.

1. Dissatisfaction? She has some, but, in a perfect example of what we discussed earlier, it is vision-driven dissatisfaction—she wants the new one because of what it can do, not because there is anything

wrong with the existing one (this fact drives most of the new cell phone purchases).

2. Vision? Yep. She knows what the new one will do. She has read the reviews. She knows what it looks like. She has played with it in a showroom, and much more. The vision piece is definitely strong for her.

3. First steps? You bet. She knows the way to the dealer, and the dealer has contacted her many times about upgrading. This component is strong too.

So if all of these things are true, why hasn't she upgraded?

4. Cost. As strong as the other three are, she hasn't decided (yet) that all of that is worth $7,500 (minus the value of her trade in).

Sometimes we literally don't have the money to cover the cost of a change, and many other times we just see the cost as too great. In the case of Kevin's mom, the cost is in the form of real dollars.

Although real costs of change often impact us in our personal lives, in our organizational settings there is a different, and possibly bigger, cost issue. And it isn't related to our pocketbooks. Most of the changes you will be leading won't cost your people any of their own money.

What is the bigger cost issue in an organizational setting?

Risk, otherwise known as the *perceived* cost of change (yeah, we like calling it risk better, too).

Look back at our list of comments in this category. Most of these are a form of "What if?"

What if it isn't better after we do all this work to change?

What if it takes too long?

What if the customers won't like it?

When people (you included) are thinking about these risks, it reduces the likelihood that they will change. So as a leader trying to influence people to change (in other words, helping them make the choice), you must reduce the perceived risks or costs of the change to a level at which the dissatisfaction, vision, and first steps outweigh it.

It is kind of like a cost-benefit analysis, with a twist.

Here is the twist. Remember that if there is *no* dissatisfaction, *no* vision, or *no* first steps, people won't choose to change. Right? So the twist is that while you can help people make a cost-benefit analysis, you must make sure that there is at least a little bit of each of the

Figure 12.1. Identifying the Forces Toward and Away from Change

Toward the change	Away from the change
Dissatisfaction	Real costs
.	.
.	.
Vision	
.	Perceived costs/risks
.	.
First steps	.
.	
.	

components on the left side of Figure 12.1: dissatisfaction, clarity of vision, and understanding of first steps. These three must each be greater than zero.

Your Now Steps

Now that you understand how people come to choose change, here is how you can immediately apply this information.

1. Think about a current change you are trying to implement, big or small.
2. Reflect on and think about the communication and conversation about this change and look for which components are being addressed and which are being ignored or overlooked.
3. If some of the components are missing from the conversation, remedy the situation immediately in your communication.
4. In your next coaching opportunity, include addressing each of these components in your conversation (there is more on coaching in Part Four).

13

HOW TO DIAGNOSE WHY PEOPLE WON'T CHANGE

A few days before we began writing this chapter, Kevin was standing in line at his local Walgreens store to buy a few items. In front of him at the register was a frail looking man who was pulling a portable oxygen tank, and the tubes were inserted into his nose. As the clerk waited on him, he asked for three packs of cigarettes. Kevin's immediate thought was that the man was certainly buying the cigarettes for someone else. That thought was reversed when the customer thanked the clerk for carrying his brand while fumbling in his pockets to find the money to pay for his purchases.

Neither of us are smokers, but we realize that this scenario might not be what it seems at first. The man may not have been buying the cigarettes for himself, and his reasons for being on oxygen may not be related to a smoking habit. But then again, as graphic and seemingly obvious as this situation seems, we wouldn't be surprised if we found that the man was a long-time smoker and that the need for oxygen was directly related to his smoking habit.

We have all dealt with situations like this. We look at someone and ask ourselves: "Why won't this person change? It seems obvious!" Obvious was exactly how the scenario at this Walgreens store struck Kevin. So let's use that situation as a way to help you understand how to use the four change components to diagnose why someone isn't changing.

- ○ *It could be lack of dissatisfaction.* Looking from the outside, it is hard to see how the person at Walgreens isn't at least somewhat dissatisfied—who wants to tote an oxygen tank all of the time?

We'll guess there is at least a little dissatisfaction, but we can't be completely sure of that. There may not be enough dissatisfaction because...

- *It could be lack of a vision.* Perhaps our guy doesn't think it is possible for his health condition to change—he thinks that it is too late to change anything. Perhaps he has been a lifelong smoker, his friends are all smokers, and his parents were too. Perhaps he can't even see a world without cigarettes.

- *It could be lack of first steps.* Maybe he tried the gum and the patch. Maybe he tried cold turkey and everything from the late-night infomercials. Maybe he has tried them all or maybe none of them. Maybe people he knows weren't successful with quitting and so he doesn't see a believable way for him to quit either.

- *It could be that the costs are too high.* Here is just one possible objection he could have: "What if I stop but nothing gets any better, and then I gave up something I love for no reason?" (*Note:* This particular thinking, barely modified, is common thinking about risk and on-the-job change; it is the "why do it if it won't get better" objection.) Of course, his view of cost and risk could come from a variety of other perspectives.

Notice that this diagnosis is pretty "soft." In each case we said this "could" be the reason. Since we really don't know what he is thinking or perceiving, we are just guessing.

There are three important points for us all in this example.

1. Using the four components, we can find possible or plausible reasons someone isn't choosing to change. When we are dumbfounded by someone else's choices, using the four components helps us see what is possible, even if his choices don't make sense to us. Remember, since the other person is making the choice to change (or not), it is how *that person* perceives the elements of the four components, not how *we* see them that matters.

2. Once we have used the components of change to understand what his challenge *could be,* it opens up our minds to possibilities, and it helps us communicate with him more effectively. But we still don't *know* what his challenge is. If we really wanted to know why our guy keeps smoking as he is constantly on oxygen, we would have to ask him!

3. With the components of change as our tool kit, we can, with open minds, ask someone how he sees a change. We can use questions to help us diagnose which of the components is in the way for him, and then, if we are trying to help him make a different choice, we can use our more accurate diagnosis (aided by our new understanding) to help change his perspective on the most important, or most easily moved, components.

People choose to change for their reasons, not ours, and we can use the change components to better understand their reasons.

For a list of questions to use to help you diagnose which components are challenging people, go to the Bonus Bytes page at BudToBossCommunity.com and click on the Change Questions button.

Beyond Diagnosis

We've hinted at the next step beyond diagnosis, which is a conversation with the other person or group to truly understand the source of their reluctance to change. Let's say that you have this conversation and you understand their perspective on the change better now, but you are not sure what other steps you can take as a leader. Here is a complete, seven-step process you can use when you have people who don't want to make the choice to change.

1. *Understand the source of the reluctance.* You can use your analysis and the components of change to help in this understanding. Even if they have shared their reasons in the past, it is important to ask them about their concerns and reservations *at this time*. Do this in the most authentic and nonthreatening way that you can. Your goal is to truly understand what they are thinking and feeling about the change. In order to do that you must . . .

2. *Shut up and listen.* Your goal isn't to convince them or influence them at this point. It is to listen to their responses. Respond only with follow-up questions designed to truly understand where they are in regard to this change.

3. *Determine their level of resistance.* After asking and hearing them you will understand how big of a deal this change is for

them and for you, and how significant their resistance is for the change effort overall. If they don't share on their own, be willing to ask them exactly how big of a deal this change is to them and how strong their resistance is. Recognize that asking this may, in itself, be tremendously valuable. You show your concern for their perspective, and you give them a chance to describe their thoughts and feelings. The chance to verbalize their thoughts and feelings often helps them understand them better themselves so that they can overcome their own resistance.

4. *Acknowledge how they feel.* Notice we didn't say "agree with them." People appreciate being heard in a nonjudgmental way—it happens so rarely. People need to be acknowledged for their opinions. Sometimes you can move past their concerns by "agreeing to disagree." Once they have been heard and understood, they are often ready to move on with the change, *even if it isn't what they would have done had they been in control.*

5. *Get others to help influence.* If they still need help deciding to change, you may not be the right or best person. Maybe you don't have a communication style match (much more on this in Part Three). Maybe they don't want to hear from their supervisor, or maybe there are other reasons. Whatever the reason, encourage them to talk to their peers or others who are on board and might be able to relate the benefits of the change more successfully to them.

6. *Determine your next steps.* This is contextual to the change itself. Perhaps their reluctance isn't a show stopper. Perhaps they are whining about the change but doing (or will do) the new procedure. Or on the other extreme, maybe they are a major roadblock. Whatever the situation, recognize that although we need to be patient with people, not everyone will come on board with any given change at exactly the same time; and, at some point, their resistance or reluctance becomes a performance issue. When the situation is a performance issue, use your coaching skills as appropriate (again, more on coaching is coming in Part Four).

7. *Let it go.* If the issue is small, or is more of an irritant to you than a roadblock to the change, let it go. Or if the coaching doesn't work and the people are still resistant, take the necessary disciplinary actions. The reality is that not everyone will like or want to work under the changed scenario. If you have a large enough group,

there will always be people whose minds won't change, regardless of your competence with the first six steps. At that point, you must be willing to either let it or them go without blaming yourself.

Your Now Steps

1. Practice your use of the components of change by looking at situations you don't understand.
2. Start with a nonwork situation and diagnose where people could be getting stuck—use this as practice (even though you might gain valuable insights!).
3. Diagnose a real-life work situation—working through the plausible reasons a person hasn't chosen to change yet.
4. Have a conversation with the person to better understand his or her perspective regarding the change, using the steps above as your guide.

14

WHY ALL CHANGE ISN'T CREATED EQUAL, BUT THE PRINCIPLES STILL APPLY

At this point you might be saying, Well this is all well and good, and it may apply to personal change for others in the organization, but it doesn't apply to *my* change situation. . . .

Before we dive into those "special" cases, let's talk just a bit more about your personal change situations. Why? Because as a new leader you are probably dealing with a ton of change—it's coming at you from all directions. Often when that is the case, we forget about what works.

Your Own Changes

Our best advice is to use the principles you've read about in the previous chapters for yourself personally. We tried to write those chapters to make it clear that the change components applied to everyone (not just those we want to help choose to change). And when you are the one experiencing the change, it is easy to forget that they apply to you as much as they do to others. If you struggle with a given situation in your leadership transition (or with any other change in your life), use the components to help you better understand the situation. Why are you resistant? What is in your way? What should you do next? The change components will help you diagnose yourself, just like we talked about using them to diagnose the resistance you see in others.

Now, Those Special Cases

We understand your perspective that your team or organizational change situation is *different* (we've heard it many times before). So we decided to share some of the types of change we most often get a push-back on and help you see how the change components and principles still apply.

When the Change Is Thrust on You (or Your Team)

How can you use these change components when the corporate office (or accounting, marketing, the federal government, and so on—insert your own favorite scapegoat) has already decided on the change for you? In this case you might feel as though you have no choice. How do you work through the idea of choosing change if there seems to be no choice available to you?

When you are in this situation, you must always remember two things:

1. You still have a choice.
2. All change has an emotional component.

When we say that you always have a choice, we mean that you can always choose to leave the situation or job (or whatever else). If the change being thrust upon you is in conflict with your values or morals, or if, for some other reason, it is untenable for you, you have the option to leave. Just reminding ourselves that we have a choice, even if the alternative of leaving is worse than staying, can improve our outlook. Having said that, once you decide to stay, you must work to understand, accept, and abide by the change. (Remember what we said about disagreeing in private and then agreeing in public in Chapter Seven?)

This is the point where your emotions come into play. You must get past the emotions of feeling stuck, feeling forced, and feeling that this change is not a good thing. As long as you feel that way, you can't accept, abide by, or work successfully in the changed situation.

If you choose to stay and work with the changed situation, then the best way to understand the situation and the fastest way to work through your emotions is through the use of the four change components. Here is one example.

○ "But I'm satisfied with the status quo."

Perhaps this is true; after all, you didn't initiate this change. But it is likely that there were at least a few small things about the status quo that you didn't like, that bugged you, or that caused you frustration. Remember these points, perhaps even write them down. Focus on these points rather than your points of disagreement. The point here is that when we are forced to change (yes, this point includes us as well), we generally get artificially happier about the way things were, we wax nostalgic, and we forget the things that bugged us before. If the change is coming (or here) anyway, recognizing how things weren't perfect before will raise your hopes for something better and open your mind to the possibilities. This may not be a huge lever for you, but as long as you can get your dissatisfaction with the way it was above zero, you are heading in the right direction.

ROMANTICIZING THE PAST

In June of 1984, Guy left sunny, warm North Carolina for Naval Officer Candidate School in Newport, Rhode Island. When he arrived, he was greeted by a number of people he had never met before who spent several hours telling him how worthless he was as a human being and that he was lucky the Navy had given him the opportunity to redeem himself. As he entered his cold, damp "space" for the night, he looked out the window to see snow falling. Sitting on the edge of his bunk, he thought: "Four years, 364 days to go."

He finished Officer Candidate School, Nuclear Power Training, Submarine School, and qualification on a submarine. He enjoyed both the opportunity and what he learned while serving as a nuclear-trained officer, and he never lost sight of his eventual goal to leave the Navy, get married, and pursue a civilian career. He was willing to serve, and he wanted to learn. He did not want to make the Navy a career.

In May of 1989, he received his discharge orders. On the day that he checked out of his submarine for the last time, he made his rounds to say good-bye, and he left the boat. Walking down the pier toward the gate, he stopped short and turned to face the submarine that had been his home for the last three years. Looking at his old boat, he thought: "Wow, I'll never be on a submarine again." And he was overcome with sadness about what he was losing.

His thoughts and feelings are really funny when you consider that he had just spent the last nine months doing the paperwork and completing the steps necessary to resign his commission and that he didn't really *want* to be on a submarine again.

You see, even when we make a change happen, we can romanticize and focus on the past despite our desire for a better future. How real is this tendency when the change is forced upon us?

○ "I don't see the vision of the future."

Often when change is thrust on us, we haven't been given a picture of the future, or aren't looking at it because we are so frustrated with the fact that we are being forced to change. The best antidote here is to focus on the desired future as seen by those promoting or implementing the change. How do you do that? Ask them, with an open mind, to help you see the "why" for the change and the planned end state. Once you see both the reason and the goal, you can begin to mentally create how that future can be better for you or how it can help you in some way or both. In the worst case, knowing the real end goal of the change will help you see that "it won't be *that* bad."

○ "But how are we going to get there?"

Again, when change is thrust upon us, we often shut down mentally and emotionally. Make sure you understand the steps in the change that have been outlined. If a change has been forced on you for you to implement, beginning to develop the first steps will help you improve your attitude about the change, and it will help you get moving.

○ "What about the costs and risks?"
You are likely to see many risks and much cost—in fact this may be where you are spending all of your mental and emotional energy. As you work to better understand and work through the other three components, the impact of the costs may begin to lessen.

Is it ever a perfect situation when change is forced on you? Probably not! Imperfect changes will continue to happen to you in your career (and life), and understanding how to handle these situations is far more important once you are a leader than it was before you became a leader.

Remember, there may be times when *you* are the one instituting changes on others. When this is the case, being able to help others apply these lessons will accelerate the timeline toward successfully implementing the change.

When the Change Is Unexpected

Sometimes change just happens! Maybe the economy changed, the regulations in your industry changed, your competitor introduced a new product, you name it; changes can come externally and unexpectedly. In this case, how we feel about these kinds of changes is much like how we feel when the change is thrust on us. If you are in this situation, reread the section above, as it will provide you with the roadmap you need. And there is one additional important consideration.

When it is unexpected, you must allow yourself to view the change as real. Too often, people resist and delay action around an unexpected change because they are in denial. As a leader, you must see the landscape clearly. If an unexpected change is real, you must help your team move forward. This is both your responsibility and your opportunity!

Your Now Steps

If you are dealing with any of these situations

1. Apply the ideas from above to your situation.
2. Consider talking the situation through with a trusted advisor, rather than trying to do it mentally.

3. Write down your thoughts, insights, and next steps in your learning journal.

If your team is, or individuals on your team are, dealing with any of these situations:

1. Share the change components with them.
2. Open up a conversation about their concerns and challenges.
3. Help them determine some next step actions they can take to move forward regarding that change situation.

15

HOW TO COMMUNICATE CHANGE MOST EFFECTIVELY

Though change affects all parts of your life, when you become a leader you are often the mouthpiece for change or the instigator of it. These are two of the most important reasons that change is one of the major sections of this book and why we have spent time to help you understand the components of it. Everything we have talked about up until now is vitally important—but from a leadership perspective the real bottom line often comes down to this: How well can you communicate the change to those you wish to influence?

This question combines two of the six major parts of this book: change and communication. To address this important concern, we've developed ten specific steps to help you. These steps can be a lesson plan for your growth in these areas, but more immediately they can be a checklist to help you with a specific situation of communicating about change.

To make this chapter most useful for you, think about a change you are now trying to communicate or anticipate communicating in the near future. Here are the steps:

- "Sell" individuals.
- Help people take ownership.
- Let people in on your process.
- Call it a journey.
- Ask questions.
- Sell small—build a new status quo.
- Ask questions.

○ Give it words.

○ Celebrate progress.

○ Take responsibility.

Now let's look at each step in this list in more detail.

"Sell" Individuals

Up to this point, we haven't emphasized the word *sell,* but if you are trying to influence people to make a choice that is what you are doing. You may not like thinking of yourself as a salesperson, or you may embrace it. Regardless of your feelings about that word, it is the reality of your life as a leader, and this is a perfect time to see yourself in a sales role. The bottom line is that you are trying to sell others on your change idea. (By the time you try to sell it, the change should be yours even if it didn't start that way.) The good news is that the components we have discussed become the levers and the keys to your conversations on your way to the sale.

While most of the time we think of leaders introducing change with fanfare and a great speech (think Dr. King's "I Have a Dream" speech in Washington D.C. or Ronald Reagan's "Tear Down That Wall" speech in Berlin), that isn't what we are talking about here. We also aren't talking about the well-rehearsed PowerPoint® proclamations of a CEO to introduce a change. Don't get us wrong, those types of talks are necessary and can be very helpful to set a tone and a direction, outline a global vision of the future, and provide some clear first steps. Making those types of talks just isn't the point of this chapter.

If you do need to give one of those talks in your career, the things you have learned to this point in this section and will learn in this chapter will help you. But that isn't what we are talking about, so don't let visions of those types of talks scare you.

To sell change requires one-on-one, personal conversations. Remember, people choose to change based on their perceptions. So, to help them feel the dissatisfaction, see the vision, understand the steps, and reduce the risk requires less PowerPoint and more conversation. Spend time with individuals and small groups asking them questions and answering theirs. Take the time to understand their concerns. Their concerns may reveal something that needs to change about the change plan, or they may reveal something your message has been missing. As you understand their concerns, you are also reducing their apprehension. When you take the time to hear people out with an open mind, you will be surprised how much their resistance may be reduced—possibly more than you could imagine.

Regardless of when in the change effort these conversations take place, you have two major goals:

1. To listen to them first
2. To get them "in the loop"

Too often people delay getting engaged with a change because they don't feel a part of it and don't feel like they know what is going on.

By the way, did you notice that this selling process we have described is more about dialogue and less about a presentation?

Good—because that should be your goal.

When you are done with any change conversation, you want others to be ready to change (or be closer to that decision) and to feel that they are a greater part of the change.

 For some additional thoughts about why you are a salesperson as a leader, go to the Bonus Bytes page at BudToBossCommunity.com and click on the Salesperson button.

Help People Take Ownership

When people feel that they are a part of the change, and when they are more engaged, they will accelerate the decision to accept the change. The goal of your change communication should be to create that feeling. The goal of your behavior should be for that feeling to be more than just a perception, it should become reality. How do you do that?

People must take ownership of the vision of the changed state. Remember that one of the keys to a successful change vision is that it is personal. You must help people create their own vision of the personal benefits for the change situation.

Often the organization has set a change in motion and provided a plan of steps at a high level. And then those steps must be translated down to specific tasks for a given team or individual. Many leaders, with good intentions, try to work out these details on their own.

Whenever possible, engage your team in detailing out the steps. By engaging them in the process, you are communicating how much you value them and their opinions. When people are working *their* plan, they are more engaged!

Let People in on Your Process

One of the biggest mistakes in communicating change that leaders make is waiting too long to communicate. We have both spoken with many leaders, at all organizational levels, who are challenged by this timing issue. The traditional thinking is: "Don't communicate until you have all the answers." However, given that you can never have all the answers in a change situation, that thinking doesn't really make sense. Beyond the mistaken "get all the answers first" thinking, there are some additional mistaken justifications that people use for waiting to communicate about the change:

○ Mistake #1: Thinking people will respect you more when you have all the answers.

The reality is that most people will respect you more when you don't have all the answers and you promise to get them. Plus, by speaking earlier, you have another way to engage them—asking for their input and feedback, rather than attempting to deliver everything in a completed package.

○ Mistake #2: Thinking that by waiting to communicate you are managing the communication more effectively.

This couldn't be further from the truth. And if you think about it, your experience proves it. Have you ever "known" a change was coming, but there was no official word available? Did you notice that everyone in the organization was talking, speculating, and gossiping about it despite the absence of information? And they probably filled the gaps in their knowledge with negative assumptions. Now think about this from a leadership perspective. Wouldn't it be better to avoid as much of this negative speculation and counter-productive talk as possible? By sharing what you know (and what you don't know) early and often, you reduce the destructive talk and have a better chance to communicate your message.

○ Mistake #3: Thinking that by waiting you will come up with the perfect way to describe the change.

This delay is typically caused because you are afraid the group won't like the message. Waiting isn't going to help. In fact, the sooner you talk about it the sooner people can begin their transition to the change. People don't want or need perfect words. They need a genuine, honest, and authentic leader. The longer you wait, the more you erode that reputation.

One of the big worries of many new leaders is how to deal with the grapevine. Although the grapevine conversations aren't always about change, they usually are. One powerful way to prevent the grapevine from getting out of control is to communicate more—more frequently and more openly.

 For more advice on dealing with the grapevine, go to the Bonus Bytes page at BudToBossCommunity.com and click on the Grapevine button.

Call It a Journey

Call it a journey, because it is. Especially if the change is big and relatively complex, help people see that this won't be like a light switch. Let them know that the change will take time to implement and that they will have time to learn and to adjust to the changes. When people see the change as a journey, it will help reduce their fear and the risks they see in it.

Ask Questions

As we have already said, stop thinking about communications about change as a presentation, and start thinking of them as a conversation. Use questions to open others up and to get them talking about the change. Ask questions to understand their feelings about the change (frame your questions around the four components of change). Talking openly about the change often helps people adjust more quickly. Their answers to your questions will be instructive to you about their response to this change and will help you frame other communications with your team more effectively.

Sell Small—Build a New Status Quo

Especially if the change is big, there will be opportunities to build small changes along the way. An army doesn't usually take the battlefield immediately but advances methodically by securing one new area at a time. This should be your model of action in a large-scale change. Help people make small changes. Advance the status quo a little bit at a time.

Not only is this approach the easiest way to help people through changes, but it makes the sell easier too. Remember to be authentic and honest though—always put the small change in the context of the larger change for people. If you don't make this connection or show your understanding you may be seen as out of touch or insensitive to the needs of the team. Each small change must be positioned as one step in the larger process so that people don't try to "rest" or get too comfortable with the temporary status quo too much along the way.

Ask Questions

We know. We already mentioned this. Why it is here again? Because you must ask questions to be an effective change communicator, and you must do it throughout the process. Ask more often and listen more carefully. Do it early, do it late, and do it often. When you do this, everyone wins, and the change will be on more solid footing.

Give It Words

When you can label the change, you help people grasp it and make it easier for everyone to communicate about it.

Companies often label new products by names so that they stick in the minds of their customers. Why not do the same thing for your change? Help it stick in the minds of your team. Though this step may be done for many reasons, one is that it gives people a way to talk about the change. Give the change a label, a slogan, or a statement that describes or hints at the postchange vision. The people on your team will be likely to give the change a name anyway. Why not influence what the change is called?

Celebrate Progress

One way you can communicate is through celebration. Notice we are saying to celebrate *progress,* not just completion. If you want to maintain and build momentum, if you want to keep people on track, if you want to show your commitment to the change (which is almost always questioned by people during an organizational change effort), you must celebrate progress.

Celebrations of progress are rare for several reasons:

o Leaders are waiting for final success (it's too late to build momentum after the change).

o Leaders don't think it matters (it does).

o Leaders think people know how things are going (they probably don't have the same picture of the progress that the leader has).

o Leaders don't know what to do to celebrate (it doesn't matter that much—just do something!).

o Leaders don't think a celebration is in the budget (if it is genuine, it doesn't have to be a big thing to be successful).

o Leaders think celebrations are for children (we all have a child inside!).

None of these are reason enough to not celebrate progress. The good news is that you are now a leader and you can make simple celebrations and acknowledgments of progress happen.

 For twelve keys to creating successful celebrations of progress, go to the Bonus Bytes page at BudToBossCommunity.com and click on the Celebration button.

Take Responsibility

Change communication won't happen automatically, and you can't assume that the communication that comes from above will be often enough, specific enough, or helpful enough. As a leader, you have a responsibility for making your change happen. You can play a bigger role in this than you realize, and it starts with how you communicate with your team.

Your Now Steps

1. Apply one or more of these steps to a current change effort today.
2. Even if you are unsure or anxious, give one or more steps a try.
3. If you aren't sure where to start, simply talk with someone about the change, asking that person questions about how he or she feels about it.

16

BUT WHAT
ABOUT RESISTANCE?

We can't leave the subject of change without talking about resistance. Although we haven't talked about it directly, everything in this section on change equips you to deal with resistance successfully and to use it to your advantage.

That is right, we said *use resistance.*

First things first.

Most people think of resistance in negative terms. They try to reduce resistance, overcome resistance, and even combat resistance. We believe that is the wrong approach.

Rather, we suggest you recognize resistance as neither inherently positive nor negative; it just is. Resistance to change exists in nature because homeostasis—the tendency for living things to remain stable—tries to hold things the same.

But instead of going all biological on you, let us give you two definitions of resistance.

The first definition comes from Peter Block as quoted in Rick Maurer's book *Beyond the Wall of Resistance:* resistance is "a reluctance to choose." When you think about resistance that way, in light of what you have learned in this section, it gives you a new mental hook for resistance. Doesn't it?

The second definition comes from Kevin's book *Remarkable Leadership.* In that book, Kevin said: resistance = engagement.

Couple Peter Block's definition of resistance with Kevin's and you get a totally different view of it. Resistance could actually be a *good* thing. After all, would you rather have people apathetic about a change or resisting it? If they are resisting it, they care about the organization, the status quo, and more. Don't they?

When you frame resistance as a natural thing, as simply a reluctance to choose, and you recognize it as a sign that people care, you allow yourself the chance to use resistance. Rather than complain about it, you can actually transform it into acceptance.

 Although this may all make sense to you now, we know that the prevalent thought about resistance is negative. You can get a special report on *Seven Reasons We Avoid Resistance* by going to the Bonus Bytes page at BudToBossCommunity.com and clicking on the Avoid Resistance button.

Also in Kevin's book *Remarkable Leadership,* he outlined five steps to working with resistance:

1. Surface it.
2. Honor it.
3. Explore it.
4. Build a plan for overcoming it.
5. Map the solutions.

That set of steps is valuable for dealing with resistance, and for now we want to focus you on one other important point.

 Resistance to change will come from one or more of the change components.

When you remember this principle, and use the lessons you have learned in this complete section on change, you have the fundamentals to translate resistance into a positive force for change.

Your Now Steps

1. Think about a current situation in which you are sensing or dealing with resistance.
2. Use the ideas in this chapter to redefine it, understand why the resistance exists, and identify the causes.
3. Take no other communication actions with regard to this resistance until you have done step 2.

PART III

COMMUNICATION

As we showed in the chapter on the critical components of your supervisor role (Chapter Six), much of what you need to do as a leader calls for the skills of interacting with people. Those skills include many things that we cover in other parts of this book, and all of those skills require you to communicate with people.

You cannot help others see the importance of change without communicating. You cannot coach others without communicating. You cannot collaborate without communicating. You cannot engage others in goal setting without communicating. Communication is such a vital skill for leaders that if you take this skill away, everything else we discuss in this book becomes irrelevant or nearly impossible.

As we dig further into communication skills, remember what we said about leadership being a complex skill set. On your first reading, look for ways that you can improve your communication skills immediately. Then go apply what you have learned. When you experience challenges or struggles, come back and review this section or the Bonus Bytes content for subtleties or insights you might have missed in your first reading. As you gain experience applying the concepts in this section, you will gain deeper understanding of the finer points that could easily be missed in a single reading.

In this section, we share a number of key concepts you can use to become a more skilled communicator. Before we get too deeply into the material, let's stop for a moment so that you can reflect on and assess your current skill level. As we have stated in other sections, this assessment will help you focus your attention and more quickly learn to apply the concepts presented here.

Self-Assessment

Using the scale below, think about your current communication skills and approaches:

1   Almost never
2   Rarely or seldom
3   Occasionally
4   Sometimes
5   Usually
6   Frequently
7   Almost always

I use a communication model to help me communicate more clearly.   _____

(Chapter 17)

I know how to describe common behavioral traits in an objective way.   _____

(Chapter 18)

I can clearly see and use the dynamics of interactions between people.   _____

(Chapter 19)

I know how to create an environment that meets the needs of people on my team.   _____

(Chapter 20)

I know how to adjust my communication style to better connect with others.   _____

(Chapter 21)

I communicate in powerful, persuasive, and memorable ways.   _____

(Chapter 22)

I listen actively and effectively.   _____
   (Chapter 23)
My presentations produce the desired results.   _____
   (Chapter 24)

Based on your self-assessment, you now have a starting point for understanding where you need to focus your attention as you read this section. We have said this before, and the thought is worth repeating. Read carefully in the areas in which you are weaker, *and* resist the urge to skim the other areas. Leaders are learners, and they are always on the lookout for how they can improve all skills—even the ones in which they have a high degree of competence.

Thoughts About Effective Communication—From Others and Us

> *The two words "information" and "communication" are often used interchangeably, but they signify quite different things. Information is giving out; communication is getting through.*
>
> —Sydney J. Harris, journalist for the *Chicago Daily News*

As a leader, you will often have to share information with other people. Always remember that sharing information is not the same as communication. You have not communicated the information until you make sure that the information is "getting through."

> *I know that you think that you understand what I just said, but I'm not really sure that what you think is what I meant for you to understand . . . understand?*
>
> —Scottish commander of a multinational force in Bosnia speaking to his troops

When you speak or write to another person, you know what idea you meant to convey. They know what they heard or read. Until you check in with them, you do not know if what they heard or read is what you meant for them to understand.

Nothing can be so clearly and carefully expressed that it cannot be utterly misinterpreted.

—Fred W. Householder, linguist at Indiana University

Before we get into this section on communication skills, we want to acknowledge that no amount of work or study to develop better communication skills *guarantees* that people will understand and act on your communications every single time. Even carefully thought out and well-crafted communications can be misunderstood. We don't say this to discourage you. Rather, we hope that it will encourage you to know that communication is difficult for nearly everyone.

17

WHY YOU NEED A COMMUNICATION MODEL

As you moved from childhood to adulthood and as you have grown in your career, you have probably noticed that not everyone has exactly the same perspective or communication style. These differences can sometimes seem complicated and unpredictable. When this is the case, finding a way to communicate effectively becomes a real challenge.

For example, Guy once had a colleague ask him for input on a business decision. In the process of discussing the various alternatives for action, they came to a conclusion about his colleague's next logical step. Almost immediately, his colleague expressed concern about being able to invest the money to take the needed steps.

When his colleague raised this concern, Guy asked: "How much money do you have?"

His colleague replied: "I don't know for sure. I just don't feel like I have enough."

Guy wanted to say (but didn't): "How much you *feel* like you have was not the question. I asked, how much *do* you have?"

He did say (going totally against his factual nature): "Well, how much do you *feel* you can invest?"

Using the word "feel" rather than the word "think" was really difficult for Guy in that moment. From his perspective, the amount of money in your checking account has nothing to do with feelings. It is just a number—a fact. And you *think* about facts, you don't *feel* about them.

One challenge in communication is getting your message through in such a way that it is understood by the other person. When you speak, you take the mental picture that is in your head, pass it through your mental filters, and turn it into words that describe what you see. Then you speak those words to a person who hears them, passes them through his or her mental filters, and turns them into a picture in his or her head. At the end of the process, you hope the pictures match. If both of you have the same mental filters, your pictures are probably the same, and you have communicated clearly. If you have different filters, your pictures may be very different, and the communication won't be successful—you have given information out, but you have not gotten through.

In the example we gave above, Guy applied a mental model to improve his communication. A mental model is simply a structured and organized way to think about, analyze, and diagnose complex problems. The concept of using mental models to solve complex problems will come up again as we address other parts of your transition to leadership. For now, we will focus on the power of using a mental model to improve your communication effectiveness.

Based on his understanding of this model, Guy consciously chose the word "feel" instead of "think" to make a better connection. Guy thinks about almost everything. His colleague feels about almost everything. Guy could have attempted to force his perspective that you think about your checkbook balance rather than feel about it, and his efforts would have fallen on deaf ears. Or he could, as he did in this case, choose a different word that better fit the perspective of the person receiving the message.

Without the model, he would only have his perspective—his filters—to work with in trying to find the best word to connect with his colleague. With the model, he could use the word with the greatest likelihood of "getting through" the other person's filters.

Let's go back to where we began this chapter.

Despite the apparent complexity of understanding people, there are actually predictable patterns in how people speak, think, and act. It is from these patterns that a model emerges to explain how people see, process, and interact with the world.

We already said that communicating requires us to get through another person's mental filters. If our filters are the same, it's pretty easy. If not, what do we do?

Without a mental model, you have to use trial-and-error with each individual person to figure out how to best connect with him or her. If you work with a person long enough, you will eventually learn things about her that simplify your trial-and-error efforts. And, there is a faster, better way to close the gap between how you see things and how she sees things. That faster, better way starts with the use of a proven mental model.

Speeding up this process and improving your ability to communicate successfully with more people more of the time is critical to your success (and sanity).

Before we begin the description of the model we use, there are a few qualifiers that we want to share with you to make our perspective clear about the use of models in general without regard to the specifics of any one model.

- *Behavior style models are a guide to understanding people.* We do not advocate using any model to "box people in" or to "label" people; we simply want to understand their perspective.

- *Behavior style models do not "define" a person.* Knowing a model is a good starting point to understand another person. However, you do not know everything about a person simply because you know his primary communication style(s).

- *Think about style blends not style boxes.* Behavior style models can define a language or an alphabet to use for objectively describing behaviors and starting to understand what might be behind them. However, very few people will exactly match any of the individual style descriptors. Most people use varying degrees of all of the styles described by any model. While individuals tend to gravitate to one or two styles more than the others, almost everyone uses and relates to more than one of the styles. Your job as a leader is to understand your style and the styles of the people on your team so that you can connect with them more effectively.

> **Remarkable Principle** Communication style models are good guides for understanding other people. They are *not* rules that define other people.

Before we leave this chapter, let's finish the story about Guy and his colleague. When Guy asked his colleague how much money he felt that he could invest, his colleague almost immediately decided on a number that he *felt* comfortable investing. By choosing one word carefully, Guy helped move the discussion from stalemate to solution in a matter of seconds. When you learn to apply a mental model to your communications, you will be able to do the same thing.

Your Now Steps

1. If you are already comfortable with a communication style model, commit to learning how to apply it more effectively. Review the resources you have or get additional resources to strengthen your knowledge of it.
2. If you do not have a communication style model already in mind, keep reading, we are about to share one with you.

18

USING THE DISC MODEL OF HUMAN BEHAVIOR TO UNDERSTAND PEOPLE

While we have both studied many ways of describing the behavior patterns we mentioned in the last chapter, we tend to rely on one descriptive model more than we do the others. We like this model because of its simplicity and practicality.

Since you might already have a model that you use, our purpose is not to create a book about the DISC model. We just want to heighten your awareness of the importance of understanding this issue of different communication filters as you transition to leadership. If you have a model you or your organization use to understand these dynamics, we encourage you to learn everything you can about it and its practical application to your situation. If you do not have a working mental model, we hope to share enough information about the DISC model to help you get started in the process of applying it.

A Brief History

People who carefully observe and study human nature and human behavior long ago noticed that we tend to follow predictable patterns in our behaviors. In fact, observation of these patterns shows up in documents that are nearly 2,400 years old. So although what we are about to describe is incredibly useful and powerful information, it is not exactly new.

In more recent times, a wide range of psychologists, psychiatrists, and behavioral analysts have proposed various models for describing the range and variability of normal human behavior. Many of the models taught today trace their origin back to the work of the Harvard-educated psychologist William Moulton Marston in the 1920s and 1930s. Marston observed four basic behavior styles that he called Dominance, Inducement, Steadiness, and Compliance. His work formed the foundation for what became the DISC model of human behavior.

Marston's terminology does not use terms common to our language today. So researchers have modified and updated his terminology with new findings and more current language. The more current and simplified version of this model, based on the work of Dr. Robert Rohm in *Positive Personality Profiles,* is what we use here.

The Model Defined

The DISC model considers two basic drivers for our behaviors:

1. The Pace drive
2. The Priority drive

The Pace drive relates to the speed people move through life. You will often see it show up in terms of how quickly people move, speak, and make decisions. You can also see it in how visibly or intensely people express their emotions.

As shown in Figure 18.1, we speak about the Pace drive using the words *outgoing* and *reserved*.

Outgoing (high pace) people tend to move fast, talk fast, and decide fast. They often process their thoughts by "talking them out."

Reserved (low pace) people often move more methodically, speak more slowly and more softly, and make decisions carefully. They often process their thoughts by "thinking them through."

The shading of the arrow from light to dark illustrates that different people can have varying intensities of this drive in either direction.

The other drive is the Priority drive. This drive reveals the direction people tend to think most naturally. This drive is often harder to see in people than the Pace drive. You will probably see it in how they react to situations and in what they focus on first.

We speak about the Priority drive using the words *task-oriented* and *people-oriented*. As with the Pace drive (Figure 18.1), we represent this drive graphically (Figure 18.2), with an arrow drawn between

Figure 18.1. The Pace Drive

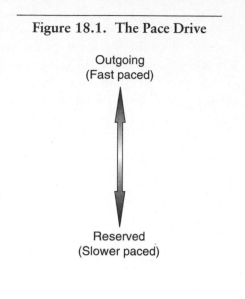

Outgoing
(Fast paced)

Reserved
(Slower paced)

Figure 18.2. The Priority Drive

Task-oriented ⟵⟶ People-oriented

the two extremes of the drive where the shading represents varying intensities of it:

Task-oriented people tend to process the world through a "task" filter. This means that they tend to think *first* in terms of facts, figures, results, and actions and *then* in terms of how those facts, figures, results, and actions affect people.

People-oriented people often process the world through a "people" (you could also say "relationship") filter. They generally think *first* in terms of how people might be affected by a given decision and *then* about the facts, figures, results, and actions necessary in a given situation.

As with the Pace drive, the shading of the arrows represents that different people can have different degrees of these two drives.

Looking back at the example we used of Guy and his colleague in the previous chapter, Guy represents the task-oriented perspective—he "thinks" about things. His colleague represents the people-oriented perspective—he "feels" about things. There is nothing inherently right, wrong, good, or bad about either perspective. They are just different ways of processing the inputs we get from the world around us.

ANOTHER EXAMPLE OF THE PRIORITY DRIVE
Here's a personal example. We knew as we were writing
Chapter Six, and talking about the components of your
leadership role, that based on your Priority drive you
would be likely to read that in a particular way. Some of
you will be excited that a larger percentage of your work
is now people focused, while others will be worried that
the work won't be as task focused as it was previously. We
took care to select words that we hoped would "work" for
everyone.

When we combine the Pace and Priority arrows into one drawing,
we get a graphical representation of the DISC model of human
behavior (Figure 18.3).

Notice that each quadrant of the combined drawing has a descriptive word that relates to key behavioral characteristics you would
be likely to see in people who have that combination of drives. The
descriptive words only show *traits* or *tendencies* that describe these
quadrants. Although there are other words we could use to describe
each behavioral quadrant, we have only shown the main characteristic
traits here: Dominant, Inspiring, Supportive, and Cautious.

Figure 18.3. The DISC Model of Human Behavior

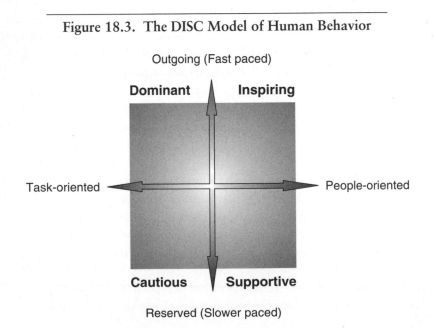

In conversation, we sometimes use verbal shortcuts for the purpose of discussing the different behavioral types:

○ The Dominant type is also known as High-D (a high level of Dominant traits)

○ The Inspiring type is also known as High-I (a high level of Inspiring traits)

○ The Supportive type is also known as High-S (a high level of Supportive traits)

○ The Cautious type is also known as High-C (a high level of Cautious traits)

Since all people actually have a blend of the four traits, the shortcut terminology we use when we say that someone has a high style in any of the four quadrants refers to a person who has a relatively high level of traits in that quadrant in her overall style blend. We don't often speak of the model by referencing low-intensity traits, but it is also true that an individual's low tendencies in a given quadrant could be helpful in understanding and communicating with her as well.

Here are some additional descriptive words for each of the four primary behavior styles:

Outgoing and task-oriented—Dominant style

- Determined
- Decisive
- Directive

Outgoing and people-oriented—Inspiring style

- Interactive
- Influencing
- Interested in people (and stories)

Reserved and people-oriented—Supportive style

Reserved

- Status quo
- Seeking security
- Sensitive

Reserved and task-oriented—Cautious style

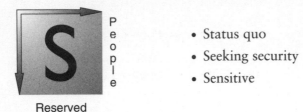

Reserved

- Careful
- Consistent
- Contemplative

 You can be a remarkable leader with any style. There is no good, bad, right, or wrong behavior style.

Behavior Style Blends

The model can help you understand yourself and other people by describing the four main, or primary, behavior styles. However, *you and everyone you lead will probably display some of all four behavior styles.* This blend of styles within each person is called his or her *style blend.* Each person's style blend will have more of some traits and less of others. The types that are strongest in a style blend are called high styles. The types that are less prevalent in a style blend are called low styles.

> **MORE ON STYLE BLENDS**
> Only a very small percentage of people have a behavior style blend that has only one high DISC type and none of the other traits. Most people (about 80 percent) have two

high DISC types and two low DISC types in their style blends. This means that one DISC type may be highest in a given individual's style blend, and that person probably also has a secondary DISC type that is also high. The secondary high type usually supports and influences the predominant type in his or her style blend. The shorthand notation we use to write these blends lists the strongest DISC type, a forward-slash, and then the secondary DISC type. For example:

o A person who has the D type highest and C as a secondary high type, would be a D/C style blend.

o A person who has the D type highest and I as a secondary high type, would be a D/I style blend.

Although both of the people in the example have strong Dominant traits, the difference in their secondary traits would make them behave, communicate, and interpret the world very differently.

Another type of style blend occurs when people have one predominate trait and two strong secondary traits (for example, D/CS, I/SC, S/CI, or C/DI). These types of blends happen for approximately 15 percent of people.

When you consider blending of the four main behavior styles and the different possible intensities of the behavior styles in each person, you can see how using four basic style descriptors can help you understand all of the different people you will encounter.

In reading the behavior style descriptive words, many people can relate to some of the words in several, in rare cases all, of the DISC type descriptions. Most people notice that they relate well to the words in one or two of the style quadrants and do not relate well to the descriptive words of the other quadrants. This is completely normal. It is just a reflection of their unique style blends.

If there is one style that definitely does not describe your perspective or your most common behavior and communication style, that quadrant is most likely your lowest style trait and the diagonally opposite quadrant is *probably* your highest style trait. (For example, Guy absolutely does not relate to the Inspiring trait description, and his highest style traits come from the Cautious quadrant—and Kevin is just the opposite!)

We hope our explanation of the model makes it clear that we see these drives as *tendencies* and not as *absolutes*. We do not present this model as a way to label, box in, or categorize people. Rather, we offer it as a way to get a better understanding of people who have different viewpoints and perspectives from our own so that we can find better and more effective ways to connect and communicate with them.

Go to the Bonus Bytes page at BudToBossCommunity.com and click on the Free Assessment button to take a quick, free behavior style assessment.

For specific insights on how you can use this free assessment with your team, click on the Team Style button.

Your Now Step

1. Take the free assessment mentioned in the Bonus Byte above so that you get a clear picture of your primary style traits.

19

HOW YOU CAN CONNECT AND COMMUNICATE BETTER WITH PEOPLE

Although it is fun and interesting to learn about the DISC model and to start learning about ourselves and other people, the model becomes useful when we begin to look at what it shows us about the interactions between people. Specifically, the interactions we focus on here are the communications that involve the various aspects of your role as a leader. Here are four specific examples:

○ Task assignments
○ Goal setting
○ Performance management
○ Conflict resolution

Each of these situations will have better outcomes when you learn to understand and apply a practical mental model such as the DISC model to understand style differences between you and those you are communicating with.

For example, the common approach to task accomplishment for each DISC style is

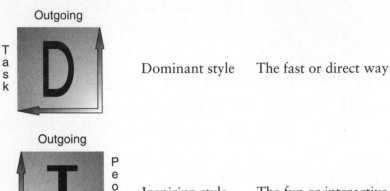

Dominant style   The fast or direct way

Inspiring style   The fun or interactive way

Supportive style   The easy or proven way

Cautious style   The right or proper way

Lack of understanding about these differences can lead to misinterpretations and negative labeling of people and their motivations. For example, people with Dominant traits who want to do things the fast way might view people with Supportive traits who want to do things the easy way as "weak." And in return, people with Supportive traits might view people with Dominant traits as "rude."

Notice that the interpretations are negative in both cases. This tendency toward negative labeling of people who are different from us extends to all of the other style interaction combinations. This negativity often comes from a simple misunderstanding about the other person's drives and motivations.

 For deeper insights into the how each style trait tends to interpret the world and what that means about the way we interact with each other, go to the Bonus Bytes page at BudToBossCommunity.com and click on the DISC Interactions button.

Beware of how the differences you might have with other people can be misunderstood and misinterpreted on both sides of the interaction:

○ How you interpret others and their motivations
○ How others interpret you and your motivations

UNDERSTANDING DIFFERENCES IN STYLE AND PERSPECTIVE

Kevin has significant levels of both Inspiring and Dominant traits. Guy has high levels of Cautious, Supportive, and Dominant traits.

We share Dominant traits. So we both like to get things done and get results. Kevin likes to interact and to make work fun. Guy likes to isolate himself and work alone. Both of us do what we do with the desire to reach our common goal. However, if we did not understand the differences in our work approaches, our interpretations could start to sound something like (this is purely hypothetical) this:

Kevin thinking of Guy: "Why does he go off on his own so much and act so serious all the time? Can't he just relax and go with the flow?"

Guy thinking of Kevin: "Why does he make decisions so quickly? Doesn't he ever consider all of the facts before he decides?"

Fortunately, we do understand our differences, and we find ways to appreciate and respect what the other person brings to the table rather than judge and criticize. So instead of the negative interpretations of each other's actions that could develop without this information, we actually think like this:

> Kevin thinking of Guy: "He must be tired from training and interacting with people all day. I think I'll give him a chance to reenergize and recoup. I'm sure he will reengage when he has had a chance to rest a bit."
>
> Guy thinking of Kevin: "I really like the fact that Kevin can decide on a course of action and get results quickly. It's good to work with someone who has fresh, creative ideas and doesn't overanalyze every situation."

Remember that differences in perspective can lead to negative interpretations of intention or character. To guard against this tendency:

1. Unless you have definite, concrete knowledge that someone had a negative intention for his behavior, choose to make a positive interpretation of his motives and drives. (This connects to our earlier discussion about the reticular activating system—do you see what you are looking for?)

2. Take proactive steps to communicate in ways that improve the odds of connecting with the other person. Learn to change your approach to better fit how she communicates.

As a leader, it is important to do this for yourself, model this behavior for others, and use these insights when coaching others, helping them work through conflict, improve their team interactions, and more.

Connecting and Communicating with Different People

As a new leader, you will be called upon to work with people in ways that might be new to you. One of the skills you need to become a great leader and to successfully make the transition from Bud to Boss is connecting and communicating effectively with a wide range of people. This range is probably broader in both number and variety of people than you probably had to work with as an individual working on a team.

Some of the people you may be called upon to connect and communicate with are

- Your team
- Your peers

○ Your supervisor

○ People in other departments

○ Customers

○ Suppliers

While each of these relationships has a different dynamic and might call for different specific approaches and techniques, the basic principles of effective communication apply to all of them, and the DISC model provides a powerful tool for growth in this area.

When you look back at the DISC model, you see four primary behavior styles. Not surprisingly, each of the four behavior styles has a corresponding preferred communication style.

Most people communicate in the ways that are most comfortable for them. While there is nothing inherently wrong with this tendency, it does present a bit of a challenge to you as a leader.

 If you only use the communication style that is most comfortable for you, you reduce the likelihood that you will communicate effectively with other people.

For example, Guy once worked in a position that required him to travel to Germany or to work with people from Germany on a frequent basis. He usually found that trying to speak with German people in German, even if he did it badly, was more effective than insisting that they speak with him in English. He also found that when he at least attempted to use German, the other people reciprocated by speaking with him in English (they usually knew English much better than he knows German).

A similar thing is likely to happen for you when you learn to apply the DISC model to your communications with other people. Although not as obvious as German and English, when you attempt to speak the DISC "language" of the other person, he will probably listen better, understand your intentions more clearly, and cooperate with you more because you have spoken with him in the way he prefers.

When Guy travelled to Germany, he knew in advance that many of the people he would see did not speak English as their first language. He could prepare in advance for the trip by practicing some German words and phrases. Your situation as a leader is similar to Guy's trips to Germany, and it is also different. It is similar in that you are interacting with people who effectively speak a different "language" from you. It is different in that you might not know what "language" to prepare for in advance of every conversation.

So let's look at another analogy to help you improve your communication effectiveness.

Imagine that you are taking a trip in your car to a place you have never been before. When you make plans to visit this new place, you will probably want a map to help you get there. Let's say that you go online to a Web site that prints maps and driving directions. When you get to that site, it will require you to enter two critical pieces of information: where you are and where you want to go. If you don't have the endpoints well defined, you cannot plan your trip. Once you know your endpoints, the Web site can then calculate your route and tell you how to get from where you are to where you want to be.

You can apply the same strategy as you apply DISC, or another mental model, to your communications with the number and variety of people you will interact with as a leader.

Your natural behavior and communication style is your starting point. The other person's behavior and communication style is your destination. The DISC model is your map for getting from where you are to where you want to be.

The concept of adjusting your communication style to match the other person's sounds pretty simple in concept. In practice, it can be quite difficult to do consistently. To help you apply the model most effectively, here's a step-wise process you can apply:

1. Estimate *your* primary behavior style(s) to identify your natural communication style and how it might differ from those of other people.

2. Make your *best guess* about their primary behavior style(s). (We'll share some tips on this step in just a moment.)

3. Think about how they might naturally speak and how they might hear or perceive your natural way of speaking.

4. Adjust your pace, tone, and wording to better fit how they hear and perceive spoken messages.

You can apply this approach to written communications also. For specific insights on how to use the DISC model to improve your written communications, go to the Bonus Bytes page at BudToBossCommunity.com and click on the Writing Style button.

To make this process work, you have to understand both your primary style(s) and the other person's primary style(s). Though it would be great to have DISC profile assessment results in hand for everyone you work with, that option might not be practical in your situation (without a good understanding of how to apply the model it can also lead to labeling and oversimplification). To make your best guess about another person's style, just answer two questions about what you see in her behavior:

1. Is she more outgoing (moves fast, decides fast, and engages quickly in conversation) or more reserved (contemplative, careful, and slower to engage in conversation)?

2. Is she more task-oriented (focuses on facts, figures, and results—uses the word "think") or more people-oriented (focuses on people, relationships, and emotions—uses the word "feel")?

By using your answers to these two questions you can make a *guess* about her style, or about how she is behaving and communicating at this moment. Even if you guess wrong, you will probably be pretty close. (You could be wrong, but at least you're moving in the right direction!) If you find that your guess is a little off, just notice how she responds to your communications and use your knowledge of the DISC model to make further adjustments.

Your Now Steps

1. If you don't know your style, you can go to the Bonus Bytes page at BudToBossCommunity.com and click on the Free Assessment button to take a quick, free behavior style assessment.

2. Identify two people you would like to connect with better. Write their names down, and make your best guess about their primary behavior styles. (We'll give you more steps for connecting with these people better in the next few chapters.)

20

BEYOND BEHAVIOR—USING THE DISC MODEL TO UNDERSTAND WHAT MOTIVATES PEOPLE

In describing the DISC model, we use behaviors as a way to make the differences between people more clear. We talk about behaviors for a number of reasons. The biggest reason we focus on behaviors is to keep our description focused on what we can clearly see and observe.

The model also gives us other insights to use in all of our communications with other people. As you understand more about what the model can teach, you will develop clearer and deeper insights to make your goal-setting, coaching, performance management, and motivation efforts significantly more effective.

For example, let's consider a difference that might develop between a leader with Dominant traits and a team member with Supportive traits. What the Dominant style leader sees as a challenging and exciting obstacle to overcome or defeat, the Supportive team member might see as insurmountable and discouraging. Understanding this difference in perspective could help the leader coach, train, and encourage the team member in more effective ways by realizing that what motivates the leader could demoralize the team member.

Similar perspective differences can occur on a wide range of issues for all of the style interaction combinations. In looking at this example, please remember that we do not recommend using the model to label people. The model is simply a starting point for deeper understanding of an individual. It should never be used to *define* an individual.

In the example above, the difference in perspective comes, at least in part, from the main needs and concerns of the individuals involved. While you can see the behavioral differences, you cannot see the differences between their needs quite so easily. However, the DISC model does offer some insight to help you with this issue.

To dig further into this topic, let's first look at what we mean by needs and concerns. To make our perspective clear, we start with a look at one of our physical needs—air.

If someone asked you to hold your breath until you were told that you could release it and breathe again, you could probably hold it for somewhere between 45 seconds and 2 minutes. If that person tried to get you to hold your breath for 5 minutes, you would still probably only last about 45 seconds to 2 minutes.

If the person attempted to stop you from breathing altogether, you would probably fight against him in order to get air. Air is a physical need. Since air is a need and not just a strong wish or desire, you—and everyone else—will fight to get it. We all act in ways to get our physical needs met. Whether the need is air, water, food, or sleep, we all behave in ways to get those physical needs met. When those needs are not met, we find it difficult to remain focused on other tasks.

The same thing happens with our emotional needs.

We all have emotional needs that are as important to our emotional and relational well-being as air is to physical well-being. Anything in an environment that challenges, limits, or prevents those emotional needs from being met creates a "fight" response that makes it difficult for people to stay focused on team and business goals.

> Remarkable Principle
>
> **People with unmet emotional or relational needs will not work to their full potential.**

When you understand the common needs and concerns associated with each of the four behavior and communication styles, you will be better able to make conscious (and maybe "unnatural") adjustments to your communication style. These adjustments will improve your ability to meet the emotional needs of and connect with other people, including your peers, your boss, and your team.

Basic needs and concerns drive our communication styles in pretty much every environment. In the discussion to follow, we focus on how understanding these needs and concerns affects you as a leader communicating with your team. As you read this section, keep in mind that the same principles apply to your communications with your peers, your boss, and your customers.

In order to keep people focused on accomplishing goals and moving forward, you will, as a leader, want to find the best ways to communicate and work with your team that both respect and meet their needs. When you create an environment that challenges people's needs, they struggle against you. When you create an environment that meets people's needs, you develop greater influence and they will generally cooperate with you. (Do you see the connection to the circle of influence mentioned in Chapter Nine?)

To create an environment that meets the needs of your team, you first need to understand the basic needs of each behavior style. Understanding the basic needs of each style allows you to do at least these two things:

1. Beware of how your needs affect your response so that you can maintain emotional control more effectively.

2. Adjust your delivery to better connect with others.

Your Now Steps

1. Stop for five minutes to reflect on the power of unmet needs to drive behavior. Ask yourself these questions (and any others that come to you as you think):
   • Does our explanation make sense to you?
   • Can you see how unmet needs can create a fight response in people?
   • Have you ever felt that response inside you?
2. Take a minute to record your thoughts and answers in your learning journal.

21

THE NUTS AND BOLTS
OF COMMUNICATING WITH
EACH STYLE

This chapter serves as a quick reference chapter to help you connect and communicate with people better. We recommend that you use this chapter in two ways:

1. Read through it one time to get a quick overview of some communication strategies that you might use with the people on your team.

2. Come back to it later when you need a quick refresher on how to communicate most effectively with a particular person.

Dominant Behavior Style—Outgoing and Task-Oriented Style

Needs
- Choices
- Challenge
- Control

Strategies
- Let them choose when possible.
- Give them big goals and challenges.
- As much as you can, let them control their work environment.

When communicating with them
- *Do*—Speak confidently and directly.
- *Don't*—Speak indirectly or "beat around the bush."

Understanding their perspective
- Thinks in terms of: *What?*—What's the point? What do you want? What do you want me to do?
- They generally want to do things the *fast* way.
- They want you to *respect* them. This is more about respecting their work and productivity than it is about liking them personally.
- Often communicate in a direct, bottom-line fashion. They want you to be direct and bottom-line with them.

 If this is your style and you want specific tips on how you can improve your communication effectiveness, go to the Bonus Bytes page at BudToBossCommunity.com and click on the Dominant Self button.

 If you would like more insights on how to communicate better with a person who has this style, go to the Bonus Bytes page at BudToBossCommunity.com and click on the Dominant Other button.

Inspiring Behavior Style—Outgoing and People-Oriented Style

Needs
- Recognition
- Approval
- Popularity

Strategies
- Notice them and what they do. If possible, make the recognition public.
- Verbally approve of them and their work.
- Interact with them. Show that you like them.

When communicating with them

- *Do*—Smile, listen to their stories, and ask about their families. Use stories and experiences to communicate complex concepts.
- *Don't*—Use too many details or strictly data-driven approaches.

Understanding their perspective

- Think in terms of: *Who?*—Who said so? Who do I get to work with? Who else thinks this way?
- They generally want to do things the *fun* way.
- They want you to *like* them. This is about how they feel when you are around them.
- Often communicate using stories and experiences. They want you to be friendly and interactive with them.

 If this is your style and you want specific tips on how you can improve your communication effectiveness, go to the Bonus Bytes page at BudToBossCommunity.com and click on the Inspiring Self button.

 If you would like more insights on how to communicate better with a person who has this style, go to the Bonus Bytes page at BudToBossCommunity.com and click on the Inspiring Other button.

Supportive Behavior Style—Reserved and People-Oriented Style

Reserved

Needs

- Appreciation
- Assurance
- Security

Strategies

- Show that you appreciate them at least as much as people as you do for their work.
- Verbalize the importance of what they do for both you and the team.

- Speak with them side-by-side rather than face-to-face. (This approach generally feels less aggressive to them.)

When communicating with them

- *Do*—Speak softly and listen carefully for their concerns. Give them a chance to process what you have said.

- *Don't*—Push for immediate action or ask them for a quick decision.

Understanding their perspective

- Think in terms of: *How?*—How would you like this done? How will we accomplish this? How will this affect other people?

- They generally want to do things the *easy* way.

- They want you to *appreciate* them. Although respecting their work is important, appreciation for them and their contribution is often more important than respect for their task accomplishment.

- Often communicate with empathy and understanding. They want you to slow down and take your time with them.

 If this is your style and you want specific tips on how you can improve your communication effectiveness, go to the Bonus Bytes page at BudToBossCommunity.com and click on the Supportive Self button.

 If you would like more insights on how to communicate better with a person who has this style, go to the Bonus Bytes page at BudToBossCommunity.com and click on the Supportive Other button.

Cautious Behavior Style—Reserved and Task-Oriented Style

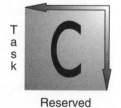

Reserved

Needs

- Quality answers
- Value
- Excellence

Strategies

- Provide data and logic to support your decisions.
- Explain your reasoning for decisions.
- Give them time to finish what they start. They seldom like interruptions.

When communicating with them

- *Do*—Provide facts and data to support your perspective or decision. Be prepared to give the reason that something is happening the way it is.
- *Don't*—Try to inspire them with an emotional appeal.

Understanding their perspective

- Think in terms of: *Why?*—Why are we doing this? Why is this important? Why do you say that?
- They generally want to do things the *right* way.
- They want you to *value* them. They are often less concerned with whether you like them than they are with you liking their work. They often view their work as an extension of themselves.
- Often communicate with logical explanations and by asking many questions. They want you to be logical and factual.

 If this is your style and you want specific tips on how you can improve your communication effectiveness, go to the Bonus Bytes page at BudToBossCommunity.com and click on the Cautious Self button.

 If you would like more insights on how to communicate better with a person who has this style, go to the Bonus Bytes page at BudToBossCommunity.com and click on the Cautious Other button.

Figure 21.1 is a quick summary to help you quickly find the information you need when you come back to this chapter for insights and perspective.

Figure 21.1. DISC Model Quick Reference Guide

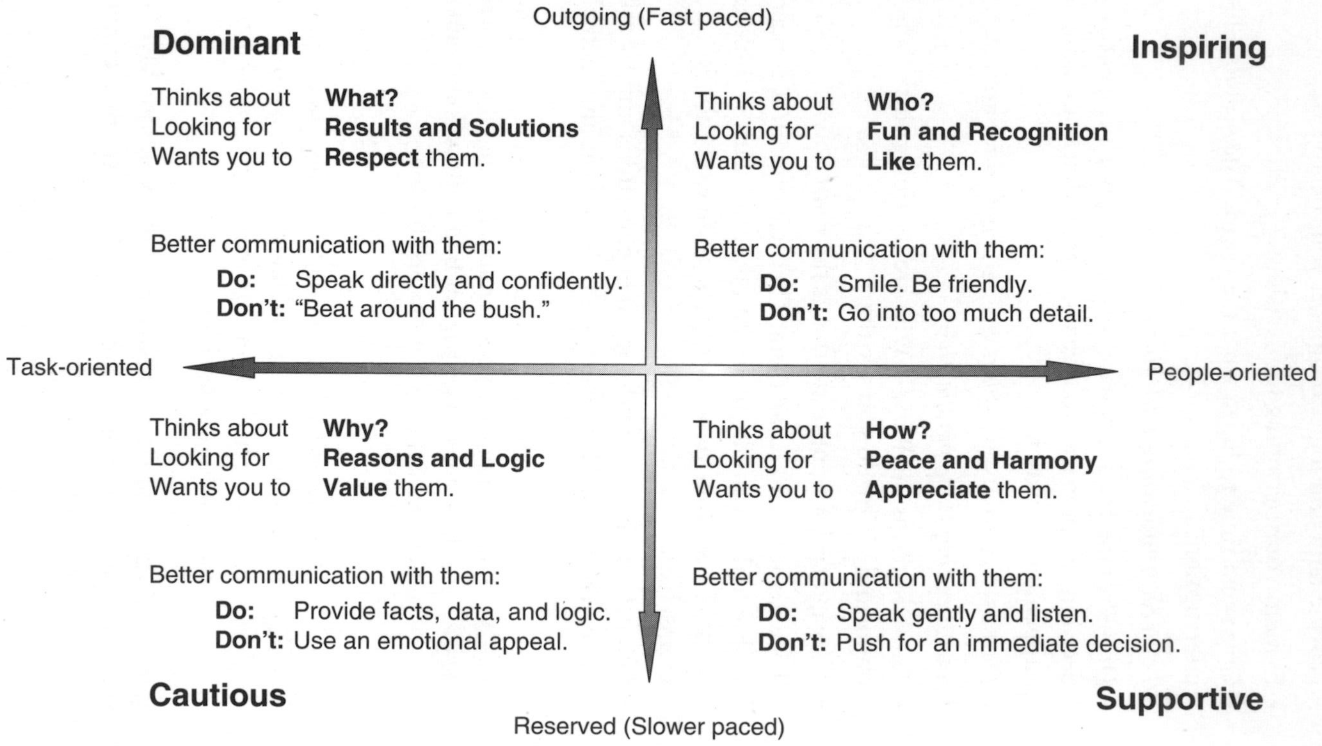

Outgoing (Fast paced)

Dominant

Thinks about   **What?**
Looking for   **Results and Solutions**
Wants you to   **Respect** them.

Better communication with them:
   Do: Speak directly and confidently.
   Don't: "Beat around the bush."

Inspiring

Thinks about   **Who?**
Looking for   **Fun and Recognition**
Wants you to   **Like** them.

Better communication with them:
   Do: Smile. Be friendly.
   Don't: Go into too much detail.

People-oriented

Task-oriented

Cautious

Thinks about   **Why?**
Looking for   **Reasons and Logic**
Wants you to   **Value** them.

Better communication with them:
   Do: Provide facts, data, and logic.
   Don't: Use an emotional appeal.

Supportive

Thinks about   **How?**
Looking for   **Peace and Harmony**
Wants you to   **Appreciate** them.

Better communication with them:
   Do: Speak gently and listen.
   Don't: Push for an immediate decision.

Reserved (Slower paced)

Two reminder Bonus Bytes...

Go to the Bonus Bytes page at BudToBossCommunity.com and click on the Free Assessment button to take a quick, free behavior style assessment.

For specific insights for how you can use this free assessment with your team, click on the Team Style button.

Your Now Steps

1. If you have not already done so, estimate your primary behavior style(s) to identify your natural communication style.

2. Make a list of everyone on your team and write their primary behavior style(s) by their names.

3. Using this chapter and your experience working with each person, add one or two communication tips beside their names.

4. Apply what you have learned here in your next communication with each person.

5. Observe their responses to your approach and adjust as necessary.

22

HOW TO MAKE YOUR COMMUNICATION MORE POWERFUL, PERSUASIVE, AND MEMORABLE

Would you have a larger circle of influence if your communications were powerful, persuasive, and memorable? We think you would. That's why we have included our top communication tips in this chapter. We believe that you can learn the skills of a master communicator and apply them to your leadership role, and we hope this chapter helps.

In our discussion of the DISC model, we talked about some great insights for adjusting your communication style to match that of a specific person. Now we are turning our attention to general tips for better communication with all people regardless of their DISC styles.

Speak *with* People and Not *to* Them

Ask open-ended, nonaccusatory questions and make fewer statements. Open-ended questions engage people and invite conversation. Be careful with "why" questions. They can often sound as though you are interrogating the person rather than engaging her. Try to move to dialogue and away from two people each having their own monologue aimed at the other person.

Speak with People the Way That They Want to Be Spoken With

Remember to use the suggestions we mentioned in the last chapter regarding behavior and communication styles.

 People generally want you to speak with them the way that they want to be spoken with.

Demonstrate Unqualified Respect

Always show respect for people regardless of their behavior. When we say "unqualified respect," we mean that you do not require that they earn the right for you to communicate respectfully with them. Remember that you can treat people with respect and still hold them accountable for their behaviors. We will discuss appropriate coaching and performance management approaches later. For now, realize that treating people with respect (that is, avoiding the use of sarcastic comments, personal criticism, and anything else that might be perceived as degrading) generally gets a better response from them. If a difficult conversation about performance becomes necessary, you will be better positioned to hold them accountable because you will have removed the possibility that you triggered their behavior by treating them poorly.

SOME ADVICE

Kevin's dad always said (and you may have heard this too), "If you don't have something nice to say, don't say anything." This seemingly simple advice isn't so easy, but when followed, it will pay you huge dividends in your communication with others.

 Always treat people with respect, regardless of their behavior toward you.

Speak About What You Want Rather Than What You Don't Want

It is easy to notice what people do wrong. In fact, it takes almost no effort to notice and comment on the wrong way to do things. To really make your communication powerful and persuasive, say what you *do want* people to do rather than what you *don't want* people to do. You will see this idea and further application of it in Chapter Twenty-Seven.

An example we often use to make this point in training comes from the scenario in which a young child is walking through the kitchen with a cup of milk. "Please be careful with that cup" would be saying what you want. "Don't spill your milk" would be saying what you don't want. The first statement is more powerful and persuasive than the second one.

Remember the reticular activating system? It works here, too. You will probably get more of what you speak about. When you speak about what you don't want, you just might get more of it rather than less of it. When you speak about what you do want, you improve the odds that people will be focused on *doing* the right things rather than on *not doing* the wrong things.

Use *And* More Than *But*

Imagine that you are in a conversation with someone and that you have just shared your opinion with him.

Compare these two possible responses:

1. "You know, that's a good point, but..."
2. "You know, that's a good point, and..."

With the first reply, it almost doesn't matter what he says next. By using the word "but," he probably triggered your defensive mechanisms. Even if what he has to say is positive, you will probably have a bit of a defensive posture as you listen.

The second reply creates a more positive lead-in to the second part of his statement. Even if he offers an interpretation of the facts that is different from yours, he has avoided triggering your defense mechanisms early in the process so that you might receive what he has to say with an open attitude.

The same is true for other people. When you use *and* rather than *but,* you bridge from one thought to the other rather than negating the first part of your statement.

Tell Them, Give Them "What's in It for Them"

When you communicate with your team members, you will often be asking them to take an action of some kind. When they take the action, it will cost them something in the form of time, effort, and energy. In return for that investment, they are looking for a corresponding benefit. (This concept is related to the cost-benefit analysis we mentioned in Chapter Twelve.) As a result, the question often running through a person's mind when she listens to you is this: What's in it for me?

Remember that the motivation to act generally comes from a desire for a benefit to the person acting. It might be either avoiding pain or pursuing pleasure. In either case, the motivation to act comes from the anticipation of avoiding personal pain or gaining personal pleasure.

When you communicate in direct and specific ways about how a decision, corporate goal, organizational objective, or request for help affects people personally, you improve the odds that you communicate in a powerful and persuasive way.

When you really know your team and your boss (this tip goes both directions), you will learn how to adjust your communications to show people "what's in it for them."

 For specific tips on how to do this for each DISC style, go to the Bonus Bytes page at BudToBossCommunity.com and click on the WIIFM button.

Engage Them in the Conversation by Listening to Their Responses

When you have a dialogue with people rather than two simultaneous monologues, you improve your persuasive power. Applying some of the other tips here will help you in this effort. Add active listening to your communication strategies, and your skill will grow remarkably quickly.

Dialogue engages people in actively thinking about and processing your suggestions. Active listening demonstrates to people that you care about their inputs. Showing your concern tends to reduce natural defensiveness and increase your persuasive power.

Your Now Steps

1. Reflect on your communication habits and preferences. Which of these tips do you violate the most? (Remember that we all mess them up. We're not trying to beat you up. We are asking you to be honest with yourself.)
2. Within the next 24 hours, write two or three ways you can improve on that communication strategy. Keep this note in a place where you can see it frequently to remind yourself of the strategies you plan to employ.

23

THE OTHER SIDE OF COMMUNICATION—BECOMING A BETTER LISTENER

As we said in the previous chapter, listening helps you create dialogue so that you can communicate more clearly. Listening, rather than a natural talent, is a skill you can develop. Listening takes focus and concentration. Hearing and listening are related and still separate issues. You can hear a person's words without listening to what he has to say.

Hearing is the ability to perceive sound with your ears. Listening is the work it takes to hear and then understand what was said. Hearing is a passive activity; it is simply the *ability* to perceive sounds. Listening is an active pursuit. It relates to the *effort* you put into hearing. This effort takes place in your thinking—the effort you exert to control how and what you think so that you can focus your attention on the speaker.

According to reports cited by the International Listening Association (www.listen.org), the average person speaks at about 125 to 175 words per minute. We can hear and process at speeds up to 450 words per minute, and some researchers estimate that we might think even faster (possibly as high as 1,000 to 3,000 words per minute). This speed mismatch between speaking rates and our processing rates might explain why most of us are distracted, preoccupied, or forgetful about 75 percent of the time that we should be listening. This preoccupation and distractedness might then explain why we usually recall accurately only about 20 to 25 percent of what we hear when another person speaks.

Frankly, active listening is an unnatural and difficult act for most people. The speed mismatch mentioned above and our natural tendencies toward distractedness contribute to some common barriers to listening that you have to overcome in order to listen well.

According to research reported in *Communication Research Report* (Watson and Smeltzer), the three most common barriers to listening are

1. External distractions—other people talking, phone ringing, and so forth

2. Internal distractions—headache, hunger, thinking about something else, and so on

3. Rebuttal tendency—the tendency to develop a counterargument while the speaker is still speaking

We're guessing that your experience tells you these barriers to listening are real. To overcome them and become a remarkable leader and listener, you need a plan. Here are the five steps we recommend so that you can overcome the barriers and become a great listener.

Listen to Understand, Not to Respond

Watch out for your natural "rebuttal tendency." Remember that we all have this tendency, and it is so much a part of human nature that it shows up in one form or another in literature and proverbs from many cultures all over the world. As newspaper editor and author Edgar Watson Howe is reputed to have said, "No man would listen to you talk if he didn't know it was his turn next."

This listening tip is really more about your attitude than it is about your behavior. Many people seem to think that a dialogue is like a verbal tennis match in which the two parties square off and hit the conversational "ball" across the net to each other. This approach to conversation leads to a sort of adversarial approach whereby both parties are trying to "score the point."

To listen effectively, we suggest that you view dialogue more like a game of catch between a pitcher and catcher. The pitcher (speaker)

throws the ball for the catcher (you) to receive it. The catcher only throws the ball back after he has it firmly in his grasp.

In other words, listen to receive the meaning. Once you understand, then you can respond.

Be Quiet—Externally *and* Internally

The obvious interpretation of this tip is to not speak while the other person is speaking. The additional insight is for you to also quiet your internal dialogue—what you are saying to yourself while the other person speaks.

Being quiet gives you the opportunity to both hear and understand her words and tone of voice. It also helps you understand the meaning *behind* the words.

To help you remember this tip, here are two quick statements to remember:

1. When your mouth is open, your ears are closed.
2. *Listen* and *silent* have the same letters.

To effectively listen, you must be quiet while the other person speaks.

Let Them Finish Their Thoughts

In other words, do not interrupt the speaker. From the previous tip, this idea seems obvious. However, many arguments and misunderstandings start with interruptions. When you are excited about a topic or emotionally invested in the outcome of a conversation you may struggle to remain silent while someone else speaks. Still, letting him finish is critical to good listening.

This idea will come back again as we discuss conflict resolution concepts, and it fits well here. When you let someone finish everything he has to say on a given thought before you speak, you improve the odds that he will in turn listen to you.

As Patrick Lencioni says in *The Five Dysfunctions of a Team,* "Reasonable human beings do not need to get their way in order to support a decision, but only need to know that their opinions have been heard and considered."

When you let people completely finish their thoughts, you demonstrate that they have been heard and understood. You create an environment that *influences* them to listen rather than trying to *make* them listen.

Stop All Other Activities

Can you really listen to someone while you are doing something else? Probably not. When you need to fully listen to another person, stop everything else that you are doing. Place your total focus and all of your energy on the act of listening.

Look Like You Are Listening

Effective listening goes beyond hearing someone's words. It extends to creating the right environment for mutual understanding. When you look like you are listening, you send nonverbal messages that let people know that you care, and you show your intent to understand their perspective.

- ○ Maintain eye contact. Effective listening calls for more than just hearing. It also means observing the speaker's unspoken message. People communicate at least as much with their body language as they do with their words. Good listeners learn to "listen" with their eyes as well as with their ears. If you are working on something else while a person speaks (checking your voicemail, sending a text message or e-mail, completing paperwork, and so on), she will not feel that she was heard.

- ○ Take notes (if appropriate). Taking notes when the situation calls for it will help you remain silent and focused on the other person's message. It can help you to block out distractions and to remember what he said more accurately. To avoid any misinterpretation of your intent, we recommend that you say something like this before you take notes: "If it's OK with you, I'll be taking notes while you speak so that I can make sure that I understand and remember your main concerns." This statement communicates two things:

    1. What the person has to say is important, and you want to remember it.

2. You are not just doodling or working on something else while the person speaks.

Ask Questions to Ensure That You Understand

Just hearing a person's words and observing her body language do not guarantee that you properly interpreted her intended meaning. If a point is even partially unclear to you, ask questions to clarify it before you respond.

You might say something like the following:

- "Just to make sure I understand you, let me repeat back to you what I heard you say."
- "I heard you say _____. Is that correct?"
- "If I understand correctly, your concern is _____?"
- "What else can you tell me about _____?"
- "Could you give me some insight on _____?"
- "What do you think (or feel) about _____?"
- "Correct me if I am wrong. Did I hear you say _____?"

When you clarify, remember to let the other person correct your understanding without entering into a debate. You do not have to agree with her perspective. You do have to make sure that you understand it.

Make sure you understood the message that she *intended* to send rather than the one that you *wanted* to hear. Ask good questions to clarify and amplify what she said. When you clarify, you build understanding.

> **Remarkable Principle** **Your desire to listen is at least as important as, if not more important than, your listening skills.**

In most of our workshops, people tell us that they have already heard or read suggestions for better listening, and still they struggle with it. This observation tells us that knowing how to listen is not really the issue. Wanting to listen is the issue.

To prove our point, think about a time in your past when you really wanted to get to know someone. Maybe it was your future spouse.

Maybe it was your future boss. We don't know who it was, but we are guessing you have had this experience with someone at some time in your life. Now think about how you approached listening to that person. We bet that you naturally did most of the suggestions in this chapter. Since you have already applied these tips, you must already know them. Right?

So, why do we even bother to list them here?

Because knowledge and action are two different things.

We believe you know how to be a great listener and have done it in the past (we bet we just proved that). Listening, however, is an issue of habits. When you incorporate these ideas more of the time, you are creating new listening habits.

Your Now Steps

1. Go back to the list of team members and their styles that you created in Chapter Twenty-One. Now write your listening level on a scale of 1–10 with each person, beside his or her style blend. (1 = I don't listen at all and 10 = I listen to him or her perfectly.)

2. For every person that consistently gets at least an 8 from you, give yourself a reward. For every person that gets less than a 7 from you, identify and write down the barrier you face in listening to that person.

3. Within 24 hours, write a minimum of two things you can do to listen better when people who get less than a 7 effort from you speak with you, and, if possible, apply these ideas.

24

YOUR KICK START TO WINNING PRESENTATIONS

Moving into a leadership role sometimes means that you need to make presentations to groups of people. Though this is not often a major part of the job, we find that many participants in our workshops and consulting work are interested in developing at least some basic presentation skills.

The ability to make presentations is an important leadership skill. In general, people with the ability to stand before others and speak well are perceived as more powerful, persuasive, capable, and intelligent. When you invest the effort to develop better presentation skills, you will

○ Improve your ability to drive change, create a vision, and inspire your team

○ Increase your odds of further career advancement

Entire books have been written on this particular topic, and we have no intention of going into great depth about presentation skills for new leaders. We have narrowed our experience down to six important points to get you started if you find yourself in the position of having to make presentations to your team, your peers, or higher-level managers and supervisors.

Use Purposeful Stories

One rule of sales is stated this way: "Data tell and stories sell." People generally remember stories and experiences better than they do data. When you convert your points into stories, you reinforce people's recall of your presentation's main points, and you communicate in a way that is more personal (to those receiving the message). You make it easier for them to relate to what you are saying.

This point is so important. We heard one professional speaker say this: "If you tell a story, it should make a point. And when you make a point, tell a story."

 For a special report on how to tell better stories, go to the Bonus Bytes page at BudToBossCommunity.com and click on the Stories button.

Simplify Statistics and Data to Make Them Memorable

Even when you use stories to communicate points for people to remember, you will sometimes need to quote data and statistics. When you do, here are three ways to make them more memorable:

- *Reduce.* Reduce the number of statistics or data points you share with people to the minimum necessary to communicate your idea. Remember it is all about your idea!

- *Round.* If possible, round statistics to make them easier to remember. For example, say, "About eight out of ten people think _____" rather than "Seventy-seven percent of people think _____." The second version might be more precise; it is not as memorable (if you are near our age you remember the ads that said "four out of five dentists surveyed . . . ").

- *Replace.* Another way to make statistics more memorable is to deliver them in the form of a picture or analogy. For example, you could say, "The number of people who will buy this product is roughly equivalent to the number of people in a city the size of Indianapolis" rather than "We expect to sell 800,000 units."

Show Less PowerPoint, More You

Have you ever sat through a presentation in which the presenter read the projected slides to you? If you have, you know how extremely painful the experience can be for the audience. Projected slides and other multimedia type tools are wonderful complements and supports to a well-planned presentation. If you use slide shows to show data or pictures, use them to support you rather than to replace you in the presentation. (This is why they are called visual *aids*.)

For specific suggestions on how to use PowerPoint most effectively, go to the Bonus Bytes page at BudToBossCommunity.com and click on the PowerPoint button.

Make It Personal

If you can tell a personal story related to the presentation, you will make it more memorable and more persuasive. This suggestion is related to our suggestion about telling stories to make points. When you share your personal experience in place of theoretical considerations, the points become much more believable and memorable.

Close Strong

Never close with a question-and-answer (Q&A) period. While it may be near the end of your presentation, you want to close with something memorable and actionable. Q&A sessions can take that energy out of the room. So, do your Q&A before your well-planned summary. If you need to make time for a Q&A, open the floor for questions after your final point, take and answer questions, and then go into your summary and your . . .

Call to Action

If you don't want people to do something, why are you presenting? Every presentation should include a strong, clear call to action that communicates exactly what you want the people listening to your presentation to do as a result of what they heard you say. While you may say it more than once, your call to action should be the last thing people hear you say.

The purpose of a presentation is to move people to action. Always include a call to action.

Your Now Step

1. The next time you make a presentation, come back to these points and review your presentation to make sure you are hitting the key elements for success.

PART IV

COACHING

Coaching is a big word, and it carries lots of different meanings for different people. Some people think of a coach in athletic terms, whether coaching a full team or an individual. Others don't have that experience, so they think of a coach in some other context. Inside the idea of coaching are the closely related concepts of mentoring, feedback, and more.

In our experience working with new leaders from around the world, coaching is an area of leadership that concerns people greatly, in part because they will be coaching their former peers. Yet this is a skill people often have some experience in, even if they don't readily recognize it. Think about it—you have probably been a coach of something in your life. Maybe you coached in school, as a parent, as a peer in the workplace, or in some other setting. In addition, most of us have had experience with at least one person we could look up to as a great coach.

One of your opportunities in this section is to recognize what you already know and apply your existing skills to the situations you will be facing as a leader in your organization.

Of course in your new role you may be thinking about this mostly from the perspective of the (annual) performance review. You have experience on one side of that table, and now it is likely that you will be the reviewer, rather than just the reviewee. This too is a part of coaching.

In Kevin's book *Remarkable Leadership* he talks about all of these skills as a part of the competency of developing others. For the purpose of this book we refine that bigger competency to the skills required for coaching. In this section we give you the insights and tools to begin your path toward becoming a great coach.

Like we've done for all the other sections, let's start with a self-assessment.

Self-Assessment

Here is a quick assessment to help you think about coaching and your comfort with it in your new role. Use the following scale of 1 to 7 on each question:

1   Almost never
2   Rarely or seldom
3   Occasionally
4   Sometimes
5   Usually
6   Frequently
7   Almost always

I am comfortable with my ability to give feedback that will be well received.   _____
   (Chapters 26, 27, 28)

I am confident in my ability to coach and develop others.   _____
   (Chapters 25, 31)

I am comfortable in receiving feedback from others.   _____
   (Chapter 28)

I can successfully lead performance reviews.   _____
   (Chapter 29)

I am supportive of those I lead.   _____
   (Chapter 30)

Based on your self-assessment, you have an initial glimpse into your strengths and weaknesses in these areas. Use those insights as you read the pages that follow. We have said this before, you will want to read carefully in the areas in which you are weaker, *and* resist the urge to skim the other areas, for the nugget we share (or you extrapolate) may be the single insight or idea that takes you to even higher levels of skill and achievement.

Thoughts About Coaching—From Others and Us

> *A good coach will make his players see what they can be rather than what they are.*
>
> —Ara Parasheghian, Hall of Fame college football coach

We open with this thought because it is critical (and it is the focus of the next chapter). To be a great coach requires that we believe in the potential of those we are coaching. As a former peer, this presents a unique situation. You probably know very well those you are now leading—both their strengths and their flaws. In order for you to coach people successfully you must see their strengths and potential, because when you can see it, you can help them see it too.

> *A coach is someone who can give correction without causing resentment.*
>
> —John Wooden, Hall of Fame college basketball coach (and player)

For a variety of reasons, Kevin, especially, is a big fan of Coach Wooden's philosophy and success. This thought captures a key point of Coach's philosophy and reminds us of our role as coaches. We may need to correct behavior or actions, but we can only be successful if the correction can be viewed in a positive light by the other person.

It is easy to correct someone. Coaching comes when someone can hear, accept, and take action on that correction, counsel, or advice.

> *Probably my best quality as a coach is that I ask a lot of challenging questions and let the person come up with the answer.*
>
> —Phil Dixon

We don't know who Phil Dixon is (we found this quote in several places in our library and online), but we love the thought. Well-formed questions, asked at the right time, are some of the most powerful tools we have as leaders, especially in our coaching role. Questions allow us to engage other people by allowing them to problem solve and learn. Although leading questions can be seen as self-serving or just a silly ploy, questions that get people to think and explore their approaches and thinking can be incredibly powerful.

Good, thoughtful, well-timed questions indicate curiosity about and concern for the other person and her perspective. Statements and direct advice often sound uncaring and condescending. The best coaches use questions rather than just statements to help the people they coach.

25

COACHING—THE ABCs OF COACHING SUCCESS

Coaching touches many parts of your leadership role, and many skills are required to do it successfully. In the course of this section we want to help you think about this pervasive topic in some practical ways. As a way to get practical, let's go back to the starting point of successful coaching. Just as the letters of the alphabet are the building blocks of all reading and language, so are the building blocks of effective coaching—we'll call them the ABCs—that we share here. Though we go beyond these building blocks in the coming chapters, these concepts alone can help you be a better coach. And as you understand and master these three specific concepts, all of the other knowledge and skills that you layer on top of these building blocks will be more successful as well.

Let's get right to them.

A: Accountability

As a coach we want those we are coaching to be successful and to develop good skills. Great coaches care and think about the skills that lead to successful performances. And yet the best coaches know that ultimately, performances don't belong to them, but to the performers. This may seem like a delicate tightrope, and it can be in one way. As a coach you may feel responsible if someone doesn't perform well. After the less-than-desired performance, you may think about what else you could have taught him, another way to have inspired him, or any number of other things.

While it is important to think about what else you could have done, in the end great coaches know the final accountability for performance lies with the performer and not with the coach.

As we discussed in Chapter Nine, great coaches are keenly aware of what is in their control and what is only in their circle of influence. The best coaches also realize that their circle of influence is large and they always work to expand it.

As you keep this accountability clear in your mind, you will be a more effective coach. Great coaches promote the confidence, skill, and proficiency of the other person, and always keep the performer clear on his ultimate accountability.

In the end, coaching is a selfless act of helping the other person become more productive and successful. When you keep the accountabilities clear, those you coach, and by extension you, will be more successful.

B: Belief

When someone believes in you and your abilities, you can tell. Can't you? Of course you can. You tend to work harder and perform better when people believe in you. Don't you? You know the answer to this, too.

Now let's flip the equation around. If you believe in someone's ability or potential to succeed, will you work harder to help her? Will you do just a little bit (or perhaps a whole lot) more than you might otherwise do?

When you put these ideas together you get this resulting principle:

 In order to coach others to their maximum potential, you must believe in their potential.

Here's the bottom line: *if you don't believe people can succeed, don't coach them.* You are doing both them and yourself a disservice if you do. Your innate belief in the potential of those you coach (even more than your skills, knowledge, and experience) is the most important factor you bring to the coaching relationship. We know we discussed these ideas in Chapter Ten. They are too important not to repeat. After all, repetition is the mother of learning.

That advice may sound good, but what do you do in real life? For example, what do you do when you are leading someone you don't believe in? In this case, to be fair to that person, to yourself, and to the organization, you must do one of three things:

1. *Look closer and see the potential that is there.* (Remember our conversation about the reticular activating system? Ask yourself whether you are looking for clues to the person's potential greatness.) Once you find that potential, coach him toward that.

2. *Find him a new coach.* Find a way to transfer the person to another team, or have someone else coach him—someone who does believe he can succeed.

3. *Find him a new work home.* If his potential isn't clear to you, and if you can't help him find another coach, his chances for success are severely handicapped. Perhaps that opportunity is elsewhere in your organization, or perhaps not.

C: Conversation

To be a good coach you must be able to communicate with the people you coach. (Sorry for the obvious statement.) An important part of the communication skills required for coaching are the skills of conversation. Good coaches are good communicators. Great coaches create conversations.

Too often, in an organizational setting, coaches want "to give some feedback" or worse, "to set someone straight." They go into a coaching situation well prepared for what they are going to say, so the coaching session is decidedly one-sided and, most likely, not very successful.

Great coaches ask more questions and work to learn more about those they coach in order to get the other person's ideas, thoughts, and opinions. As they do that they are doing more than creating conversation, they are creating common ground, deepening the relationship, and cultivating engagement of the person being coached.

There will always be situations in which a coach might need to provide direct advice or very specific counsel. And even in these cases, when you create conversation you create something more powerful.

Coaching is a complex task. When you recognize and capitalize on the basic building blocks—the ABCs—you will become a more effective coach immediately.

Coaching is more about "we" than "me," more about conversation and discovery than advice.

We had so much fun with the ABCs that as we finished the book we identified key building blocks D, E, and F. If you want those thoughts, go to the Bonus Bytes page at BudToBossCommunity.com and click on the Coaching Alphabet button.

Your Now Steps

1. Think back to your last coaching session. Determine how much of each of the ABCs was in play.

2. Determine what you can do differently, based on this analysis.

3. Plan (and schedule if necessary) a coaching session today so you can practice these ABCs more effectively right away.

26

FEEDBACK—THE HEART OF ALL COACHING

Now that we have settled into the concept of coaching and our leadership role in developing others, let's talk about feedback. Ken Blanchard, best-selling author of *The One Minute Manager* and many other leadership books, said, "Feedback is the breakfast of champions." With all due respect to Wheaties®, we agree. Feedback is required for anyone to continue to improve his or her performance in any skill and in any setting.

Though coaching is more than just feedback, feedback is an integral part of coaching. In this chapter we explore feedback from a variety of angles, helping you understand it and, more important, helping you use it effectively and confidently in your leadership role. There are two additional benefits you will gain from this chapter—you will be better able to give feedback in any situation (not just with those you lead), and you will be better equipped to receive feedback as well (don't you want to have every resource available to you to continue to improve *your* skills too?).

Three Sources of Feedback

Let's start by looking at the three sources of feedback. By this we mean the perspectives from which most people seek out, look for, or, at a minimum, expect feedback. When feedback doesn't come from one of these sources, people are usually taken aback by, less open to, or even openly skeptical of it. Given these truths, it is worthwhile to understand these sources. Don't you think?

Position or Power

People expect feedback from people in a place or position of power—
from their supervisor, for example. It isn't unusual to get feedback from this perspective, and if a person is looking to improve, gain
a promotion, or get a new assignment, feedback from this perspective
will be highly valued.

Generally speaking, a leader's ability to be heard when giving
feedback is granted by his or her role. Other examples include
positions such as teacher, judge, minister, and parent. Depending on
the individual this could also include lawyers, doctors, and others.
Paradoxically, in terms of inspiring willing and positive cooperation,
this may be the least powerful of the three feedback sources.

Expertise

People seek out or expect feedback from people with expertise. If
you want to be a better runner, you want feedback from an expert
in the mechanics of running or training. If you want to create a
more effective blog, you ask for counsel from someone who has been
blogging for a long time and is successful. If you want to be a better
listener, you seek advice from the best listener you know. This is
true for all of us—when we want to improve we want to learn from
someone with more expertise or experience than we have. Recognize
that in this case, expert status isn't something that we can claim, but
rather something that must be conferred upon us by other people. The
other people judge our expertise, and, in this case, their perception is
the reality that drives their receptiveness.

Expertise can show up in a variety of ways, and before
others can see it, we must recognize it ourselves. For more
perspective on how to recognize your own expertise, go
to the Bonus Bytes page at BudToBossCommunity.com
and click on the Perspective button.

Relationship

Have you ever gone to someone for advice, not because of what
she would know about the situation but because she cared about
you? Most people have confided in and asked for feedback about a

work-related situation from a friend or loved one, even if that other person knew nothing about the work, industry, or people involved in the situation. Why did they seek this feedback? Because of the relationship.

> **HOW THESE THREE SOURCES WORK**
> Here is a quick example to better understand these three sources. At the time of this writing, Kevin's oldest child, Parker, is eighteen, has just graduated from high school, and will soon be off to college. As his dad, Kevin has the first feedback source with Parker. Since Parker also works for Kevin, Kevin has positional power as his boss. Because they have a strong relationship, Parker values and sometimes seeks advice from Kevin based on their relationship. However, as previously stated, Parker is eighteen, and, like most eighteen-year-olds, he doesn't really think his dad knows much at all about the things that matter to him (things like taste in comedy, music, or movies, and college experiences, for example). Kevin hopes that as Parker gets older he will regain the expert status, at least in some areas that he once had in Parker's eyes.

These three sources ultimately come down to trust—can people trust your feedback and your motives for giving feedback or not? Consciously or otherwise, these three sources are the lenses through which people make that trust determination about you as their coach.

Trust is a critical ingredient for feedback and coaching success. If you want to be a great coach, you must constantly and consistently work to build trust with those you coach.

This information is important to you for several reasons. First, only one of these three sources is yours automatically as a leader (position, in case you missed it). You may think you have earned the expertise source, but that is far from automatic. Consider the following possible scenarios:

- If you are a new supervisor and came from another area or company, people may not know your experience. When you come from "somewhere else," without information to the contrary people will assume that you don't know their jobs.

- If you were literally a peer, doing the same work as those you now supervise, one of two very different scenarios could play out for you. Either people grant you expertise status because they know you know the work, or they resist giving it to you because they don't feel you know any more about it than they do (after all, they may have trained you when you started—how can you possibly know more than they do?). This scenario further complicates the expertise source, because people may perceive it based on your actual knowledge or on your relative knowledge, compared to what they know. Either way, *they* make the call.

The relationship source is complex too. Consider these possible situations:

- As a former peer, you know someone well, and your strong past relationship provides you with the ability to use this source.

- As a former peer, people see your relationship as having changed, and so tapping this source could be challenging, because people aren't clear about your motives.

Relationships take time and personal investment, thus it may take time before you can lay claim to and use this feedback source.

As an aside, the juxtaposition of these sources is often fuel for an ongoing debate. Would you rather have a supervisor who has great people skills and knows how to lead (position and relationship sources) or a person who knows your job well (expertise). If you are like us, you have heard this argument many times. In some ways everyone's perspective is correct. The argument is about which of these sources people personally value the most. Although people may never come to an agreement on which source is most important, everyone is likely to agree that in most situations the best scenario is when all three sources are present. When people can say their supervisor (position) has excellent leadership and interpersonal skills (relationship) *and* has enough knowledge about the work of the organization to have credibility (expertise), they are much more likely to receive feedback well.

If you believe you are lacking in both expertise and relationship from the perspective of those you lead, keep in mind the quotation we've seen attributed to many different people: *People don't care how much you know, until they know how much you care about them.* The message is clear: work on relationship first. In most cases that will be easier to establish than expertise (especially if you don't know people's work), and it is more highly valued by most people anyway.

We humbly submit that if you want to be an exceptional or remarkable coach, you must aspire to earn all three types of feedback.

 For details on how these three types of feedback connect to people's communication styles, go to the Bonus Bytes page at BudToBossCommunity.com and click on the Feedback Sources button.

Four Types of Feedback

Beyond the sources of the feedback, there are four specific types or forms of feedback.

Negative Feedback

You are certainly familiar with this type. Sadly, when people at work talk about "giving feedback" this is typically what they are thinking about. The reality is that this is just one type. What is negative feedback, then? It is any comment about past performance that didn't go well. In shorthand it is a negative comment about past performance.

Positive Feedback

Although it may not be the first thing that comes to your mind, you are certainly familiar with positive feedback. Even though we don't give or receive enough of this (more on that later), we do know what it is. It is a comment about past performance that did go well. In shorthand—positive comments about past performance.

You may be thinking there are really just these two types of feedback, but we said we would share four with you. Now let's talk about the two you might not have thought about.

While most people think of feedback as positive or negative, that tells only part of the story. As important as it is to learn from the past, we only look at the past as a guide to adapting, changing, or improving *future* performance.

Instead of focusing only on the past, why not make your intentions perfectly clear and use the past to give people advice about what to do *the next time*? Or look at it this way: if we are giving feedback or coaching to help people to do better in the future, shouldn't we focus on the future? After all, past performance is past and outside of anyone's control. But future performance can be controlled by the performer and influenced by the coach (that is you!).

Given this, let's consider the other two types of feedback, or rather, feed*forward*—which we define as future-focused advice and counsel.

Negative Feedforward

This type of feedback helps people see what not to do in the future. It refers to past performance as context for advice about the future. It is especially effective in emergency or crisis situations. It is the "whatever you do, don't push that button" kind of feedback. It is advice about things not to do in the future. In shorthand it is explicitly stating things to avoid or to not do in the future.

Positive Feedforward

The final type of feedback helps people see what to do in the future. It, too, refers to past performance as context for future performance. It provides advice about what to keep doing or start doing that will lead to better results. In shorthand it is speaking about things to start or keep doing in the future.

FIVE REASONS TO CONSIDER FEEDFORWARD
No translation required. If you have ideas about what to do—or not to do next time—why not share them? From your place of expertise, the tendency is to give feedback assuming that people will know what or how to change or adapt next time. When you give clear feedforward you aren't assuming, so there will be no translation required.

It can be faster. Sometimes leaders spend a long time trying to give the feedback in a way that people will accept and understand. In these cases it is often much faster to just give some clear directions on what to do next time. You know this is true because in a crisis or overloaded work situation this is what you probably do—and it works. Remember that feedforward isn't only effective, it can also be faster.

It can be more readily accepted. There can be lots of defensiveness and denial when people keep hearing about their past performance. People are usually less defensive when receiving advice about what to do in the future. Because it is future focused, feedforward is often accepted—and therefore used more readily than past-focused feedback.

We can't change the past. Maybe this should have been first on the list. People can learn from the past, but they can't change it. This is why feedback is still important—if we focus solely on the future our advice may become too directive (do this and this, but not that). Yet if you only think about the past, you aren't creating the desired future either. Focus some of your conversation and coaching on what you *can change*—which is the future. In other words, in order for feedback to be constructive (which everyone professes to want), it must be about what you can do next time.

Feedforward creates an upward spiral. You are having a conversation about performance because you want people to grow, to succeed, to be more productive, and to be happy in their work. Right? Using feedforward as a tool helps you move people in an upward, engaged spiral of performance.

Your Now Steps

1. Analyze the recent feedback you have given, noting how balanced between positive and negative, past and future it was.

2. Recognize your weakest areas.

3. Give someone feedback today, consciously making it more balanced than it would have been before you read this chapter.

27

HOW TO USE THE FOUR TYPES OF FEEDBACK

Now that you know the four types of feedback, the obvious question is, How do you use that knowledge to give better feedback and help people create better results?

We are glad you asked. Here are several suggestions.

Not One, But All

As you might have guessed, the key to your maximum success with feedback is to use all four types—a balance of positive and negative, feedback and feedforward. Timing and placement of these will come with practice and thought, but all four play a crucial role in people's understanding the entirety of their performance and how to continue to improve.

 To get deeper insights into how to use all four types of feedback, go to the Bonus Bytes page at BudToBossCommunity.com and click on the Four Types button.

A Caution About Negative Feedforward

Having said that all four types of feedback have their place, negative feedforward does have an Achilles' heel. As mentioned before, it is a great tool in times of urgency, crisis, or safety issues and the like. At the same time, it can create a focus problem. Let us explain.

If you have a small child who wants to play outside, you are probably happy to let him, and you want him to be safe. One of the cardinal rules we all know about outdoor safety is where to play—namely, *not* in the street. With this thought in mind, there are two ways you can give a child feedback in this area. You can use negative feedforward—"Don't play in the street." Or you can use positive feedforward—"Play in the grass." If your child follows either piece of advice he will be safely away from the street, right? This is true, but these two statements aren't received the same way by our brains. (Remember this concept from Chapter Twenty-Two?)

Since our minds have a hard time decoding the opposite of any idea (for example, "please don't hesitate to call"), it is a more difficult mental process. When people hear "stay out of the street," they hear "street" first and then have to process the "not" part of the message. When the negative feedforward is repeated, we are actually implanting a repeated message that we don't want ("street" or "hesitate"). Negative feedforward should be used judiciously, and when used, done in tandem with positive feedforward (in other words, "Stay out of the street *and* play in the grass")—and the positive feedforward should be used far more frequently.

Use (Much) More Positive

Tons of research, and our intuition, tell us that we need to give more positive feedback and have more positive conversations in the workplace (more on this point in Chapter Thirty, "How Do You Show Your Support?"). Here are the compelling results from research done by Marcial Losada and Barbara Frederickson, both noted researchers in Positive Psychology. Losada calculated that a ratio of positive to negative comments of 2.9013:1 (let's call it 3:1) is an important benchmark. The research indicates that it takes about three positive feelings, experiences, expressions, thoughts, pieces of feedback or observation, and so on to fend off the languishing effects of one negative. This 3:1 tipping point is called the *Losada Line*.

Their research found that "high ratios of positive to negative affect (emotion) would distinguish individuals [and teams] who flourish from those who [languish]." These higher levels of positivity above 3:1 are linked with "(a) broader behavioral repertoires, (b) greater flexibility and resilience to adversity, (c) more social resources, and (d) optimal functioning." In terms we can all understand, more positive feedback, conversation, and emotions lead to greater flexibility, greater determination, better relationships, and better performance, among other things.

These findings beg the question: Is it possible to have too much of the good thing?

Apparently so—Losada also found an upper limit of the positive influence at about 12 positives to 1 negative (12:1). Beyond this point, the enhanced flexibility, determination, relationships, and performance no longer improved with more positive feedback. Why? The implication is that being too positive can be perceived as false.

The reality is that in any workplace we have experienced or consulted with, there is little danger of getting anywhere close to the 12:1 ceiling. Given that observation, we suggest that you first get above the 3:1 minimum and not worry too much about the 12:1 ceiling.

Arguments for and Against More Positive Feedback (and Feedforward)

We think we have just given you a very powerful reason for giving more positive feedback, and we suspect there are still doubts and questions in your mind. We've heard the concerns hundreds of times. Let us address them now.

- ○ *People already know.*
  "I don't need to give them positive feedback. They already know they are doing a good job." Maybe this is true. Even if they do, the positive reinforcement is valuable and keeps their momentum and focus high. Being recognized is a deep human need.
- ○ *Why do I need to give them positive feedback for doing their job?* To which we respond, you don't have to unless you want them to continue doing their job and to keep striving to do it better.
- ○ *People don't want/need to hear it.*

This is a combo excuse of the previous two. Just because people work hard and don't ask for positive feedback doesn't mean they wouldn't appreciate it. Two reasons people don't ask:

- The sparse positive feedback they get is so vague that it is unhelpful and sometimes perceived as insincere.
- They've never seen really consistent and plentiful feedback at work, so they don't know it is even possible.

○ *I don't want them to get big headed.*

The argument here is that we don't want people to become complacent or that we don't want to exceed the 12:1 ratio mentioned above. But let us ask you three questions.

- Do you do your best work when you are confident and feeling good about your potential for success?
- Would more specific details about what you are doing well help you in this area?
- Is your workplace close to exceeding the 12:1 positive:negative ratio?

We think the answers to these questions are: yes, yes, and no. The reality is that people receive so little positive feedback that you are far from having to worry about complacency (at least from this cause).

○ *I don't really notice the positive things others do.*

This is the most insidious of all the reasons. Remember the example of the RAS in Chapter Four, "How to Get the Most from This Book"? Here is how your brain works: you see what you are looking for. So we ask you, "What are you looking for?" If you want to give more positive feedback and feedforward, you must look expectantly for what people are doing well. Don't worry, you won't miss or ignore the opportunities for negative comments—they will show themselves too.

Your Now Step

We'll make it really simple.

1. Give more positive feedback and feedforward. Start building that habit today.

28

HOW TO GIVE FEEDBACK

With the sources and types of feedback as background, let's get practical! What follows are nine specific tips for giving feedback that has the best chance to be understood, accepted, and applied.

Honest, Genuine, Sincere

None of the rest of these tips will matter if your feedback is seen as a ploy or a manipulative technique. Your feedback must be honest, and it must be viewed as your honest assessment. You should be tactful, honest, genuine, and direct. Recognize that if the feedback is negative in nature it might be hard for the person to receive. This doesn't mean you should be less honest or sincere. On the flip side when people don't perceive positive feedback as honest or sincere, you would have been better off saying nothing at all.

Specific

All of the feedback and feedforward you give—both positive and negative—needs to be specific: behaviors, words, results, and so forth. Although we are typically better at making corrective feedback specific, too often our positive feedback sounds like a vague "nice job." It may be harder to make your comments specific, but that is why you are the leader—you can handle it.

Balanced and Complete

You may have read or heard that you should "sandwich" your negative feedback between positive feedback at the start and finish. This is really good advice, *if done correctly*—which it rarely is. In theory, the concept gives you a 2:1 ratio of positive to negative, but it often falls short because the negative is typically very specific, whereas the positive is usually vague, or worse, insincere. The goal should be complete and balanced feedback, in a great ratio of positive–negative and past–future.

To get a complete look at the Feedback Sandwich and how to make it most appetizing and healthy (sorry, we couldn't resist), go to the Bonus Bytes page at BudToBossCommunity.com and click on the Feedback Sandwich button.

Constructive, Helpful

You now know what makes your feedback more constructive—when you talk about how people can apply it next time. When you use feedforward appropriately, you will be providing helpful and constructive feedback.

In Context

Feedback will also be more helpful and more easily accepted and understood when it is given in the proper context. Help people understand the situation as you see it. Make the feedback about workplace behaviors, not personality or style differences. Certain behaviors might make sense or be effective in one situation but not in another. If this is the case, point it out. When you give feedback that acknowledges these things you will be more successful.

With Clear Intention

Make sure your intention is clear for yourself first. Then make it as clear as you can for the other person. Do all you can to give feedback with the intention of helping someone succeed and feel good about her growth and progress. If you keep your intention pure and focused on helping the other person, your feedback will be far more successful.

With Data

It will be easier for people to accept your feedback (though it is no guarantee) if you can share data. Do you have mistake logs, productivity reports, quality indicators, or timeliness data? Providing hard data that can start the conversation and begin to build a need for a change or recognition of a problem (or grand success) will be enormously helpful. Data can also come in the form of first-hand observation. You can and should include your thoughts on the person's performance. When you include data, too, you make it much more effective by removing the perception of subjectivity. (There is more advice about sharing your thoughts in Chapter Forty on assertive communication.)

Focused on Behaviors

Feedback should always be focused on what people did or said, not what you thought they were thinking, your assumptions about their intentions, or the way they have "always performed." This one is always important and is especially so as a new supervisor of your former peers. Your feedback needs to be based on their actual behaviors, and not on their reputation, or historical success or failure.

From the Accepted Perspective

Remember the three sources of feedback in Chapter Twenty-Six? For your feedback to be most effective, it must be given from a source that makes sense to the receiver. Back to our example of Kevin and his son Parker in that chapter. . . . If Kevin wants his feedback to Parker to be heard, he shouldn't start with, "You know Parker, I remember when I started college, and so you might want to consider . . ." Since (right now) he doesn't have credibility with Parker from the expertise source on this issue, he will be more successful if his feedback comes from a place of relationship or possibly even position. Remember, it doesn't matter that Kevin really does have expertise regarding college life; from Parker's perspective, that source is questionable.

Beyond these nine keys there are some other considerations that are very important as well. Keep these in mind, too, whenever you are giving feedback to others.

Physical Environment

The physical environment and situation for the feedback can make a big difference in the impact the feedback has. Here are a couple of examples.

- ○ *Where.* Where you give your feedback can make a difference. Is it noisy? Are there lots of distractions? There are enough challenges with communication in general, and feedback and coaching specifically, that you will want to reduce the noise and distractions. If you work on a factory floor, for example, you might want to move to a different location to give feedback whenever possible. Or if you are giving feedback over the phone, it might not be best when one party is driving or in an airport. (Don't get us started on all the places we have seen people having what seem to be serious conversations on their cell phones.)
- ○ *Public or private.* The prevailing wisdom is to give praise or positive feedback in public and negative feedback in private. Generally speaking, this is a fine rule of thumb. A better piece of advice is to consider the receiver and his wishes. There are some people (Kevin's wife Lori comes to mind) for whom praise in public isn't truly valued. If a person doesn't like to be singled out or if he might get embarrassed by that praise, don't give it in a public forum. Simply stated, give people any type of feedback in ways and locations that will work best for them.

Timing

In most cases, the closer the feedback can be given to the performance the better. When you shrink the time between performance and feedback, you allow for clearer memories and more specific details of the past performance to be analyzed by both parties. In addition, in the work environment, behaviors are often repeated. So delaying feedback means that someone may continue to do something incorrectly or ineffectively (or be unaware of what she is doing well). The worst case here of course is the annual performance review. (More on that in the next chapter.)

Given that rule of thumb, life and work situations can sometimes get in the way of immediate feedback. Here are some considerations relating to the timing of your feedback.

- ○ *For them.* Is the timing right for them? If the performance just ended they may be stressed, excited, or unable to focus on feedback at that time. For example: a colleague just finished giving a presentation in front of senior executives. Pulling her aside when she sits back down is too soon!
- ○ *For you.* Make sure you give the feedback when you are ready. If you are stressed, exuberant, or upset, now might not be the best time. Give the feedback when you are in a position and a frame of mind to give the feedback successfully.
- ○ *As soon as possible.* All that being said, it is still important to give any feedback as quickly as possible.

 For some further thoughts on the differences between feedback and advice and how to use both as a leader, go to the Bonus Bytes page at BudToBossCommunity.com and click on the Advice button.

How to Receive Feedback

One more thing. The best coaches also receive coaching. And one of the best ways to give better feedback is to get better at receiving feedback. When that happens, you are better able to put yourself in the shoes of the other person and give more helpful and successful feedback.

 For more details on receiving feedback successfully, go to the Bonus Bytes page at BudToBossCommunity.com and click on the Receive Feedback button.

Your Now Step

1. Select one of the keys for giving better feedback and practice it within the next two days.

29

PERFORMANCE EVALUATIONS IN THE REAL WORLD

Both of us have a good deal of experience with formal performance evaluations—we have both received them as employees of large multinational companies, we have both given them, and we have both worked with and consulted a variety of companies who use performance evaluations.

Although we have all of that experience, we obviously can't speak to the specifics of your organization's process or form. And that doesn't really matter, because while some of the details of your process may differ, the majority of performance evaluation processes are the same in the most important ways. So if you let go of the details of your form and the timeline of when they are due, you will get more from this chapter.

Consider this the nondenominational approach to using performance evaluations effectively.

Here is what we do know, with some degree of certainty, about your process.

- There is an annual cycle. Your process may suggest or require quarterly or semiannual meetings, but the focus is probably on an annual cycle.
- There is a form. Too often this form becomes the focus or goal of the process. No one designs the process that way, but far too often, someone is making sure that every supervisor is turning in the form for every employee. When that happens, the deadly shift in focus has begun.

Effective performance reviews must be focused on performance, not on forms. Forms can facilitate discussion and clarity, and may be needed for other organizational purposes, but as leaders you can't allow the form to take precedence over the performance.

- There is a meeting. You probably received some training about how to conduct "the meeting." All of us have experience as the employee at "the meeting," and if you are a new leader you may not yet have experience on the other side of the table. If you don't yet have that experience, or if your experience on either side of the table has been less than stellar, read on—that is what this chapter is about.
- We all (as leaders and employees) have experience and opinions about the process, and they are probably not all great.

With all of that as a backdrop, let's talk about how to make your annual performance review process work for you and for those you coach and lead.

Warning: Any internal grumbling, cynicism, and victimization should end here. Regardless of your organization's process and how messed up it might be in your opinion, we are going to talk about six steps you can take to make it work for you and your team. Everything in this chapter is in your ability to influence if you choose to make it so, and it will all work within the confines of your specific process.

Six Keys to Making Performance Reviews Work for You

By this point in the book, you probably realize that our focus is on giving you practical insights and observations rather than long, drawn-out theoretical discussions. There are entire books written on this one topic. So, as is the case in other parts of the book, we are giving you, from our perspective, the six most important things to consider as you plan for and deliver performance reviews.

Make It Ongoing

The single biggest problem with the annual performance review is with the *annual* part. How can anyone improve or adjust his course successfully if he only receives feedback once per year? If your kids only got feedback on their writing skills once per year, you'd be picketing the school. If the coach only gave the basketball players feedback on last year's performance at the start of the new season, they'd be mocked on talk radio and fired. Is once a year really often enough to give people feedback on their work performance?

Yes, you have to fill out the form at the end of the year, and you can also have ongoing conversation about people's success and challenges all year long. Whether formal or informal (and a good rule of thumb is that there should be some of each), you should think about your feedback and coaching as a process and not as an event.

Avoid Surprises

If you are doing the ongoing-process suggestion correctly, there is nothing that shows up on the "final" performance evaluation that should surprise the receiver. If you are having ongoing conversations, why would there be? The only possibility would be if something new happened with someone's performance on a project or with a customer in the short time since the most recent conversation. Make it your goal that there are no surprises.

NO SURPRISES

Guy once had a workshop participant tell him about one of her performance review experiences. After about twelve months on the job, she walked into the first performance review meeting with her boss. She had received many verbal thanks and congratulations on her work. So she was expecting to receive a positive review.

As she sat down with her boss, he immediately confronted her with a report showing that she had violated one company policy twenty times in the past year, and there was no mention of the positive things that she had done. This was the first time she was notified of the policy or that she had violated it. Her boss did not give her the opportunity to fix her mistakes. He just kept track of them and dropped them on her at the end of the year.

Though she didn't quit on the spot, she also didn't stay with that employer very much longer. She moved on to become a good worker (eventually promoted to supervisor) with a different employer.

Her boss let the *same mistake* happen nineteen times too many, and he allowed a good employee to leave the company.

Make It a Conversation

Most performance reviews end up being the leader sharing a bunch of feedback and the employee making a few comments at the end. While we have never seen a process designed with this as the intention, it typically ends up this way. We'll share much more about this in Chapter Thirty-One ("A Practical Coaching Model..."), but in short, good performance evaluations are a conversation. If it is all about the other person's performance, why wouldn't that person be doing *at least* half of the talking?

Create Ownership

In the end, don't you want employees to own their behavior, their results, and their plans for improvement? The best way to promote ownership is to create conversation in your feedback and coaching sessions. When people are sharing their ideas and are involved in a conversation about their performance, they can't help but own the outcome.

Want more help with this idea? Learn about five specific ways to create greater ownership with your coaching or performance management process by going to the Bonus Bytes page at BudToBossCommunity.com and clicking on the Create Ownership button.

Reduce Fear and Anxiety

Another one of the biggest problems with most performance evaluation processes is that "the meeting" is filled with anxiety. If you had a meeting once a year, knew that you might get some surprises about your performance, and expected to get lectured by your boss (from a position of power) as she walks through comments on a daunting form—wouldn't you be a little stressed? Or put another way, have you ever been stressed about a performance evaluation in the past?

If you follow the other suggestions in this chapter you will reduce this anxiety significantly. But recognize it won't go away immediately. Acknowledge how people are feeling before and during the meeting. Do everything you can to make them feel more comfortable and more engaged in the process. When you do that, everyone wins.

See the Form as an Outcome, Not the Purpose

Repeat after us. "It isn't about the form." Your form may be either unwieldy or elegant. And it doesn't matter. It isn't about the form. Yes, the form must be filled out. As you are doing the other things in this chapter, the form *will be* filled out. More important, what is on the form will be more meaningful and will have greater positive impact on people's future performance—which is why we do it anyway.

 For more thoughts on how to use your performance management form as a part of a successful conversation, go to the Bonus Bytes page at BudToBossCommunity.com and click on the Review Form button.

Some Final Notes

1. Everything in this chapter probably seems like common sense to you. It is. But common sense, as it is often said, isn't common practice. You, as a new leader, have the chance to apply this wisdom, even though it may not be common or expected by those you lead. Prepare to encounter initial resistance, because what you will be doing will be new. Use what you learned in the change section as your guide to moving through that acceptance. The changes we suggest in this chapter are in your control. Take control.

2. As you do these things, you will get better results, and your team members will appreciate it, and probably start to talk. Don't be surprised if you become an organizational star in this regard. If so, any acclaim you receive will be well earned. Smile and accept it.

3. As you make this work as a leader, you can then model these things as an employee. It is also in your ability to influence your review process.

Though this is likely to go beyond the scope of your control, you might be interested in an article Kevin wrote suggesting the abolishment of formal performance reviews. To get your copy go to the Bonus Bytes page at BudToBossCommunity.com and click on the Performance Review button.

Your Now Steps

There is plenty to work on in this chapter, but here is the easiest and most immediate place to start.

1. Give someone some feedback informally today.
2. If you have a situation in which some more specific conversation might be needed, schedule a more formal meeting with that person today. Get it on the calendar. Even if the formal review was last month or last week, schedule a meeting. Remember you are now thinking *process,* not *event.*

30

HOW DO YOU SHOW YOUR SUPPORT?

If you ask ten people to give you descriptors of the best coaches they have experienced, chances are seven or more will mention feeling supported by their coaches. Underline and highlight the following fact in your personal thinking about coaching.

The best coaches are supportive.

Knowing and agreeing with that idea is one thing. Knowing what that means, and being able to identify and consistently exhibit the behaviors, is something else entirely. That is the point of this chapter: to identify and explain ten specific behaviors that will be seen as supportive by others, and therefore to help you be a better coach.

Ten Supportive Behaviors

As you read this list of supportive behaviors, think about how you can apply these ideas in your interactions with the members of your team. Think about both the informal, frequent, everyday interactions and the formal, infrequent, coaching and performance review interactions.

Collaborate

As a leader or supervisor, you cannot do everyone's work, or do their work for them. You must, of course, delegate and empower others to do their work. And yet as a leader you must create a sense of shared ownership. You need to see yourself (and the team needs to see you) as a part of the team. While your role may be different, you are still a part of the team. When you see yourself as part of the team and consistently act that way, others will feel supported in their actions. Remember that delegation isn't the same as abdication. To keep that difference clear in you mind, you must see yourself as a collaborator.

Help, Assist

Along this same line, we support others when we are willing to lend a hand. Kevin's earliest and best experience with this was with his father. Growing up on a farm that raised hogs commercially meant that there were some (very) unpleasant jobs to be done. On many occasions he remembers being given these unsavory jobs while his dad was away at a meeting or attending to other farm-related business. In most every case, if he returned from the meeting while Kevin was still at the unsavory task, he changed his clothes and picked up a pitchfork or shovel. Perhaps you lead a team or individuals with tasks you can't do directly. If that is the case, you can still assist. Find out what you can do to help the team when the timeline is short and the work is long. Make sure your help is really helpful, welcomed, and seen in the spirit it is intended (and not seen as micromanaging, checking in, hovering or something else with a negative connotation).

Empathize

To empathize is to understand how the other person feels. One of the most valuable things you can ever do is to let people know that you understand how they are feeling. You may not agree with their perspective. You may think there are actions they could have taken to avoid the situation they find themselves in. These may be points of coaching at the appropriate time. But to empathize first is one of the most supportive things you can do for another person or group.

Recognize Someone's Value

The best and fastest way we know to describe this idea is this—our children don't always exhibit behaviors we approve of, yet we will always love our children. When you let people know that you value them as individuals, you are supporting them. And when you have to give negative feedback about their performance, remember to separate their performance from who they are. You are supportive when you care about people and show it (and don't just say it).

Recognize Their Goals and Interests

People are more than their on-the-job performance. When you know something about people's strengths, interests, and long-term objectives, you can often help them reach those objectives and support those interests. This recognition isn't about giving people complete freedom to do whatever they want to do on the job. To the contrary, you are supportive of others when you help them succeed in their current job and help them reach toward their personal and professional goals too.

Listen

We know we have already talked about listening. The fact that it shows up again proves how important it is! One of the most supportive things you can do for anyone is to (really) listen.

Stop what you are doing.

Remove the distractions.

Be quiet, and listen. When you listen, you show that you value her feelings and opinions. When you listen, you communicate that you care.

This idea may seem basic, but it is so powerful because most people are rarely truly listened to. When they are, it is meaningful and memorable. When the person listening is their leader or supervisor, it is even more supportive and more powerful.

Always remember the power of listening, especially when you are in a position of power or influence with the other person.

Give Positive Feedback and Feedforward

Do you want to be more supportive? Tell people more often what they are doing well and what they are doing right. Almost no one hears this type of feedback often enough. (Remember the Losada Line from Chapter Twenty-Seven?) Nearly everyone we know has a story about a specific piece of positive feedback they received in their life—often in their distant past. These positive events are so memorable for most people because they are so rare. Ask people to tell you their stories.

You'll be able to tell in their words and their eyes how powerful and supportive specific and genuine positive feedback can be.

Be Encouraging

Dictionary.com lists three definitions for the word *encourage:*

1. To inspire with courage, spirit, or confidence.
2. To stimulate by assistance, approval, etc.
3. To promote, advance, or foster.

We talked about definition #2 when we covered the ideas of collaboration and helping. When you recognize the goals and interests of others, you are far down the path of promoting, fostering, and advancing them—definition #3. This leaves us with definition #1. We can encourage others by sharing our confidence in their abilities to give them the courage to attempt new things. Showing your confidence in them can inspire their inner confidence. When you do these things you are clearly supporting both who they are and who they can become.

Create Positive Exchanges

Do you know people who seem to light up the room . . . when they leave? That is the opposite of what we are talking about! Make it your goal that every conversation, exchange, and encounter you have leaves the other person feeling good or better about himself, his situation, and his life in general. Though this benchmark may be very difficult to live up to, making this your goal will allow people to see you as a more supportive person.

Be Accountable

Yes, other people are ultimately responsible for their behavior and results. And yes, it is important that you cultivate that accountability in those you lead. At the same time, if you truly see yourself as on the same team as your employees, you have a responsibility, too. When a person is looking at her failures or shortcomings, you can take responsibility for helping her, providing resources, and doing what you can to help her succeed as you work with her to think about her next steps.

When you exhibit these behaviors in a genuine, authentic way you encourage and support people to become the very best they can be. And isn't that the goal of coaching anyway?

 Great coaches are supportive of those they coach.

Your Now Steps

You can put these ideas into practice immediately. Here's how:

1. Pick one of the behaviors from the list above to be your focus today. Exhibit and use that behavior in as genuine and sincere a way as possible.

2. Allow yourself to fail! It may not go perfectly, but don't let that deter you. Get started!

3. If you don't know the goals and interests of individuals on your team, make that a priority too. Pick one person and get started on learning that person's goals and interests before the end of the week.

31

A PRACTICAL COACHING MODEL TO HELP YOU SUCCEED AS A COACH

Up until this point of this section we have talked about many components of coaching and how to use those pieces and parts. Now we want to tie it all together for you with a model.

In real life, most coaching happens in some sort of meeting, whether formal or informal, long or short. And as you will see in Chapter Thirty-Two, one of the most important keys to any meeting is to have a plan. The model we are going to show you is that planning tool for coaching.

Consider this model a roadmap for your success in coaching others. It can be used in a micro way to help you determine what you need to do right now in a conversation, and it can be used in a macro way as a roadmap for helping an individual improve (or overcome a performance issue) over a period of days, weeks, or months.

In *Remarkable Leadership,* Kevin introduced a practical and simple coaching model. This is a model he has implemented with organizations to use both from a supervisor perspective and for peer coaching. Our goal for this chapter is to introduce this model to you and to give you some insights as to how you can use it.

About the Model

Before we look at the specifics, notice the layout of the model in Figure 31.1.

Figure 31.1. A Coaching Model

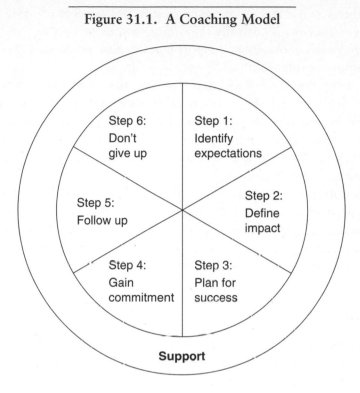

It Is Circular

Real life isn't typically linear. This model is circular to show that while there are steps, coaching and learning are more fluid than that. In a given moment you may recognize you need to move to a different place in the model. That is OK. We built it in a circular way to remind you of and reinforce that fact.

It is also circular to match how we learn, which is in a circular and upwardly spiraling way. As we learn new things and apply them, we set new expectations, we raise our potential, and we build on those past successes.

The Outer Ring

The six steps sit on top of a bed of support. We talked specifically about support in the previous chapter. The steps individually and collectively work better when done in supportive and caring ways.

Whether you use this exact model or not, this concept of using supportive behaviors is critically important to your success in coaching. We won't talk more about support here because we already devoted a complete chapter to it!

In many ways we hope that you see this model as a way to apply many of the skills you have learned through this book so far. To execute these steps successfully requires your communication skills—including thinking about the style and approach of the other person, your listening skills, and more. To coach successfully requires understanding why people choose to change and how to help them do so. Integrating and applying those lessons here will help you at every step of this model. You will see that this is meant to be a collaborative process (more on that to come in the next section of the book). Finally, this model gives you a preview of goal-setting ideas that we will elaborate on in Part Six: Commitment to Success.

About the Steps

Rather than giving you all of the details of how to do these steps (that just might be the next book!), we urge you to take what you already know and apply what you are learning from this book to this model as you continue to master the craft of coaching.

We believe in you, and we believe that what follows will get you off to a great start.

Step 1: Identify Expectations

In order to coach someone successfully, you must be clear on where you are coaching her to. What are your expectations for her performance, her behavior? What are your near-term and long-term expectations for her? You need answers to these questions, but you need more than this—you also need to understand her expectations. Until each of you knows exactly what the other person expects and you have mutual agreement on those expectations, how can you hold her accountable for reaching them? Here are some tips for identifying and creating agreement on expectations:

o Create clearly defined expectations from your perspective.
o Find out her picture of success and her expectations of her performance.

- Share your expectations *after* hearing hers.
- Be specific and descriptive.
- Gain mutual understanding and agreement on those expectations.
- Focus on one expectation at a time.
- Use "I" language as a way to communicate expectations more clearly. (For more details, see Chapter Forty.)

Step 2: Define Impact

This step comes directly from what we know about change. If you are coaching people to improve their performance (whether it is currently below needed standards or it is good and you are trying to take them to even higher performance), you are suggesting that people change. Since you already know that they must choose to change in order to change, you must help them make that choice. Remember that people do things for their reasons, not yours (and not the organizational reasons either). The key is to help them develop personal benefits for moving to the new level of performance.

Since these are personal benefits, the best place to start is by having them identify the benefits that they see. Once they have established the personal benefits as they see them, you can suggest others and reinforce what they have already described.

One challenge you may find at this step is complacency. Let's say that you have tried everything you can think of to define an impact and create a new future in their minds, and they still don't see a need to change (either because they don't share your expectations or they are pretty happy with the way things are—no dissatisfaction). Once you identify this lack of dissatisfaction, use what you have learned about the components of change to continue looking for ways to help them move forward.

 To learn some additional ways to overcome complacency (for yourself or those you are coaching) go to the Bonus Bytes page at BudToBossCommunity.com and click on the Complacency button.

Step 3: Plan for Success

Now you have clear expectations and a reason to move toward them. The next logical step is to build a plan to get there. The best plan will be one that is co-created with the people being coached, because it is harder for them to resist or defer a plan they helped create. Going one step further, we encourage you to have them lead the planning discussion, with you helping rather than you laying out a plan and saying, "What do you think?" The former will be more accurately viewed as their plan, while the latter is likely to be seen as your plan. As with every other step in this process, you want to engage the people being coached, because all the effort is about and for them. We will talk more about this step in Part Six: Commitment to Success.

Step 4: Gain Commitment

Once a plan is in place, you want to gain their commitment to follow it to its intended results. The only way to gain commitment is to ask for it. If you don't get it, or if you sense there is hesitancy or resistance, stop, slow down, and explore the resistance. Consider a question such as, What do we need to adjust in this plan in order to deepen your commitment to achieving it? (Your actual questions will be personalized, of course, but this gives you a starting point.)

Your goal is for them to state their commitment to you. This step crystallizes the communication so far and removes all ambiguity about responsibility and accountability (but only if they state their commitment). Though all of the steps in this coaching model are important, without the commitment to action, the rest of your coaching efforts could be little more than an exercise in futility and the creation of frustration for both parties.

Step 5: Follow Up

You have a plan and a commitment, but we know that even with the best intentions, there is no guarantee the plan will be followed. The reasons can vary widely, and at some level the reasons don't matter (at least at first). Performance is a process. Coaching is a process, too—the best coaches always follow up. Once a plan is in place and there is commitment to implementing it, it is your responsibility to check in, to see how things are going, and to offer assistance and feedback as necessary. This is your chance to provide encouragement and reinforcement. You may find in your follow-up that you encounter fresh or renewed resistance. If so, this is your clue to roll back in the model to step 2 to redefine the impact and help reinforce the person's choice to change his or her behavior.

This follow-up isn't a one-time "check it off your to-do list" kind of thing either—follow-up is ongoing until the new expectations are consistently met, and you start the process over again.

Step 6: Don't Give Up

The logical step beyond following up is to not give up. Your people are worth your best efforts. You need their performance, and when you know they are capable of it, you will stick with them. People may start to lose momentum or hope. Their attention or focus might get diverted, but by following this process you should minimize this likelihood.

This step implies more than just scheduling another meeting. Great coaches have patience, courage, and discipline. Keep believing in people even if they begin to lose belief in themselves. This commitment will prove your compassion and caring, provide you with relationship benefits, and help people reach their performance goals. It is also one of the most meaningful things you can do as a leader.

More on How to Use the Model

Now that you have seen and understand the model a bit more, let's talk about some ways you can use it.

Planning for a Meeting

If you are planning for a coaching meeting (whether a performance evaluation meeting or otherwise), using this model will help you be well prepared. If you are planning for a performance evaluation, your form will help, but this model may be of additional assistance in the process. If your session isn't using that form, thinking through these steps, especially steps 1 through 3, will help you be better prepared for your coaching session.

During a Meeting

During a coaching meeting it is easy to get off track. If you have your model in front of you (or the plan you created from it), it can help you stay on track and on target for the most effective conversation.

As a Bigger Process

This model can be used as much more than a planning or meeting tool. As you now know, some of the steps take place outside of a single meeting anyway. One way to look at this model is as a philosophy of coaching that you build out of your learning, practice, and available tools. Then, as you add new skills and tools, you will be able to fit them into these steps (much like what you have already learned about how communication and change fit in).

Your Now Steps

1. Think about one of your employees who you feel isn't performing to potential (even if he is meeting job requirements).
2. Schedule a coaching session with him.
3. Prepare for it.
4. Use this model to coach him to even higher performance.

A Special Note

Two of the questions we receive regularly in workshops, and that we promised to answer, belong in this section. We decided to provide them as Bonus Bytes so we could go into greater depth than we would have been able to do in the book. Here they are:

 For insights on answering the question, "How do I discipline my friends?" go to the Bonus Bytes page at BudToBossCommunity.com and click on the Discipline Friends button.

 To answer to the question, "How do I get lazy people to work?" go to the Bonus Bytes page at BudToBossCommunity.com and click on the Lazy People button.

PART V

COLLABORATION

In this section, we give you greater understanding of the process a group goes through as it grows from being a group of individuals to becoming a team. We also cover some of the important skills you will need to develop for yourself and in your team to help your team achieve better results.

We address the following:

○ Ways to lead better meetings
○ Team dynamics
○ A model for diagnosing the current condition of your team
○ Conflict resolution

In previous chapters, much of what we have covered addressed your personal mind-set, your personal behaviors, or your interactions with one other person. This section shifts the focus a bit to include the skills and mind-sets it takes to work with a group of people. Many of the skills in this section will also apply to one-on-one interactions, but we are adding a layer of complexity by including, and in some cases focusing on, situations in which multiple interactions happen simultaneously. The additional complexity does make these skills a bit more challenging. Don't worry, though, you can learn to successfully apply these concepts.

As we have done in previous sections, let's take a moment for you to do a quick self-assessment to help you focus your efforts as you read this section.

Self-Assessment

Answer these questions about your current team-building and collaboration skills and approaches using the following scale of 1 to 7 on each question:

1   Almost never
2   Rarely or seldom
3   Occasionally
4   Sometimes
5   Usually
6   Frequently
7   Almost always

I know what to do to make my team meetings productive.   _____

  (Chapter 32)

I understand my role as team leader in meetings.   _____

  (Chapter 32)

I know how to accurately and objectively assess my team's performance.   _____

  (Chapters 33, 34, 35)

I know how to help my team achieve success as a team.   _____

  (Chapters 34, 35)

I understand how conflicts start and escalate.   _____

  (Chapters 36, 37)

I know what to do to stop conflict escalation.   _____

  (Chapters 38, 39)

I understand how to quickly and effectively help my team resolve conflicts. _____

(Chapter 38)

I understand and know how to use assertive communication techniques. _____

(Chapter 40)

Based on your self-assessment, you now have a starting point for understanding where you need to focus your attention as you read this section. Remember to read all chapters in this section without skimming through the areas in which you have greater strength.

Thoughts About Collaboration and Teamwork—From Others and Us

The way a team plays as a whole determines its success. You may have the greatest bunch of individual stars in the world, but if they don't play together, the club won't be worth a dime.

—Babe Ruth, baseball player

Although it is possible that the people you lead are a group of individuals with their own respective tasks that do not depend on working cooperatively with others, it is more probable that they actually need to work together to get things done. If that is the case, you are likely to be evaluated, at least in part, on the level of collaboration and teamwork that you can create.

Individual commitment to a group effort—that is what makes a team work, a company work, a society work, a civilization work.

—Vince Lombardi, Hall of Fame football coach

Teams are, at their core, a collection of individuals with a common goal. Your job is to connect with individuals in a way that leads them to develop a commitment to the common goal. This is in many ways what this part of the book is all about.

Coming together is a beginning. Keeping together is progress. Working together is success.

—Henry Ford, industrialist

As individuals grow together to become a team, the group goes through a series of predictable stages. One of the stages creates a great risk of the team coming apart before it gets to high-level performance. When you understand the process and have the skills to navigate the trouble spots, you can keep the group together until it becomes a high-performing team.

HOW YOU CAN APPLY THE SEVEN KEYS TO BETTER MEETINGS

Do you like to attend or lead meetings? If you're like most people we have met in our workshops and consulting work, you have been in your share of bad meetings. It seems that meetings are the one thing that almost everyone loves to hate. Jokes about bad meetings show up almost everywhere you look. In movies and on television shows, people love to ridicule meetings. And we still must have meetings for teams to get information, solve problems, and plan for the future.

Here's the good news, meetings do not have to be boring, unfocused, and long. They can be on-target, efficient, and productive. When you apply the Seven Keys to Better Meetings, you will put yourself on the road to leading these types of positive meetings.

If you already have successful experience leading meetings, this chapter will serve as a refresher for you. If you didn't lead meetings before you moved into your new role, this chapter will introduce some tips for making your meetings more productive.

The Seven Keys to Better Meetings

1. *Plan them in advance.* Remember this axiom: proper prior planning prevents a poor performance. If you plan the meeting, you improve the odds of success. Your planning should include thoughts about
   - What's the purpose?
   - What do we want to accomplish?

- Given the answers to the first two questions, is a meeting the most effective way to reach these goals? (That is, should we meet at all?)
- Who is responsible for bringing information to the meeting?
- What role will each person play in the meeting?

2. *Have a written agenda.* The meeting agenda should be available to attendees prior to the meeting, and it should include at least these items:

- What are the desired outcomes?
- How will each desired outcome be addressed?
- Who is responsible for presentation or other tasks?
- Time allotted for each outcome?

For a template of a meeting agenda with a description of how to use it go to the Bonus Bytes page at BudToBossCommunity.com and click on the Agenda Button.

3. *Have the right people in attendance.* Your meetings should include anyone

- With important information to offer
- With the power to decide
- With the power to block a decision
- Who is directly affected by decisions made at the meeting

As a general rule, plan to meet your objectives by including as few people in the meeting as possible.

4. *Create meeting rules.* People need to know what is and is not acceptable at your meetings. We have seen everything from three taps on the table with a pen to penalty flags thrown to keep the meeting on track. Depending on your team and their perspectives, you and your team can create any rules that keep the meeting in order and moving forward toward its goals. These rules will be most successful when they are understood and agreed to by everyone on the team. Your code of conduct can include these types of items:

- How to make and who makes decisions

- How roles are assigned and the expectations of each role
- What behaviors are and aren't appropriate during a meeting (side conversations, starting on time, and so on).

5. *Establish clearly defined roles.* Role assignments help people know how they can best contribute to the success of a meeting. Clearly defined roles also help you minimize some of the natural problems and challenges that develop during meetings:

- Traffic issues—Who speaks, and when do people speak?
- Procedural issues—these include questions such as, How long will we talk about a given topic? How do we address agenda changes? How do we decide a particular issue? How will we move forward if we can't reach agreement in a reasonable amount of time?
- Goal or content issues—What is the scope of the problem we are discussing? What is our decision-making authority?
- Record keeping—Who does it and what does it look like? (Make sure your record keeping includes capturing and maintaining the action items from the meeting.)

Not every meeting will have exactly the same role assignments. Different size meetings call for different arrangements. In general though, we recommend assigning the following roles for every meeting:

- Facilitator—Keeps the meeting moving and manages the process.
- Leader—Stays focused on the goals of the meeting. We normally recommend that the leader and facilitator be different people so that both roles can be managed well.
- Recorder—Keeps the meeting minutes or flipchart notes.
- Time keeper—Monitors progress against the agenda and helps the facilitator stay on track toward timely completion of the meeting.
- Team member—Everyone else (and a role that most people in the other roles will play concurrently).

6. *Document decisions and action items.* In most cases, if you have no task assignments, you had an ineffective meeting.

7. *Balance the process, the results, and the relationships.* A meeting is sort of like a dance between these three things. A successful

meeting acknowledges, values, and protects all three items. At the conclusion of a successful meeting you should have

- Documented decisions and action items (results)
- A timely end, with all items addressed in a successful and productive way (process)
- A team that can still function together (relationships)

As we said in the boat wake analogy in Chapter Eight, these are not either-or objectives. You cannot have a successful meeting if you sacrifice results or relationships for process. You will probably not get results or relationships if you have a bad process. If you follow the agenda perfectly, reach decisions, and yet alienate half the team, your meeting may still be a failure in the long run.

 Successful meetings balance process and relationship needs while they get results.

 If you would like more information on how to apply these Seven Keys to Better Meetings, go to the Bonus Bytes page at BudToBossCommunity.com and click on the Meetings button.

The Role of the Team Leader in Meetings

We find that it can be really difficult to stay focused on the content and outcome of a discussion (the leader role) while you simultaneously manage the flow of the discussion, keep track of the agenda, and monitor the timeline (the facilitator role). Given that, you will typically get better results by separating the roles of facilitator and leader. This separation of roles is particularly important when there are complex issues to discuss or when people might be particularly emotional about the topic of the discussion.

Since you will probably fill the role of team leader in the majority of the meetings you hold with your team, we have a few thoughts for you to help you fill this role most effectively.

The team (or meeting) leader...

Provides the Vision

Your team will look to you for direction about where you want to go. If you don't know where you want the meeting to go, your team will struggle. Be clear, state your desired outcomes, and describe what decisions and actions you want as a result of the meeting. You can negotiate with people on the specifics of the decision or action, and you should know where you want to get to by the end of the meeting.

Acts as an Energy Model

People will take cues from your enthusiasm (or lack thereof) for the meeting and the individual topics or sections. Set a high-energy expectation by showing commitment to and enthusiasm for the outcome of the meeting.

Cares About People and Their Success

The facilitator can manage the process and make sure that everyone gets a fair chance to speak. The role of showing personal concern for success of team members falls to you, their leader. While this is always your responsibility, during meetings your engagement and positive interaction with people are fully on display and demonstrate that you care about them and their success.

Makes the Call

In some situations, the ideal decision-making model is a variation or adaptation of consensus building in which everyone participates to some degree in the decision. However, this process is often very slow and deliberate, and you might not get there in the time you have for your meetings. If that is the case, the meeting leader makes decisions based on the discussion she heard during the meeting.

 For more perspectives on choosing the right decision-making model for your meetings, go to the Bonus Bytes page at BudToBossCommunity.com and click on the Decision Making button.

Your Now Steps

1. Think back to your last meeting. Did it go well? If it did, great! If not, look at the Seven Keys to Better Meetings and determine how you could have improved it.

2. The next time you have a meeting, take action to correct the mistakes of your last one.

33

UNDERSTANDING WHAT HAPPENS WHEN GROUPS BECOME TEAMS

Groups and teams are both made up of individuals. We contend that the biggest difference between a group and a team is organization around and alignment with a common goal. Teams are focused on achieving a common goal. Groups are not.

> **Remarkable Principle** — **Every team is a group, but not every group is a team.**

One of your responsibilities as a leader is to help the group that you lead to become a team. Maybe you already have the good fortune of leading a highly functioning team that knows how to get things done. If this describes you, you are in the lucky minority! The more common case we have seen is that you have inherited a group of people that is somewhere between all individuals working totally on their own and the whole group working collectively and collaboratively as a team.

We have each been on teams, led teams, and coached, consulted, or facilitated meetings for our client's teams. Both together and separately, we have seen a wide range of behaviors—good and bad—that contributed to overall team performance. From our research and our experience, we have developed a collection of tools that we find helpful to leaders as they work with their organizations in the process of growing from a group of individuals to a high-performing team.

When we introduced the concept of adjusting your communication style in Chapter Nineteen, we used the analogy of taking a trip in your car as a way to visualize the process of adapting to better communicate with others. That analogy also applies here. The team, or group, that you have is what you have. It is where it currently is because of a number of factors. If you want to lead that team to a new way of working together and interacting, you first need to assess where it is and where you want it to go. In other words, you have to clearly define the starting and ending points of your "trip" together as a team.

Just as there are predictable patterns of human behavior that we introduced with the DISC model, there are also predictable patterns of team development. When you understand the patterns, you can use the patterns as a guide for diagnosing or evaluating your current situation more objectively and for mapping where you want to go and how you want to get there.

One of the patterns we use to better understand team dynamics comes from a model describing the stages of team development proposed by Bruce Tuckman. His model, introduced in 1965 and shown in Figure 33.1, says that small groups go through four stages of development as they start to focus on a common goal and become a team.

To paraphrase Tuckman, in the Forming stage people begin the process of coming together; learning about each other's likes, dislikes, and preferences; clarifying the tasks to be accomplished; and defining the roles to be filled. In our experience, the most significant issues before the team at this stage stem from interpersonal, or people-related, concerns.

The Storming phase is when interpersonal conflicts start to develop as people start to wrestle with the relationship dynamics; the differences in perspective, problem solving, and approach to tasks among people; the assignment of specific roles; and the tension of determining group or team expectations and rules. There is some shift toward a task focus in this stage, and we see that the biggest team issues are still interpersonal ones.

In the Norming phase, teams start shifting their focus away from each other and more toward task accomplishment. The team is getting

---

Figure 33.1. Tuckman's Stages of Team Development Model

Forming ⟹ Storming ⟹ Norming ⟹ Performing

things done, and they are still a little tentative in their approach. We have noticed that the relative tentativeness of the team's approach comes from some sensitivity left over from the Storming phase and some continuing relationship development. The focus at this stage seems to be pretty evenly split between issues of task accomplishment and relationship development.

When a team reaches the Performing phase, they have developed an approach that sounds like: "Get it done. What's next on the agenda?" Team members generally operate at a high degree of trust and cooperation, and their relationship issues have mostly been addressed. As a result, the team is now ready to focus almost exclusively on the task.

In our work with teams, we see evidence of the stages that Tuckman suggested, and offer some additional insight. We see the process as less linear and more cyclical. In keeping with the original stage nomenclature for the sake of clarity and consistency, we see the model more like what is shown in Figure 33.2.

Many behavioral, psychological, and sociological researchers have studied and written about the process of group to team formation. The debate about the "right" or most "correct" way to describe or diagram the process is far beyond the scope of this book. We just want to give you greater insights about the overall process of moving from group to team so that you can apply this knowledge to better lead your team in your situation. In general, we see that most teams go through similar and predictable stages of development, and that

Figure 33.2. The Cyclical Nature of Team Development

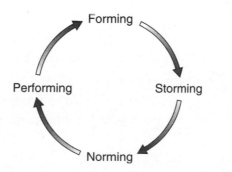

- ○ *The stages are not rigid, well-defined boxes.* Instead, they are general descriptions of what happens within a team over time.

- ○ *The phases are cyclical and fluid.* They do not happen in a linear and fixed pattern. In general, changing the nature of the task, the goal, the work process, the roles, or the team members starts the cycle over again. In other words, any change in membership, role assignment, goal, or work process can move a group that has become a team back to Forming. In our experience, team membership changes have the most significant and predictable impact. If you gain, lose, or replace a team member, you will go back to Forming. While you may move more quickly through the formation process the next time, you will go through it again.

- ○ *The stages do not necessarily happen exactly as shown.* The graphical representation of the stages is useful for helping you think about what is happening with your team. It is not a perfect representation of what happens in every situation. They are not clearly defined and distinct phases that happen perfectly in order. For example, a team operating at the Norming stage might slide back to the Storming phase if a change in task or role assignment happens before reaching the Performing stage. Or a team at the Performing stage might revert back to Storming on a given topic or situation.

- ○ *You need to focus on people issues first.* While the purpose of a team is to accomplish a common task or to achieve a common goal (task accomplishment issues), the initial factors that limit or hinder task accomplishment are mostly relational (people issues). This observation is consistent with what we observed in our discussion about the components of your leadership role in Chapter Six.

Your Now Steps

1. Stop for a moment and think about the behaviors and status of your team. Where are they in this process of team development?

2. Write down your answer and proceed to the next chapter, where you will learn how to move your team forward.

34

HOW TEAMS DEVELOP AND HOW YOU CAN HELP THEM

In the last chapter, we introduced a model that describes how groups become teams. The model is sort of interesting, and its real value comes in understanding how to apply it to *your* situation to diagnose what is happening within *your* team so that you know what to do as the leader to inspire your team to higher performance.

This chapter is focused on giving you a clear vision of where your team is at the moment and offering you practical suggestions for how to move it to the next stage of development.

Forming: The Transition from Individual to Group

What you may notice in the Forming stage:

- Members often feel anxious and uncomfortable.
- People don't know each other well yet.
- Tasks aren't clear.
- Roles aren't clear.
- Procedures aren't clear.
- Tension may be noticed.
- People don't understand leadership's role or goals.

What you can do to facilitate the transition from Forming to Storming:

○ Get to know each other and begin building relationships.
○ Discuss and build understanding of individual strengths, weaknesses, similarities, and differences.
○ Clarify the team's purpose, mission, and goals.
○ Focus all efforts on common goals.
○ Establish or clarify team operating procedures.
○ Identify tools and resources available to the team.
○ Clarify roles.
○ Determine the role of leadership and define or explain decision-making approaches.

Storming: The First Signs of Conflict

What you may notice in the Storming stage:

○ False conflicts—Behaviors are misunderstood or misinterpreted.
○ Contingent conflicts—Procedural or situational factors (such as meeting times, places, or formats).
○ Escalating conflicts—Beginning as simple disagreements, which then lead into more fundamental differences of opinion (in other words, venting personal hostilities, sharing deeply held ideas or emotions).
○ General frustration voiced during meetings and afterward.
○ Heightened levels of stress.
○ Less productivity than you (and even the team) want or need.

What you can do to facilitate the transition from Storming to Norming:

○ Surface and recognize the value of differences on the team.
○ Discuss the tension, the sources of the tension, and possible solutions.
○ View conflicts as a useful and valid part of teamwork and deal with them in an open and constructive manner.
○ Address the disagreements and provide time for appropriate conversation.

- Get everyone involved in these discussions.
- Address other issues that are causing challenges or reduced productivity.

Norming: The Cohesiveness Begins, and More Teamwork Starts Happening

What you may notice in the Norming stage:

- Conflict is replaced by a feeling of cohesiveness.
- A sense of unity or team identity develops.
- Members are highly involved.
- Members become more satisfied with the team and its progress.
- Members may experience higher self-esteem.
- Stress and anxiety are reduced.
- Members are more likely to accept or to be persuaded by team norms.
- Cooperation and collaboration begin to replace conflict as the prevalent features of team interaction.

What you can do to facilitate the transition from Norming to Performing:

- Develop (or continue to reinforce) a specific project management plan with a detailed timeline.
- Establish methods for solving problems and resolving conflicts.
- Build in feedback and evaluation mechanisms (individual and team performance).
- Establish or reinforce traditions or expectations for how the team works together.

Performing: The Goal!

What you may notice in the Performing stage:

- There is more focus on team goals and outputs than on process.
- Members understand and are loyal to each other and the team.
- Members play to each other's strengths.

- Members are clear on their roles but willing to assist others.
- Members are accountable to each other.
- High-quality work gets accomplished.
- More complex tasks can be managed.

What you can do at the Performing stage to keep forward progress:

- Push for implementation.
- Evaluate results and make adjustments.
- Learn from experience: take time to reflect on what is working and what isn't.
- Evaluate efficiency and strive for continuous improvement.
- Recognize and reward team success over individual success.
- Help the team realize how successful they are. (This will help them see how to get back there in the future!)

Your Now Steps

1. Look back at your answer to the Now Steps from the last chapter. Now look at the specific tips we offer for helping your team move through the cycle to the Performing stage. Identify two or three actions you could implement in the next 72 hours to help your team improve.
2. Schedule time to take the actions you identified in step 1.

35

HOW YOU CAN ACHIEVE
GREATER TEAM SUCCESS

When we spoke about succeeding in your transition to leadership, we said that as a leader you can compare leadership problems to the problems faced by a craftsman who has many tools at his disposal. That statement becomes even truer as you work with a group of people to help them become a team that achieves a high degree of success.

If you have ever watched craftsmen work on a project, you may have noticed that they always seem to know just the right tool to pull out of their toolbox and how to apply it for greatest effect. They always know which tool to use because they know two things:

1. How to identify the problem they want to solve
2. Which tool will work for the particular problem

Throughout this book, we have shared both general principles and specific techniques you can use to solve a wide range of leadership problems. We have attempted to collect the techniques that best fit the situation you are in as a leader making the transition from Bud to Boss. We have worked to focus our suggestions on the items of immediate concern to people like you. And still, when you look at your leadership toolbox for just the right tool to use to help your team move through the stages of team development, you might struggle to know exactly where to start for a given situation.

As we said earlier, leadership is complex. What works one time might not work the next time. It all depends on the specifics of the situation (including but certainly not limited to): the people, the nature of their relationships, how long they have known each other, their relative roles, and their skill levels.

At this point, you have a wide range of tools you can use to solve problems within your team. And, like a craftsman, you need to know which tool to use when the time is right. Unlike a craftsman, your problems are not simple. You will not apply the same tool in the same way each time you experience a problem.

For example, let's say you notice that team results are not optimal on two occasions in which there appears to be conflict between members of your team. In one case, you determine that you need to act as a leader-mediator to help them develop an action plan for moving forward, and in the other case you decide you need to get your IT department to add a computer to your work area. Both problems looked like conflict on the surface, and they had different issues once you began to investigate.

We have found that having a structured and organized way to think about, analyze, and diagnose complex problems like these speeds up the process of picking the right tool. To help you, here's a model that Kevin developed for evaluating team performance to find the most likely source of a team problem. If you can narrow your focus to one or two specific areas, you can make a better choice as you choose the right leadership tool.

The diagnostic tool we use, which we call the CARB model (commitment, alignment, relationships, behavior) is shown in Figure 35.1.

The diagram shows that team problems often start with a failure in one of four basic areas and, when all of these areas are strong, greater success and productivity will result. The four basic areas are

- Commitment to the team and each other
- Alignment and goal agreement
- Relationships among team members
- Behaviors and skills of team members

Underneath these four areas are four other ingredients necessary for highly successful teams. They are

- Leadership
- Communication

○ Support systems (anything the team needs that must be provided by the organization)

○ Trust

Figure 35.1. The CARB Model of Team Performance

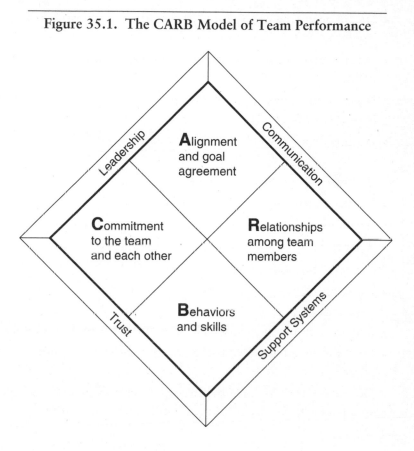

To use the model as a diagnostic aid when you evaluate your team's performance, think through each item sequentially and consider how you would answer specific questions related to each of the eight items. You might consider questions in the following areas:

○ *Commitment to the team and each other*

- Are all team members engaged in the primary work of the team?

- Will each team member assist every other team member if necessary?

- Is there a sense of pride to be a part of the team?
- Do team members feel connected to each other and value the contributions of each other?

○ *Alignment and goal agreement*

- Do all team members know the goals of the team and the organization?
- Do all team members agree that the goals are relevant and valid?
- Do team members see how their personal work aligns with the team's work?
- Do people see the connection between the work (and success) of the team and the achievement of organizational goals?

○ *Relationships among team members*

- Do team members get along well professionally?
- Are there any unresolved conflicts between team members?
- Are there any relationship issues getting in the team's way?

○ *Behaviors and skills of team members*

- Do team members treat each other with professional courtesy and respect?
- Do all team members have the necessary skills to do their jobs?
- Do team members have the skills to interact as members of a team?
- Do team members have the needed meeting skills or interpersonal skills necessary to be successful team contributors?

○ *Leadership*

- As the leader, am I modeling the right behaviors?
- Have I said or done something that indicates that they are getting the results that I expect?
- How does overall organizational leadership support teams and their success?

○ *Communication*

- Do we have open, honest communication most of the time?
- Is information getting to the right people at the right time?

○ *Support Systems*

- Does my team have the right support systems to do their work?
- Do they have all of the resources they need to do what I have asked them to do?
- Do our policies and procedures support team performance and success?

○ *Trust*

- Do my team members trust me?
- Do my team members trust each other?
- Do I show my team members that I trust them?
- What is the overall trust climate in the team and in the organization?

Questions such as these, and others, will help you find the real source of a team problem or challenge. Thinking through the types of questions with a focus on a particular area of team functioning can help you eliminate some of the noise that develops when a team is having a problem. For example, when you dig further into a problem and ask some questions, you find that what looks like a relationship issue is really a support systems issue. Applying a relationship-fixing tool will not work in this situation.

We suggest that you start by asking questions about your leadership and then moving into the rest of the possible sources of the problem. We make this recommendation because it will be easier for you to ask tough questions of other people in the other areas after you have carefully considered and addressed anything you might be doing that is contributing to the problem.

 For a more complete description of this tool and how to use it, go to the Bonus Bytes page at BudToBossCommunity.com and click on the CARB Model button.

Your Now Steps

1. Look at your team using the CARB model approach. Do you see any challenging areas? If not, great! You are a fortunate person.

If you do (we think this is the more likely situation), look back at the diagnostic questions above to pinpoint the most likely source of the dysfunction or challenge.

2. Now that you have a clearer sense about what is causing the challenge, look through the book to find the best tool for your situation (it might be in a chapter after this one). Read or reread that section to get a better handle on how to apply that tool. Within 24 hours of starting this process, write down a plan for applying that tool to your situation.

3. Implement your plan from step 2.

36

SPEAKING OF CONFLICT

(BECAUSE WE KNOW YOU'RE WONDERING ABOUT IT)

As a leader, you *will* face conflicts in the workplace. That's just a part of life as a leader. When you look back at the four stages of team development (Chapter Thirty-Three), you see that the Storming phase is a normal and natural part of the team development process. Your goal is not to avoid or suppress conflict. Your goal is to learn how to manage and resolve the inevitable conflicts so that your team can grow and improve through them.

We also know that as a former peer, thinking about the conflicts you may now have to resolve between former peers or between yourself and one of your friends may make you feel a bit ill. If you feel that way, you're not alone. Read on, because you will feel better and you will have tools to help you the next time you face a conflict.

Learning to become comfortable with conflict resolution can make you a much more effective and remarkable leader. In *Managing Differences,* workplace conflict resolution expert Dan Dana reports that one estimate is that up to 65 percent of performance issues are the result of unresolved conflict (and therefore not the result of a lack of skill or motivation on the part of individual employees).

Clearly, conflict competence is a big deal and an important skill for you to develop as a leader.

"Every conflict we face in life is rich with positive and negative potential. It can be a source of inspiration, enlightenment, learning, transformation, and growth—or rage, fear, shame, entrapment, and resistance. The choice is not up to our opponents, but to us, and our willingness to face and work through them."

—Kenneth Cloke and Joan Goldsmith, American authors on leadership and dispute resolution

Before we dive into this topic, think back to where we began. We have said that leadership is a complex skill set in a number of ways. Well, conflict resolution is a complex skill set all by itself within the larger complex skill set of leadership! We realize that helping you develop a full set of conflict resolution skills lies beyond the scope of this book, and we cannot ignore it just because it is a big topic.

Even though the full topic of conflict resolution is bigger than we can cover in detail here, we do want to share insights and observations that will help you grow your skills in this vital leadership competency. We strongly recommend that you use what we have written here to start the process of becoming more comfortable and competent with conflict resolution and that you add it to your current skill set/tool kit. We hope that you will continue the process with other more specialized resources on this critical topic.

For a full list of other resources to help you develop your conflict resolution skills, go to the Bonus Bytes page at BudToBossCommunity.com and click on the Conflict Competence button.

How Do We Define Conflict and Conflict Resolution?

Conflict is a word that often creates a strong emotional response when people hear it. It is also a word with a wide range of meanings. It can mean completely different things to different people.

From a broad perspective, people use the word *conflict* to describe situations ranging from minor miscommunications on the one end to wars and feuds on the extreme end. Since we're talking about one word with so many possible interpretations, let's narrow the focus

Figure 36.1. The Levels of Conflict Intensity

Level 1:	Level 2:	Level 3:	Level 4:	Level 5:
Everyday Stuff	Uncomfortable	Beyond Normal Skills	Formal Processes	Intractable

and make sure we are working from the same understanding and definition, and at the level that is relevant to you as a new leader.

We will use a definition of conflict proposed in *Becoming a Conflict Competent Leader* by Craig E. Runde and Tim A. Flanagan. They define a *conflict* as "any situation in which interdependent people have apparently incompatible interests, goals, principles, or feelings."

From that starting point, let's look at the issue of conflict intensity. If you drew a conflict intensity scale, it might look something like Figure 36.1, with the levels defined as

- ○ *Level 1: Everyday stuff.* You probably already know how to handle these conflicts. These are the normal, everyday misunderstandings and miscommunications that get resolved quickly and easily, or are quickly forgotten.

- ○ *Level 2: Uncomfortable.* You might already have the skills to address these conflicts. They are a little more involved, and not yet out of control. Some of what we have already discussed (for example, the DISC model) should give you some insights for resolving these conflicts.

- ○ *Level 3: Beyond normal skills.* This is when the conflict is getting really uncomfortable and calls for skills a little—or maybe a lot—beyond your current skill set. In these situations people are getting pretty angry, and we are moving into what Dan Dana calls a workplace conflict. In *Conflict Resolution,* he defines a workplace conflict as "a condition among workers whose jobs are interdependent, who feel angry, who perceive the other(s) as being at fault, and who act in ways that cause a business problem." This level is the target area for our discussion about conflict resolution. We share tools, tips, and insights to help you move these conflicts toward deescalation and resolution and away from the next higher level.

- ○ *Level 4: Formal processes.* These conflicts have escalated to the point that they require formal administrative, mediation, or legal processes. They almost always call for the involvement of third parties. This is when you would probably call your HR department or get your leader involved, or both. The time, energy, and financial costs of these conflicts climb rapidly.

o *Level 5: Intractable.* The costs in terms of time, money, and emotional investment are incredibly high. These conflicts are not likely to be resolved quickly or easily. The good news is you shouldn't have to experience many of these in your leadership role. If you find you are, you are either mislabeling them or ignoring them for far too long—because before they reached this level, there were opportunities for resolution.

The conflict management and resolution skills we discuss are specifically designed for Level 3 conflicts. These skills and approaches will help at lower-level conflicts. But if you find yourself in a higher-level conflict, they may not be sufficient to achieve success. Although they might help, you are likely to need professional advice.

To understand the process of resolving conflict, let's start with a definition so that we can speak the same language for the rest of this section. Our definition of *conflict resolution* is "a plan for future behaviors and interactions agreed to by both parties."

 Successful conflict resolution leads to a plan for future behaviors and interactions agreed to by both parties.

Two key points about our definition of conflict resolution are worth special notice:

o An emotion (anger) is included in the definition of workplace conflict, and it is not mentioned in the definition of conflict resolution.

o Workplace conflicts develop because of past behaviors and interactions, and resolution is about future behaviors and interactions.

These key points lead to two critical concepts for you to keep in mind as you work to resolve conflicts with and between people on your team:

○ Conflict resolution is not about making people like each other or helping them feel better. It is about changing behaviors that are causing a business problem.

○ Conflict resolution is about planning for the future. It is not about discussing the past.

Even though emotion is always a part of conflict and we do want people to feel comfortable in the workplace, the goal of conflict resolution is not about emotion. Other people's emotions might be in your circle of influence, but they are definitely outside your circle of control. As a result, you can take or encourage actions that influence emotions, and you cannot effectively do anything to force emotions.

Though we prefer to have the people who work side-by-side every day like each other, we realize that you have no control over this outcome. So we do not advocate or teach methods that focus on making people feel good about each other. While there are no guarantees, we have noticed that when people fix the behaviors that are creating the conflict, their feelings tend to fall in line with their behaviors.

This chapter has been mostly focused on giving you some definitions and better understanding of concepts that make the next chapters easier to digest. So rather than give you Now Steps on definitions, let's move right into . . .

37

COMMON CONFLICT QUESTIONS AND THEIR ANSWERS

From our workshop, coaching, and consulting experience, we know that new leaders have lots of questions about conflict and conflict resolution. In this chapter, we address three of the most common questions we hear.

Is Conflict Bad?

It depends. It depends on the nature, the duration, and the outcome of the conflict.

Is conflict inherently bad? No. Can conflict be bad? Yes.

As we already said, Storming—in part a conflict stage—is a normal part of team development. Good things can come from the conflicts that develop during Storming. With the resolution of these conflicts, teams grow stronger and more effective. We call this *constructive conflict*. If, however, it continues to escalate, it becomes *destructive conflict* and it destroys the team.

We believe that conflict, when properly managed and resolved (before it reaches Level 3), can be a good thing for your organization. Constructive conflict can create the opportunity for new ideas, approaches, and solutions to surface as people focus their different perspectives toward achieving a common goal.

Poorly managed or avoided, however, conflict becomes destructive. Conflict is a bad thing when it creates negative emotional energy and distraction that divert attention from doing the work of your organization. In other words, when the conflict creates a business problem, it is bad.

 Conflict is a good thing when it creates the dialogue and discussion of different ideas and solutions to move an organization forward.

Why Does Conflict Happen?

Many things can create conflict in a team. If you look back at our definition of *conflict*—"any situation in which interdependent people have apparently incompatible interests, goals, principles, or feelings"—you can see three common causes for conflict:

- *Poor communication.* Poor communication leads to misunderstandings that amplify those "apparently incompatible interests, goals, principles, or feelings."
- *Unmet needs.* Remember that people have a difficult time focusing on organizational goals when their personal needs are unmet. When people are fighting to have their needs met, conflicts can easily grow.
- *Different expectations.* This point is closely related to poor communication. When two people have different expectations about how a situation should be handled, what direction to go, or what goals should be accomplished, their interests, goals, principles, or feelings can appear to be incompatible.

The simplified conflict resolution process we describe in Chapter Thirty-Eight is designed to create an opportunity to address each of these causes of conflict, to vent the anger often associated with destructive conflict, and to develop the resolution plan needed to meet our definition of *conflict resolution*.

Why Do Conflicts Escalate?

Simply put, conflicts generally escalate because someone says or does something that triggers the "retaliatory cycle" mentioned by Dan Dana in his work on workplace conflict resolution. Shown graphically, the retaliatory cycle looks something like what we see in Figure 37.1.

Figure 37.1. The Retaliatory Cycle

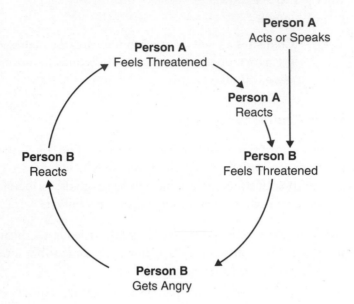

The cycle starts when person A says or does something that person B perceives as a threat to his interests, goals, principles, or feelings. It often does not matter whether person A *meant* to be threatening or not, it only matters that person B *perceived* some type of threat to his physical or emotional security. Once the perception of threat happens, person B then feels angry and reacts from that anger. This reaction by B causes A to perceive a threat to his physical or emotional security, and he reacts.

Does any of this sound like something you have experienced?

Once initiated, the cycle feeds itself until someone acts to break it. The good news is that someone can act to break the cycle. So if you find yourself involved in a conflict with another person, you can often break the cycle by asking yourself a simple question: *Did he mean that action or comment the way that I took it?*

If you stop to think, for just a moment, about both sides of the interaction happening in the retaliatory cycle—the other person's intention and your perception—you might realize that the person did not mean to send the message that you received. We have already discussed one issue that can cause misinterpreting other people's words and actions, shown in the DISC model. This phenomenon is just one of many issues that can create a perception of threat when no threat was intended. Cultural differences, regional slang differences, male-female communication style differences, and others all come into play in conflict situations.

> "If you understood everything I said, you'd be me."
> —Miles Davis, musician

We often interpret other people's words and actions in a totally different way than they intended them. When we interpret the message wrong, we misperceive their intentions. When we do that, depending on the situation, we may move toward anger and escalation rather than toward understanding and resolution. Asking this question of ourselves is one way to stop the cycle before it even begins.

Although you cannot make other people change their perception of your behaviors, you can question your perception of theirs. This technique is about keeping your focus on the things that are inside your circle of control. While the technique will not eliminate conflict from your life, it can help you move toward constructive conflict, where the focus is on discussion and resolution, rather than jumping immediately to destructive conflict, where the focus is on blame and retribution.

 For more insights on how you can act to break the conflict cycle when you are personally involved in it, go to the Bonus Bytes page at BudToBossCommunity.com and click on the Cycle Breaker button.

Your Now Steps

1. Reflect on a past conflict you have had at work or at home. Did you see the retaliatory cycle work its magic to escalate the conflict? What could you have done or said differently to break the cycle?

2. Record your thoughts in your learning journal.

38

USING A PROCESS—THE FIVE DS OF WORKPLACE CONFLICT RESOLUTION

You will occasionally find yourself in situations where the conflict has grown beyond the level at which simply adjusting your communication style or questioning your perception will be sufficient to move the conflict to resolution. Left alone, these conflicts almost always get worse. When this is the case, since we have defined workplace conflict as conflict causing a business problem, as a leader you have to take action to resolve it.

Remarkable Principle

Using a predefined process for resolving Level 3 conflicts supports you and the other parties by creating a framework for discussion that leads to resolution.

Be careful here. This is not a one-size-fits-all process. This is a general process you can use to guide your decisions and approaches to addressing conflicts in situations that have grown to Level 3. Only use this process when

○ *The conflict is causing a business problem.* In other words, the conflict between the two parties is resulting in a failure to serve customers, meet goals, produce on-time work, and so on. If the people simply do not like each other and they can still get the work done without negatively affecting the people around them, leave the conflict alone. Do not use this process in an effort to get people to like each other.

○ *The conflict is safe to discuss.* You do not expect a real risk of physical violence, and you see no evidence of influence from alcohol or drugs in either party. If these are your concerns, you should use other approaches—probably involving your boss and a Human Resources representative—to resolve the situation.

○ *You and the other parties have full authority to take action.* The people solving the conflict need to be able to take any actions agreed to as a result of the process. Never ask someone to take responsibility for something that is beyond her control.

In addition, keep both your supervisor and your Human Resources contact informed about your concerns with and approach to resolving these conflicts. They may or may not want to be involved in the resolution process. They should be informed so that you can stay within your specific company guidelines and any legal requirements.

Using this process, you are working to create an environment in which two conflicting parties come to a face-to-face meeting with the intention of looking for a solution to a business problem. You can facilitate this process as a leader-mediator for two other people, or you can use this process for resolving a conflict in which you are one of the involved parties.

As written here, the process flows with you serving as the leader-mediator for two other people who are in conflict. For more specific perspectives on how to use this process and our other suggestions to resolve conflicts in which you are personally involved, go to the Bonus Bytes page at BudToBossCommunity.com and click on the Personal Conflict button.

The Five Ds

Consider these five Ds as a high-level process to guide the overall conflict resolution process as a leader-mediator. Using these steps, along with everything in the other chapters on conflict, will improve your odds of success.

Define the Conflict in Terms of Its Business Impact

When you find a way to define the problem you want to discuss in terms of specific business results, you do a number of things to make the conflict resolution conversation more likely to produce a positive result:

- ○ You verify that you have a valid workplace conflict situation that it is worth investing your time in resolving.
- ○ You anticipate the outcome of the conversation by defining the problem in terms that can be resolved by specific actions and behaviors.

This step can get a bit complicated. Most conflicts involve a number of variables and could be defined in many different ways. The goal of this step is to find the way to define the conflict that describes it in a very specific and measurable way so that

- ○ You have a clear picture of what a good resolution plan would look like when you get to that stage of the process.
- ○ You bring the involved parties to the resolution conversation in a way that minimizes the risk that they will feel threatened or in need of defending themselves in the course of the conversation.

Here are some examples of bad conflict definition statements and some possible better statements:

- ○ Bad statement—"John ignores Sue's requests for financial reports."
- ○ Better statement—"We are not getting financial reports to accounting in time for them to meet their legal obligations."

- ○ Bad statement—"Mary and Steve don't like each other, and they can't work together."
- ○ Better statement—"Steve and Mary are both involved in the customer service process. At the moment, customer calls are not being handled in a timely fashion."

Look for the objective and observable way to state the problem that the conflict is causing, and phrase it in terms of business impact.

 For more insights on how to define a workplace conflict the way we suggest here, go to the Bonus Bytes page at BudToBossCommunity.com and click on the Define Conflict button.

Deliver an Invitation to Meet

With a well-thought-out conflict or problem definition statement, you can invite the parties to meet to discuss a solution to the problem. We emphasize the word "invite" in this statement. In some cases you might have to insist on a meeting. We suggest that you sell the meeting more than you insist on the meeting. (Remember that we said leaders often have to sell?)

If we assume that both of the involved parties have an interest in the business performing well and you phrase the invitation in a way that keeps the focus on the business problem rather than on their personal behaviors, they will probably cooperate with an invitation. Frankly, if they don't cooperate, you probably have a performance management problem and not a conflict resolution problem.

Using the definition statements above, the invitation might sound something like this:

- ○ "John (Sue), I have noticed that financial reports are not getting to accounting in time for them to meet their legal obligations. Since you and Sue (John) are both involved in that process, I would like to schedule a time to meet with both of you to find a way that we can solve that problem."

- ○ "Steve (Mary), it looks to me like our customer service support request times are increasing. Since you and Mary (Steve) are both involved in the process, I would like to schedule a time to meet with both of you to find a way to solve that problem."

For more insights on how to deliver a meeting invitation that is likely to be received well, go to the Bonus Bytes page at BudToBossCommunity.com and click on the Meeting Invite button.

Decide on a Mutually Agreeable Time and Place to Meet

Keep the goal of bringing all parties to the meeting with as little defensiveness and as much cooperation as possible in the forefront of your thinking as you engage them in a discussion about where and when to meet for the conflict conversation. Here are a few considerations to consider for good times and places:

○ Pick a time when they can be uninterrupted for a full two hours. You might not need this much time; you should schedule it though. We will explain why in the next chapter.

○ Pick a place that is "neutral territory" and protected from interruptions. You do not want to meet in a place in which either person feels uncomfortable, out of place, or at a disadvantage to the other person. You also want to protect the conversation from interruptions so that you can keep the forward momentum once you get started.

○ Let the parties know, gently, that you expect them to come to the meeting under the following ground rules:

 • Both parties will stay engaged in the conversation until a plan is developed.

 • Neither person will use his or her position to force a plan on the other.

Discuss the Problem to Seek a Resolution Plan

In the next chapter, we will share insights about the value of not rushing the conversation. For now, focus on what to plan for in conflict conversations and what communication skills might come into play. So that you are prepared for what is likely to happen during the conflict conversation, here's a typical timeline:

0–10 minutes:

Get the meeting started and define the conflict or problem for discussion, and remind everyone of the meeting ground rules.

10–20 minutes:

Involved parties start to share their perspectives. Some emotions start to come to the surface.

20–60 minutes:

People discuss their perspectives. This is when many people get stuck by speaking about the past and venting their emotions. People usually get more intense. Somewhere in the 40–60 minute range is when most people start to feel heard and understood (and a little tired) so that their emotional level starts to subside.

60–75 minutes:

> Heavy emotions ease, and people relax a bit. They generally move from resistance to a willingness to discuss future plans and actions.

75–90 minutes:

> Document the action plan and conclude the meeting.

This timeline might be a little shorter or a little longer based on many factors, including the past relationship of the involved parties, the severity of the conflict, and the specific issue being discussed, among others. The general timeline is useful for understanding why you should schedule a two-hour meeting for conflict resolution.

During the conversation, you will want to look for ways to reverse the retaliatory cycle and to trigger the deescalation cycle shown in Figure 38.1.

Figure 38.1. The Deescalation Cycle

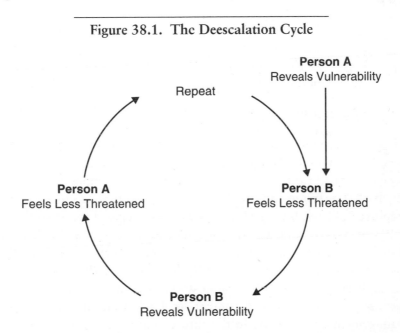

Notice that the deescalation cycle begins when one party reveals a vulnerability to the other. In effect, he or she ceases to be a threat so the perception of threat is removed.

Signs of vulnerability can include

- Apologizing (effectively, as discussed in the next chapter)
- Taking responsibility

○ Conceding a point

○ Disclosing emotional impact (felt sad, felt upset, felt threatened, and so on)

○ Expressing positive emotions about the other person

○ Initiating an opportunity for both people to "win" or gain

If you are one of the involved parties, work to trigger deescalation by showing your vulnerability in a way that does not diminish or minimize your perspective. There are many ways to do this effectively. One way to do this would be through the use of assertive communication techniques. (We share more on assertive communication techniques in Chapter Forty.)

If you are acting as a leader-mediator, work to trigger deescalation by looking for and calling attention to any show of vulnerability by either party.

 For more insights on how to consciously trigger the deescalation cycle, go to the Bonus Bytes page at BudToBossCommunity.com and click on the Deescalate button.

Document the Plan

Most of us are prone to remember our agreements in a way that best benefits us. To guard against this tendency, document the plan you have developed for resolving this conflict and give copies to everyone involved. You might consider keeping a copy of the agreement in each employee's file with your Human Resources department as well.

If you have truly reached agreement on an action plan that will actually address the inappropriate or ineffective behaviors that led to the initial conflict, you should never have to have this conversation again. If either party fails to follow the resolution plan, your conversation has shifted out of conflict resolution and into performance management or coaching. In the future, you would discuss any failure to follow the agreed-upon plan as a failure to live up to their commitments rather than as revisiting the conflict conversation.

 If you want more perspective on how revisiting a conflict resolution conversation becomes a performance management conversation, go to the Bonus Bytes page at BudToBossCommunity.com and click on the Conflict Returns button.

Your Now Steps

1. Think about a past conflict. Look at it again in light of what we have just discussed. Explore different ways to define the conflict so that it is defined in terms of business results or outcomes. Write some different conflict definition statements in your learning journal.

2. Find another leader who is good at resolving conflicts. Schedule a time to meet with her to learn how she goes about conflict resolution discussions. If helpful, share some of what you have learned here to start or extend that conversation.

39

THE SEVEN DEADLY SINS
OF CONFLICT RESOLUTION
AND HOW TO AVOID THEM

So far, we have focused mostly on definitions and background information to give you a bigger framework for understanding the specific tips and techniques we recommend for resolving conflict. Now let's talk about seven specific things that people often do with the hope of resolving conflicts that actually make them worse. We call these seven behaviors "The Seven Deadly Sins of Conflict Resolution."

Our suggestions for how to avoid these sins apply when you are the leader-mediator working to help other people resolve conflicts and when you are personally involved in a conflict with another person. When you are the leader-mediator, encourage others to apply the tips for avoiding the sins. When you are personally involved, keep the suggestions in mind so that you can apply them and move quickly to resolution with the other person.

Talking About the Past

The past is over. You cannot change it with any amount of pleading, explaining, or arguing. It's over. Forget it. You can look briefly to past behaviors to give you a better understanding of how the current situation developed. Once you have that understanding, move on. Talking about what has already happened in an attempt to explain it away only stirs up negative emotions and leads to conflict escalation rather than resolution.

> "Don't let yesterday use up too much of today."
> —Cherokee proverb

How to Avoid This Sin

Stay focused on the future. The past sets the context, but you can't change the past. Once you understand how the past brought you to the present, shift your discussion to future behaviors and interactions. When you start to make plans for the future that address the concerns created in the past, you create energy and hope. This energy and hope are what will eventually lead to conflict resolution.

Trying to "Fix" Emotions

One of the greatest challenges in conflict situations is that emotions, usually highly charged emotions, are always involved when the conflict starts to escalate. Since emotions are the result of how we interpret and respond to the world around us and not objective, measurable, and readily changeable, trying to fix or change them is like trying to put spilled milk back in the bottle.

We can control our behaviors. They are objective and observable. You can talk about them. They either happened or they didn't. Either we will make them different in the future or we won't. The changes we make to our behaviors might lead to different emotions, but the emotions themselves lie outside our direct circle of control.

When we try to fix emotions, we sink ourselves in a conversation that leads down a path of discussing things we cannot control. So we get stuck in a negative conversation spiral that tends to make conflicts worse rather than better.

How to Avoid This Sin

Keep your focus on behaviors rather than feelings. The key words to remember are "objective" and "observable." Once you understand the impact of behaviors on emotions, quickly move to the things you can observe, measure, and change.

You should acknowledge and understand other people's feelings so that they feel that you heard and understood them. Just don't try to fix their feelings. Instead, discuss the behaviors (words, actions, body language, and so on) that can be used in the future to avoid having this conflict come back again.

Trying to Rush the Resolution Conversation

If a workplace conflict has grown to the point that it calls for a focused and intentional resolution conversation, it has become a business problem. When you consider the salaries of the employees involved, the value of work that is not being done, the cost of poor decisions, the impact of poor information flow, and so forth, this business problem is probably costing you more than you realize. Unresolved conflict gets very expensive very quickly.

If you are conflict averse, you may want to have a quick conversation to get through the conflict conversation fast. You may not want to be involved in a potentially emotionally charged discussion for very long.

If you attempt to rush the conversation by doing a "drive-by" conversation in the hallway, by quickly stopping at the other person's workstation, or by scheduling 15 to 30 minutes for a brief discussion, you probably will not get good results. If you have a fast conversation you risk sending all parties back to work in an elevated emotional state. This makes them less able to do their jobs and make good decisions, and may actually make the conflict worse, not better.

How to Avoid This Sin

Before we get into how to avoid this sin, let's make sure that we are considering the same level of conflict. What we are about to propose would be far in excess of what you need to do for normal, run-of-the-mill, everyday, simple miscommunication conflicts. You also would not use this suggestion if you just had a momentary clash of perspective in a meeting that you resolved on the spot. This suggestion only fits when a conflict has become a lingering business problem.

When a conflict grows to the point that it needs a semiformal meeting for resolution, like we discussed in the last chapter, you should schedule a two-hour time block for a face-to-face discussion between the involved parties. In general, you do not want to do "shuttle diplomacy" where you act as a middleman between the two parties. Get them to talk it out until they reach a resolution plan. Resist the urge to solve the problem for others. Let them solve their own problem.

You can facilitate a conflict resolution process for others. You cannot resolve conflicts for others.

Why do we say to allow two hours for a conflict conversation? Because that's what it usually takes to get all the way through the conversation to reach resolution of conflicts that have grown to Level 3. When the conversation starts, the emotions may rise in the room, and you might be tempted to stop the conversation. Unless you see the threat of physical violence, you should normally let the conversation run its course.

If you end too soon, you never get to resolution. If you end at the peak of emotional energy, you might actually set the stage for later acts of retaliation or retribution between the two parties because they never reached the point of agreeing on their future interactions and behaviors toward each other around this issue. Make sure you commit the amount of time necessary to reach a mutually agreeable conclusion.

Don't give up too soon. Conflict conversations often get worse before they get better.

Blaming Others

Though it is a normal part of human behavior, blame really has no value in conflict resolution. Most of us want to see ourselves as good people. So even when we behave badly toward someone else, we might be inclined to find a way to make our behavior the other's fault through a process known as self-justification.

As Carol Tavris and Elliot Aronson put it in *Mistakes Were Made (but not by me)*: "Self-justification is more powerful than the explicit lie. It allows people to convince themselves that what they did was the best thing they could have done. In fact, come to think of it, it was the right thing."

With a little self-justifying sleight of hand and one simple statement, we can shift responsibility for our behavior from ourselves to other people. For example, "I yelled at you because you yelled at me." Although it feels a bit like self-defense, it actually triggers conflict escalation. Very seldom will anyone respond positively to you if you blame him. (It could happen. It's just not very likely.)

How to Avoid This Sin

Take full responsibility for your words and actions. In the example above, you might say: "I yelled at you because I got angry." That's it. End of story. No blame involved.

Trying to Justify Behaviors

Justification is blame's evil twin. It is intimately connected to blame in the process of self-justification. They often go hand in hand, and they are hard to separate. Blame is a form of justification, and justification often leads to blame.

The difference for our purposes lies in the outward expression. The self-justification that we associated with the previous sin of blame is an internal thought process. The justification we are now addressing shows up as outwardly expressed statements. In this context, justification is an overt statement that tries to explain away or rationalize our behaviors.

When we try to justify our behaviors to others, we generally look to the past (committing conflict sin number 1!) and try to explain our intentions to others in an effort to correct their perception (which is outside our circle of control). It might seem like "explaining" to us, but it sounds like "making excuses" to others.

How to Avoid This Sin

Like avoiding the sin of blaming others, just take responsibility for your words and actions. If you will own your behaviors without attempting to justify, rationalize, shift blame, or explain, justification will tend to evaporate from your conflict communications.

Refusing to Apologize

We have seen many workplace conflicts, and we have been involved in a number of conflict resolution conversations at various points in our careers. We have rarely seen a situation develop in which all of the responsibility for the conflict fell completely and totally on only one of the involved parties. We acknowledge that it could happen. It's just not very common.

Refusing to apologize for what you contributed to the conflict can have a serious negative impact on the retaliatory cycle. Failure to apologize can trigger the other person's self-justifying thought process so that you stay locked in conflict.

How to Avoid This Sin

Find the thing you did for which you can offer an apology—your word choice, your tone, your timing, something, anything you can admit that you own. Apologies, when sincerely and honestly offered, have a calming effect on conflict situations.

When you act as the leader-mediator, make sure that you notice and comment favorably about any honest apology offered by either party.

> "Never ruin an apology with an excuse."
> —Kimberly Johnson, poet

A good apology also helps remove blame and justification. For example, "I'm sorry that you feel that way" is a poor apology. In a very subtle way, it keeps blame alive and fails to acknowledge ownership for words, tone, actions, and behaviors. A better apology would be, "I'm sorry that I used such an aggressive tone of speech."

Refusing to Forgive

This is another sin that often goes together with one or more of the others. When other people have accepted responsibility for their actions, some people still want to seek vengeance or retribution against the other person. This behavior often shows itself when people want to punish others after a conflict. The punishment appears in the form of withholding information, refusing to speak, ignoring, making sarcastic comments, and a host of other bad workplace behaviors.

One subtle form of refusing to forgive happens when people confuse holding people accountable for their actions with punishing people for their actions. We fully support and promote the idea that people should experience the natural consequences of their behaviors. If what they did is an automatic firing offense, fire them. However, if future interactions are motivated by "getting even," refusing to forgive is the real issue.

Refusing to forgive creates a negative interaction pattern that dooms a relationship—either personal or professional—to failure. No plan for future behaviors and interactions will resolve a conflict if either party refuses to forgive the other.

How to Avoid This Sin

We have this concept listed as one of seven deadly sins of conflict resolution, and we have both seen whole books written on this one point. We cannot hope to cover the full range and implications of forgiveness in leadership, conflict resolution, and relationships in general. We can offer some brief thoughts about how to avoid this sin.

From a personal perspective, be willing to offer forgiveness quickly and without conditions. Conditional forgiveness sounds like this: "I'll forgive you if ____." Conditional forgiveness is not forgiveness. Remember that you can forgive a behavior without forgetting it or removing the natural consequences someone might experience as a result of the behavior.

As a leader-mediator, make sure that you notice and call attention to any show of forgiveness by either party. This is a behavior that you definitely want to encourage.

Here's a final note on forgiveness. We often hear people say, "I just can't forgive them." This statement usually means one of two things:

1. The person has confused forgiving and forgetting.
2. The person has confused "can't forgive" with "won't forgive."

Forgiving is a personal choice that does not depend on the other person.

For more perspective on how to draw the line between forgiving and forgetting, go to the Bonus Bytes page at BudToBossCommunity.com and click on the Forgiving button.

In practice, these sins rarely show up individually. They almost always appear in combinations. Our intent here is not to provide the definitive list of such sins. Rather, we hope we have stimulated your thinking about conflict and conflict resolution so that you can approach it more positively, with a greater awareness of the things that can go wrong, and with some thoughts about what you can do to better manage and resolve conflicts when you identify these sins.

Your Now Steps

1. Look back at the list of deadly sins of conflict resolution to find the one that you commit most often. (We all have one or two that creep into our behaviors.) Read the How to Avoid This Sin section for that particular sin again.

2. In your learning journal, write two actions you will take the next time you find yourself committing that sin.

3. The next time you act as a leader-mediator, look for evidence of the How to Avoid This Sin behaviors in the actions of the involved parties, and encourage them to more consistently apply the suggestions by verbally acknowledging and thanking them when they do.

40

APPLYING ASSERTIVE COMMUNICATION TECHNIQUES

To be an effective leader, you will sometimes have to take a stand on issues—issues that in the past you either could avoid or did not have to think about. You will have to apply your communication skills in a number of possibly uncomfortable and tense situations that include confronting poor performance, resolving conflicts, negotiating agreements, and other, similar situations. We have already covered a number of techniques and approaches you could use for these situations. In this chapter, we explore assertive communication—a powerful communication approach that fits a wide range of situations.

We define assertive communication as communication approaches that state your case or perspective while still respecting the case or perspective of the other person. You can view communication techniques as falling on a line within a range of behaviors that goes from passive communication to aggressive communication, as shown in Figure 40.1.

Figure 40.1. The Communication Continuum

| Passive | Assertive | Aggressive |

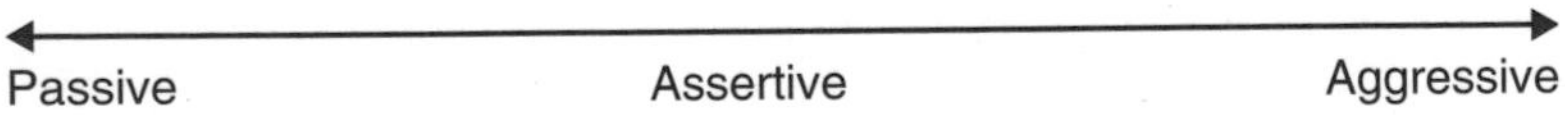

We define the areas on this communication continuum like this:

Passive communication—I let you step on me. I take whatever you offer without debate or counterpoint. I might not speak at all.

Assertive communication—I protect my concerns and interests. I explain my viewpoint and perspective in a way that respects and honors your viewpoint and perspective.

Aggressive communication—I step on you without concern for your perspective. I neither listen to nor acknowledge your viewpoint. I am totally focused on "making you" hear my point. (This is really a futile effort. Making you hear my point is outside my circle of control.)

Assertive communication minimizes conflict escalation by improving clarity and by reducing misunderstandings and misinterpretations.

Some Rules of Assertive Communication

Use "I" statements. No blame or justification. Saying, "I felt _____" is better than "You made me feel _____."

Focus only on behaviors. Be careful with interpretations of or speculation about intentions. "You raised your voice" is assertive. "You were trying to intimidate me" is aggressive. The first statement states the behavior—something that is external and observable. The second statement makes an assignment of intention——something that is within another person's mind and not observable.

Keep your responses short and focused. The longer you speak, the more likely you are to slip into a bad communication pattern.

Monitor your tone of voice. Be aware of your volume and intensity. You can cross into aggressive communication very easily by raising your voice.

Watch your nonverbal messages. Finger pointing, hand waving, and standing over people can communicate threat and aggression. Beware of their need for personal space. Make sure that you stay outside their personal space comfort zone. Consider sitting side-by-side rather than face-to-face.

"Courage is what it takes to stand up and speak. Courage is also what it takes to sit down and listen."

—Winston Churchill, Prime Minister of Great Britain during World War II

Listen! You can only respect and appreciate someone's viewpoint if you have heard and understood it.

Maintain eye contact. Steady (not glaring) eye contact generally shows respect and connection. (In North America this is usually true. Be sensitive to the culture of the other person.)

Respect the other person. This is a restatement of one of the seven tips for powerful, persuasive, and memorable communication we mentioned in Chapter Twenty-Two.

You can probably find many ways to put the assertive communication rules, like so many communication tips, into practice. Here's a general example of an assertive communication statement you might use in a conflict conversation: "When you _____, I felt _____."
Specific examples could sound like this:

o "When you raise your voice, I feel threatened."
o "When you said I was lazy, I felt that you didn't respect me."
o "When you don't share information with me, I feel angry."

For a more in-depth look at how to communicate assertively and how to encourage others to communicate assertively, go to the Bonus Bytes page at BudToBossCommunity.com and click on the Assertive Communication button.

Your Now Steps

1. Study the rules of assertive communication. Compare these rules to your normal communication approach in stressful situations. Where do you fall on the communication continuum from passive to aggressive?

2. If you are like most people, you default to one side of assertive or the other. Identify the most common errors you make that push you away from assertiveness and toward either passive or aggressive approaches.

3. Write an affirmation statement in your learning journal to help you overcome these tendencies. For example, if you tend to raise your voice in the face of conflict you might write: "The next time I feel threatened or attacked, I will respond calmly." (No, we

don't believe that writing it down will magically "fix" a behavioral tendency, nor do we suggest you read the statement the next time you feel the urge to behave in the way you are working to change. We just want you to get started on the path of correcting the behavior.)

4. Commit to reading your affirmation statement (saying it out loud is even better) three times per day for the next month.

PART VI

COMMITMENT
TO SUCCESS

The last major section of the book could easily have been the first. As a leader, you are in the business of creating success. You do your work to create something that didn't exist before. That is true for the famous visionary leaders, and it is just as true for you.

Success for you and your team may be defined by more loyal customers, creating new products, getting packages delivered on time, teaching students, healing the sick, or a thousand other things. Regardless of your business, as a leader you are in the success business.

If you are in the success business, your first order of business must be goals. Goals define what success looks like. And although there are thousands of resources available to you on goal setting, most of it is written from a personal perspective. As a leader, you can't stop there, and so, as your authors/guides, we won't either. In this section, as we focus on our *commitment to success,* we won't stop short by only discussing goal setting: we also get to the real end line—goal achievement.

Though we could have put this section first, we put it last for two important reasons:

1. We know from experience that some of the other skills are probably causing you more pain and arousing more interest. As authors who want you to read this book, we started with what we felt you see as most important.

2. All of the other skills in this book roll together to support goal setting and goal achievement, and they provide a backdrop for you in your transition to leadership.

A LIVING EXAMPLE

We hope that we are modeling what we are teaching within these pages. As leaders, we must think of our followers first. We must speak about change from their perspective; we must communicate with them from their perspective (e.g. DISC model); we must focus our coaching on them; and in resolving conflict we, too, must get out of our perspective. By putting this section last, we are trying to model that principle.

As a leader, you have the opportunity to make the world a better place. But that can only happen if you build a commitment to success and use the skills in this section to make that happen.

Like we've done for every other section, let's start with a self-assessment.

Self-Assessment

Here is a quick assessment to help you think about goal setting and goal achievement and your comfort with both in your new role. Use the following scale of 1 to 7 on each question:

1   Almost never
2   Rarely or seldom
3   Occasionally
4   Sometimes
5   Usually
6   Frequently
7   Almost always

I consider myself a successful goal achiever.   _____
   (Chapter 42)

I regularly set goals.   _____
   (Chapters 42, 43)

I am confident in my ability to help others set
goals.   _____
   (Chapter 44)

I know my role in helping my team achieve their
goals.   _____
   (Chapter 44)

I have a positive attitude at work and in life in
general.   _____
   (Chapter 45)

I provide support and focus to help my team achieve
their goals.   _____
   (Chapter 46)

Based on your self-assessment, you have an initial glimpse into your strengths and weaknesses in these areas. Use those insights as you read the pages that follow. Remember our warning: read carefully in the areas in which you are weaker, *and* resist the urge to skim the other areas, for the nugget we share (or you extrapolate) may be the single insight or idea that takes you to even higher levels of skill and achievement.

Thoughts About Goals and Success—From Others and Us

Know what you want to do, hold the thought firmly, and do every day what should be done, and every sunset will see you that much nearer to your goal.

—Elbert Hubbard, writer and philosopher

We chose this thought because it eloquently summarizes some important points: to reach your goals and achieve success you must know what you want, stay focused on it, and make progress toward it daily. This observation is beautifully written and completely true.

> *Nothing can stop the man with the right mental attitude from achieving his goal; nothing on earth can help the man with the wrong mental attitude.*
>
> —Thomas Jefferson, U.S. president

Having the right attitude for success is critical, and it is especially true for you as a leader. Why? Because people look to you, take their attitudinal cues from you, and follow your lead far more than you realize. Although some people want to ignore this or think of it as New Age thinking, it predates us, and it predates Jefferson too—by a couple thousand years at least.

> *A great leader's courage to fulfill his vision comes from passion, not position.*
>
> —John Maxwell, author

Yep, you've got the position now, but as we hope you now understand, that isn't enough if you want true success for you and your team. Do you have a vision? If so, great! If not, you must continue to develop it. Because it is that vision that you will be leading people toward. We will talk about this and give you some tools in this section.

> *A goal is created three times. First as a mental picture. Second, when written down to add clarity and dimension. And third, when you take action toward its achievement.*
>
> —Gary Ryan Blair, speaker and author

Gary reminds us that having the vision isn't enough. You must crystallize it and clarify it. And most important, you must take action toward it.

> *Believe Big. The size of your success is determined by the size of your belief. Think little goals and expect little achievements. Think big goals and win big success. Remember this, too! Big ideas and big plans are*

often easier—certainly no more difficult—than small ideas and small plans.

—David Joseph Schwartz, author

This quotation comes from the classic *The Magic of Thinking Big,* and it in many ways summarizes the book. We selected it to share the last line with you: "Big ideas and big plans are often easier—certainly no more difficult—than small ideas and small plans." Although counterintuitive, this statement is completely true. So if you are going to set goals for yourself and with your team, why not set bigger goals and achieve bigger success?

41

ARE GOALS REALLY THAT IMPORTANT?

Let us answer this question by telling you a story. This is a story that is similar to the stories of many people we've talked with. In fact, even though we are now "writing the book," we can both see ourselves in Joanna. Thankfully, we can also see ourselves in the wisdom of her mentor Tom....

Joanna was a great employee and a relatively new supervisor, just like you. She cared about her work. She worked hard. She really wanted to succeed. And even though she had gotten promoted to team leader, she felt like she was just spinning her wheels because she wasn't making the progress—personally or professionally—that she had hoped she would by now.

She talked with Tom, a person she considered a friend and mentor, and shared her feelings. Tom asked her about her goals.

Joanna paused, feeling a bit tentative. She shared some general comments about what she hoped to achieve in her work and how she hoped her work would contribute to her life.

Tom listened carefully, but she could sense he was waiting for more, and he was. After a pause, Tom quietly suggested that Joanna's goals weren't clear enough, and he encouraged her to set some more specific goals for the future. That action, he said, would be a way for her to both improve her results and create higher personal satisfaction.

Joanna walked away from that conversation resolved to set some goals. She bought a book on goal setting and read it cover to cover. The concepts in the book made sense, and she decided on the weekend she would set goals using the approach the book suggested.

But the weekend came and went, as did the whole next week. Then the next weekend passed, along with the weekend after that—and Joanna still hadn't set any goals. She rationalized that she was just too busy. She was working too hard, and she didn't have time to stop and set her goals; besides, she already knew what she wanted to accomplish.

Four months later she visited with Tom again. He asked how her goal setting had gone and about the successes he suspected she was having since they last talked. She replied with a mix of sheepishness and defiance that she didn't have time for goal setting, that she knew what she wanted to achieve, and that it would take too long to follow a goal-setting process. She knew she just needed to get to work.

We could continue the story, but at this point we are guessing you see enough of yourself in the story that you are ready for some answers. Maybe you haven't taken quite so long or been quite as stubborn as Joanna, but even if you have been, now is the time to answer the question: Are goals really that important?

Seven Reasons You Need Goals

Goals create accomplishment instead of activity. Most leaders are extremely busy—running from meeting to meeting and task to task focused primarily on how to be more productive and get more accomplished in their day. But when your focus is on the tasks and the busyness, you lose track of any accomplishment—in effect you are focusing only on the activity itself. Goals help you look beyond the activity and get clear on what you really want to accomplish. In other words, though time management is great, goals put the focus on accomplishment.

Goals give you direction. As we mentioned previously, you wouldn't get in your car to go on a trip without knowing your destination. A destination provides purpose for your efforts. A destination gives you a reason for your efforts. A destination gives you a way to monitor your progress and stay on track.

Goals capitalize on the brain's amazing powers. Our brains are problem-solving, goal-achieving machines; which means that our brains operate best when they are seeking a solution to a problem. When you have a goal, your mind sees it as a problem to be solved and gets to work (with or without your conscious influence) on achieving the goal. The only way to put this power in motion is to have a clearly stated goal. Who wouldn't want to use the full power of his or her brain?

> "Man is by nature a goal-striving being. And because man is 'built that way' he is not happy unless he is functioning as he was made to function—as a goal striver. Thus true success and true happiness not only go together, but each enhances the other."
>
> —Maxwell Maltz, in *Psycho Cybernetics*

Goals make life (and work) easier. If nothing else, the three goals just listed improve your productivity. They help you work smarter no matter what the work is. And when you work smarter, your life gets a whole lot easier. Seriously now, who doesn't want to do things that make life and work easier?

Goals help you go faster. When you know your destination you can get to it more rapidly. Yes, any goal-setting process requires some planning time, but that time will be repaid many times over.

GOALS AND SPEED

Our experience with writing this book is instructive. When we were offered a contract for the book, the writing time-line was relatively quick. We knew it would be a challenge, but that it would be doable. The goal wasn't just writing the book, the goal was turning in the manuscript July 5, 2010. By having a tight time schedule we finished the book more rapidly. If the goal had just been to write the book, it still might not be done (whenever you are reading it)! There is no question that having goals with timelines speeds up progress and achievement.

Lessons

- Make sure your goals have timelines and deadlines.
- Timelines create and support your commitment to success.
- Don't be afraid to set challenging but achievable timelines.

Goals create satisfaction. How do you feel when you achieve something you care about? How do you feel when you don't know if you're making progress? Goals create satisfaction by giving you the targets to shoot for and therefore the sense of accomplishment when you know you have reached them. Satisfaction is more than just a nice feeling, it also drives momentum—and that momentum is a powerful force for advancement and additional accomplishment.

Goals create confidence. There's hardly any greater confidence booster than achieving something you have specifically set out to do. Setting goals and accomplishing them give you the confidence to set even greater goals, thus stretching yourself to greater performance in the future.

We could return to Joanna and the choices she made, but far more practical and important is to ask you how you will finish your story. Do you set goals? If so, are they ambitious enough, and are they focused on the great accomplishments that await you? If you don't have any real goals right now, at least consider these seven reasons and the advice they suggest.

Though we have just given you seven reasons you will want to set goals, let us give you one more. Your team won't achieve the success you are hoping for without goals. And it is hard to convince people to set them at work (or to discipline yourself to do it) if you aren't doing it for yourself in other parts of your life.

 The single biggest reason to set goals is that they improve your chances for success.

Your Now Steps

These steps will probably take less than five minutes, so do them now before you read on.

1. If you don't have any clearly stated goals, get serious. (We'll teach you how to set them in Chapter Forty-Three.)
2. Review this list of reasons for setting goals and identify the one or two that are most compelling to you.
3. Write those reasons in your learning journal as preparation for getting some goals written down.

42

GOAL SUCCESS STARTS WITH YOU

We hinted at this at the close of the previous chapter. Goals are not going to set themselves. Talk to ten people and nine of them will tell you they believe in goal setting. These nine people will also tell you that goals are important, that they can help you be happier and healthier, and that they are the best and fastest way to achieve more in life (they might even be able to recite some of the reasons we gave in the last chapter).

We would agree with those nine people.

Unfortunately, eight of the nine, when pressed, will tell you they don't set many (or any) goals; that they really want to, but...

Actually, we are being a bit optimistic here. We've both read several times that only about 3 percent of people ever set and write down *any* goals. Although we did not find the specific research that shows this result, it does match our practical experience.

Back to you as a leader. If you know a behavior is important, and you know that most people don't or aren't doing it, isn't it the leader's job to, shall we say, lead the way? By this point in the book, you know our opinion, and if you are still reading this many pages in, you probably agree with us.

So we know we need to set goals, and yet most people (including you?) aren't—so there must be some reason that people don't set them. Actually, we think there are at least seven reasons.

Seven Reasons People Don't Set Goals

1. People don't know how to set goals.
2. People are searching for the perfect way to set goals.

3. People are afraid to set goals.

4. People are afraid to succeed.

5. People are afraid they won't succeed.

6. People don't want to set the goal too high.

7. People don't want to set the goal too low.

It reminds us of Goldilocks, who wanted to get the porridge "just right." After looking at and thinking more about this list we came to two conclusions:

1. These aren't really reasons. They are *excuses* for not setting goals.
2. Each of these reasons or excuses can be addressed and influenced by you as a leader. So whether you are attacking these excuses for yourself or to influence others, as the chapter heading suggests, goal success does start with you.

Go back and read the list again; this time, read them all with a whine in your voice, and look for which "reason" on the list is your personal excuse—or the ones you have heard from your team in the past. Once you understand your challenges, you are in a better position to overcome them—we've even given you some solutions to help you get started.

> *Excuse #1: "But I don't know how. . . ."* This excuse makes sense in a way. How can we do anything if we don't know how to do it? Maybe you really don't know how, but to be honest, the resources to help you learn are plentiful. And we aren't talking rocket science here. There are hundreds of books about goal setting and thousands of free resources on the Internet. (Actually, an Amazon.com search on goal setting nets more than one thousand results, and a Google search on the same phrase yields more than twenty-three million results.)
>
> *Solution:* Find a resource, read it, and get started. And there is no time like the present.
>
> *Excuse #2: "But I want to set them the right way. . . ."* This excuse is the opposite of Excuse #1. There are some people that collect goal-setting books, tools, and techniques like others collect baseball cards (or Kevin collects antique tractors). Yes, there are many approaches; and yes, some may be better than

others or work better for you. But none of them will work until you do.

   Solution: Enough collecting! Pick an approach and get started. Most any will do. Don't spend too much time trying to find the best one. Just get started! If you want to work on this as a team, pick a single resource to share with everyone and get going. Any more time spent trying to find a better approach is really procrastination.

Excuse #3: "But I'm afraid...." Afraid of what? The unknown? There is nothing to be afraid of, except the unknown of trying. Recognizing your fear is a great first step, but setting goals isn't like the unknown risks of climbing Mt. Everest or swimming with sharks. There really is nothing to be afraid of (although there are two more excuses related to fear).

   Solution: The best way to conquer a fear is to do the thing you fear. Set a goal. Start with a small, short-term one if you must, but just do it.

Excuse #4: "But I'm afraid I'll succeed...." Actually, this excuse falls into a special category because people typically won't really say it and might not even consciously think it. But in reality, it may be the biggest and most powerful excuse of all. If you set a goal, you might achieve it, and in a paradoxical way, some people are afraid of the change that might come with that achievement. Or in some other cases they don't feel worthy of achieving it. (Or both.)

   Solution: Start small. Start with a small goal, one that will help you build your confidence and show you some success that you can manage. (If you have, or sense that members of your team have, significant self-esteem issues that are preventing you or them from feeling worthy of success, we encourage you to get help. There are lots of things you can do as a leader, and one of them is to know when to get additional help.)

Excuse #5: "But I'm afraid I'll fail...." That is certainly possible; you may fail. When you do, try this thinking instead: focus on the progress rather than the failure. For example, if you set a goal to lose 20 pounds and you only lose 10 is that so bad? Or if you set a goal to increase sales by $1,500,000 and only get $1,100,000 (or $600,000), aren't you ahead of where you were?

How many pounds would you have lost, or increased sales would you have realized, if you hadn't set a goal at all? Repeat after us: "There is nothing wrong with failing. Failing is just a chance to make corrections before trying again."

Solution: Let go of your fear, just a little bit, just this once. Just set a goal.

Excuse #6: "But if I set the goal too high, I might not reach it...." This is a combo-pack of Excuses #3 and #5 (and maybe a bit of #2 as well). If the goal is motivating to you, you will make progress. Maybe the goal is massive, and maybe you won't reach it; but if you set it you will move in the right direction. Plus, imagine the big satisfaction of meeting—or even exceeding—that big goal. And remember the quotation in the opening of this section about big goals? They are often as easy to reach as smaller ones.

Solution: Set a big goal, and go for it!

Excuse #7: "But if I set the goal too low, it might not be worth the effort...." How can this be? If you set a goal and reach it, great! Then you can set another one, big or small. Just like anything else, with practice comes greater skill. Some of your goals may be easy to reach, and that is OK. Over time you will learn to calibrate the goal size that is just right for you. This is especially true as you influence a team to set goals. This will often be the resistance or excuse you hear from a team.

Solution: Set a small goal and get started.

Have you noticed a theme in these solutions?

The solution is to take action. And as a leader, that is your job. Whether you are starting with yourself or your team, remember that goal success starts with you, and it all starts when you do!

Your Now Steps

1. The best way to start setting goals is to set one. (Yes, it is just that simple.)
2. Don't worry if the goal seems too big or too small; just set one.
3. If it is a work- or team-related goal, share it with others.
4. Then get started on achieving it!

43

BEYOND SMART—THE KEYS TO GOAL SETTING

Many of the goal-setting resources we mentioned in the previous chapter talk about and teach SMART goals. You have probably heard of this acrostic before, and maybe even used it. In case you have never heard of it, it is an acrostic that suggests all goals should be

Specific

Measurable

Action oriented

Realistic

Time-bound

If you want to learn more about these very fine suggestions, a Google search will give you over 16 million references to choose from. As a leader with massive potential, you should go beyond SMART. Let's get smarter....

Nine Keys to Better Goal Setting

1. *Write them down.* Maybe this goes without saying, but we had to say it! Clarity comes in writing goals down, and this is just as true for individual goals as for team goals. Writing them down also allows you to review them more easily and more often.

2. *State them in the present tense.* Our subconscious minds, which are exponentially more powerful than our conscious minds, like to

solve problems. When you state your goals as if they have already occurred, you stimulate and challenge your subconscious mind to seek opportunities to reach the goal. For example, your goal should be stated as "Have zero billing errors in June," not "Reduce billing errors 5 percent by June 30." Always state your goal in the present tense "as if" it has already occurred.

3. *Visualize the purpose—personally and organizationally.* We referred to this concept in Part Two: our minds can't tell the difference between something real and something vividly imagined, which means that the more vivid, multisensory, and real you can make the picture of how things will be when you have achieved the goal, the more powerfully drawn to it you will be.

For more details on how to utilize visualization for an individual or team goal, go to the Bonus Bytes page at BudToBossCommunty.com and click on the Visualize button.

4. *Focus on the "Big Why."* The goal isn't enough; you need to know why you want to achieve it. It is your *why* that will keep you motivated and moving forward.

5. *Align them with your values.* If your goal isn't aligned with your personal or organizational values it is likely to be weak and unsuccessful. Chances are your goals will be aligned with your values, and as you set your goals make sure they are. You will also want to keep that alignment crystal clear in your mind. Striving for this mental clarity is another strategy to help you move toward that goal more quickly and successfully.

6. *Find the Bigness Balance.* In the last chapter we talked about big versus small goals. Although you need to find a balance, generally speaking, when in doubt, go bigger.

For more details on how to find the bigness balance for your goals, go to the Bonus Bytes page at BudToBossCommunty.com and click on the Goal Size button.

7. *Consider the timeline now.* When you set the goal, start your planning process, including a rough timeline of the steps and when you need to reach them in order to achieve your desired outcome on time.

8. *Think about barriers now.* You won't know all of the challenges you will face, but you probably know some of your barriers now. Write them down. If you have ideas for overcoming them write them down too. You don't have to have a complete plan at this moment, but by identifying some of the barriers, you expedite your planning and improve your chances for success.

9. *Commit to an action plan.* The steps up until now are the precursors to a plan. Now you must commit to completing the plan and implementing it. If you aren't willing to do these two steps, how likely are you to achieve the goal?

 For a goal-setting planning form that incorporates many of these ideas and helps you get beyond the goal statement, go to the Bonus Bytes page at BudToBossCommunty.com and click on the Goal Sheet button.

OK, we cheated a bit. Some of these concepts take you beyond just setting the goal. We aren't apologizing, though, because the only reason you set goals is to give you a better chance to achieve them. By having that mind-set at the start of the process, you can do a better job of setting them.

We hope you also notice all the connections here to the vision component of change that we discussed in Part Two. That component and goal setting are virtually one and the same. A goal after all implies change, right?

 When goals are clearer, we make it easier for people to choose to change.

Your Now Steps

1. Take the goal you set in the last chapter (You did it. Right?) and apply these ideas to it.

2. If you haven't written a goal yet, start there, and then apply these ideas.

3. Procrastinating now is a big mistake. Even if the goal isn't a big deal or isn't the goal you are really thinking about most of the time, get started.

44

HOW TO SET GOALS
WITH OTHERS

Everything in Part Six is universal. It all applies to individuals setting goals in their personal and professional lives, and it all applies to team goal setting, too. When we put other people into the mix, just as in anything else, we layer in some complexity. Because of this added complexity, having some additional tactics can be helpful.

The goal of this chapter is to help you apply these universal ideas when you are helping another person set goals (as you would in a coaching situation) or when helping a team set mutual goals.

When sharing this idea with groups, we sometimes encounter questions and resistance. They typically sound something like: "I understand the idea of helping someone else with his or her goals as a coach, but aren't team goals usually handed down from above or from me as the leader?" That question is understandable, especially given most people's experience. Team goals are often provided to people. Our response to that question is to ask a series of questions something like this:

○ How does that process work?
○ Do people feel ownership of those goals?
○ And most important, how often are those goals achieved?

Normally, the answers to these questions are "not very well," "no," and "seldom." Since the results of mandated goals are typically negative, we recommend a different approach to team goal setting.

Four Reasons to Set Team Goals Collaboratively

There are four significant reasons that you need to get others involved in creating the group's or team's goals. Any one of these is reason enough to create a conversation about the goals rather than creating a PowerPoint presentation with the goals already formulated.

1. To gain agreement
   There are actually two agreements you want to gain:

   • Agreement on what the goal actually is

   • Agreement that the goal is worthwhile and beneficial

   Once you have these agreements you will increase the clarity of the goal for everyone. Goal clarity in itself has a very positive impact on ultimate goal achievement. With agreement you will increase focus on the goal as well. Take the time to create both of these agreements and you have a stronger chance of achieving the next item....

2. To create engagement
   Notice we said engagement not buy-in. We recognize that many people talk about wanting others to "buy in" to their ideas and plans. And, given the choice between having people who are "bought-in" versus people who don't care or who actually disagree, we choose the former. However, "buy-in" is still limited and not as powerful or lasting as engagement. When people are engaged in an idea or goal, they are committed to it. They feel ownership for it. They have thrown more than their hats into the ring; they have thrown their hearts in, too. Once people are engaged in the goal you can capture what comes next....

3. To set collective consciousness
   Remember the example of seeing "your" car everywhere after you buy one? Your reticular activating system works as a filter, and it helps you notice things you are focusing on or are interested in. Here is how that helps with team goals. Once people understand and are fully engaged in achieving a goal, their subconscious minds go to work and the reticular activating system helps. People will begin to see things that they didn't see before, such as new resources, methods, or clues to achieving the goal. Sparks will fly between people on the team, and progress may be achieved faster than could be logically expected. We hope that you have experienced this at some time in your life. If you have, it may have

happened almost by chance. When you follow the steps in this chapter you can actually create and nurture that type of magic.

4. To manifest synergy

We have people work together because we know that together we can achieve more than we can separately. This is the definition of synergy. However, if you prepare your goals in a vacuum and then present them to the group, the chance for you to achieve team synergies (especially at the start) is virtually nil. Since a major purpose for creating a team goal is to capture the synergy of that group of people, doesn't it make sense to use a process that will actually create it?

As you can now see, getting others involved in the creation of goals they will be working toward is more than just a good idea, and it is more than just the right thing to do. It is the most important step you can take to improve the likelihood that your team will reach the goals you set.

BUT THE GOALS ARE GIVEN TO ME TO GIVE TO THE TEAM. . . .

We realize that unless you are the business owner or CEO, you may not have complete control in this case. Someone else may have set the goals and given you the PowerPoint slides to share with your team (or he or she may have announced them to you and the team at the same time). If this happens, don't dismay or throw your hands in the air. While you could give a copy of this book with this chapter dog-eared to your boss (we'd appreciate that), it probably won't change the fact that the goals have already been mandated.

What do you do then?

Our advice is to

○ Focus on what is in your circle of influence.

○ Acknowledge to the team that everyone needs to take the goals and make them their own, even if they didn't create them. (People generally understand that setting goals can be the prerogative of management, and your acknowledgment and plan to engage them are likely

> to be a breath of fresh air to them. It may even ignite significant energy!)
>
> ○ Use the steps in this chapter to focus on building the plans to achieve the goals and to set your subgoals and targets on the way to the mandated goal.

 If you want people to feel ownership of a goal, set the goal *with* them, not *for* them.

Creating Ownership of Goals

These strategies work whether creating ownership for an individual or across a team. The larger the group, the more complex and time consuming the process may be, but these engagement steps remain the same.

 The single most important thing you can do to create ownership of anything—including a goal—is to let the other person share his or her thoughts first.

Have Them Speak First

We've said it before, if you, as a leader, tell others you want to help them and then begin by sharing your thoughts, you are likely to cause them to disengage. Regardless of your intention, if you "go first" you are short-circuiting ownership before you even get started. Get them talking and sharing their thoughts. Encourage them. Have a few questions to jump-start their brains if necessary. Be comfortable with a little silence, because it may take a minute to get them going. Just don't give in and offer to go first. Be patient. Your patience will be rewarded.

Agree

Having them speak first doesn't mean your opinions can't be included in the conversation. As the leader, you have a perspective they don't have, and it needs to be shared. By allowing them to share first, you encourage them to be more open to your input as well. What you want is agreement on a goal or goals that you can all live with—and that they own. This means striking a balance between their needs and ideas and yours. Our advice in short? Have the final goals show as few of your fingerprints as possible.

 For help in finding this balance of getting your input included without losing the ownership of others, go to the Bonus Bytes page at BudToBossCommunity.com and click on the Create Ownership button.

Check Alignment

Remember our discussion of the CARB model (Chapter Thirty-Five) and how important it is to organizational success to align individual and team goals to the organizational objectives? You could start the goal-setting process with a question like, "Given the organization strategies and initiatives, what must we do to support and further those goals?" However, your former peers may wonder what planet you came from. Instead, we recommend a question more like: "What goal(s) can we set that will help the organization succeed?"

Though we suggest you start with that type of question, after conversation and agreement on the actual goal(s), it is worthwhile to loop back to these questions to make sure you have both alignment and ownership.

Build a Plan

Build the plan in the same way you built the goal—together. The more engaged people are in the creation of the plan, the more likely they will be to implement the plan! Here is where they may lean on you more as a leader. Even if you have only been in your role for a short time, your expertise and advice will probably be sought here. Why? Because planning is often hard—so people naturally want help—and you often have access to resources they don't have to help the plan come together (more on that in the last chapter).

Your Now Steps

While we urge you to apply the ideas of this chapter, the timing may not be perfect, and we realize doing the steps listed here will take some time. There is still something you can do right now.

1. Look at the collection of goals that your team or individuals on your team are currently working toward.

2. Assess your team's relative sense of ownership in the goals.

3. If you aren't sure about their level of engagement, informally ask people how invested they feel in their goals.

4. Take their answers into account as you plan to create future goals with others.

45

WHAT IS THE RIGHT ATTITUDE TO SUPPORT GOAL ACHIEVEMENT?

Leaders and achievers are always looking for ways to become more successful. They are constantly striving to reach goals more quickly and with greater assurance. Factors that help people reach their goals have been written about for centuries. Certainly attitude is on the list of these factors. Without question, attitude is one piece of the goal achievement puzzle. Attitude is always discussed, often downplayed, and typically misunderstood in the goal achievement puzzle. For leaders interested in creating success, these are three good reasons to explore attitude a bit further.

Let's consider two common situations.

> *Situation A.* Tom is incredibly talented and has lots of experience in his field. His goals have been set high but are considered reachable by everyone—except Tom. For whatever reason, he doesn't think he can achieve them, and he spends much time telling others how tough they are. Though he works hard and clearly has the ability to reach the goals, deep down he has significant doubt.
>
> *Situation B.* Allison is capable but doesn't yet have years of experience. Because of the company goal-setting approach her goal looks pretty big—to her and anyone else looking at it from the outside. She dives in headfirst, expecting to succeed, even though she doesn't know all of the things she will have to know to ultimately succeed.

Which situation has a better chance of success? While we have made these hypothetical situations pretty extreme, we still believe Situation B has the best chance of ultimate success, because we hold attitude in pretty high esteem.

While the right attitude alone won't create success, without it you will be severely handicapped.

In this chapter we outline what the right attitude is (to support maximum goal achievement), why it is important to us both as individuals and leaders, and how to develop it.

So what is the right attitude? We're glad you asked.

Consider the three Ps of the right goal achievement attitude:

○ *Positive.* This is where most of these conversations start...and stop. Prevailing wisdom and much research show that having a positive attitude improves the likelihood you will achieve your goal, speeds your progress, and, perhaps most important, makes you more resilient—allowing you to overcome obstacles and remain persistent in pursuit of your goal.

○ *Possibility.* The key to possibility in your attitude is belief. Do you believe you can succeed and reach the goal? Do you believe you can earn it? Do you believe the goal is possible? If you think it is possible for others, can you see it for yourself? This is more than just an extension of positive thinking. After all, if you didn't think the goal was achievable, how likely would you be to work hard to achieve it?

○ *Proactive.* The right attitude isn't about thinking and belief alone, the right attitude includes realizing that you must roll up your sleeves and do something. As you take action in the direction of your goals, you can build momentum, grow belief, and enhance attitude as you go.

We realize all of these ideas sound pretty good. But what makes this the "right" attitude, or more practically, how does an attitude that includes the three Ps help you and your team?

○ The right attitude enables the right behaviors—behaviors of persistence, discipline, creativity, and more.

○ The right attitude enables the right focus—staying on target mentally and remaining alert for opportunities.

○ The right attitude enables the right results—it improves the likelihood of your success in reaching your goals.

Behaviors, focus, and results. The right attitude can create all of them, for both you and those you lead.

Steps to Develop the Right Attitude

Now that you know what the right attitude looks like (and you realize it is more than "just" positive mental attitude) as it relates to goal achievement, how do you create it? Here are some immediate steps you can take.

1. *Set the goal.* This is the start. Before you can achieve a goal you must know what it is. This sets everything in motion. The size and nature of the goal will have an impact on all three Ps described above. The good news is you now know how to do this, and you have set at least one goal already. Right?

2. *Involve those who will be achieving the goal.* If you want others to believe in the goal, you must involve them as much as possible. The right attitude comes easier when people own the goal. (You're working on this one, too. Right?)

3. *Create greater belief.* Remind people of past successes. Reward and recognize small successes on the achievement path. As you do this, you create a momentum effect, and the greater belief buoys the attitude.

4. *Get excited about the goal.* Actually, this is a misstatement. Don't focus on the goal itself, get yourself and others excited about the *benefits that come from achieving the goal.* When you know why you are doing the (hard) work of moving toward a goal, you create the right attitude. This is another way of saying: keep reminding people of their "Big Why."

5. *Make the goals visual and vivid.* Though this point has already been mentioned, it is critical. Help people "see" the achievement of the goal. Help them make that picture as real as you can. Then, whenever possible, remind people of that vision.

6. *Keep the goal in front of you at all times.* Do you have a list of your goals that you read often? Do you have team goals written down and visually available to people in multiple places? Do you open team meetings by reminding people of the goals? When people are reminded of their goals, they are excited about achieving them. The reminder helps people manage their attitudes and keeps them "right."

We all know that the right attitude will make a difference. Now you know some reasons, and you know how to influence and nurture that attitude in yourself and in those you lead. Once you get the attitude right, you are fast-forwarding your progress toward achieving your goals!

Your Now Step

Keeping a positive attitude is a lifelong challenge for everyone—even if some people seem more "positive" by nature than others. Here is a little-known fact for some of you. Those who are "more positive" know it is a challenge. Those who aren't often assume there is no hope for them. Regardless of your attitude, inclination, or past habits, as a leader who values achievement and results, you don't really have a choice. Develop the right attitudes to support goal achievement. The step below can help you get started.

1. Determine one of the steps above to focus on today. As you read them, you will know which one your inner voice says you need to work on. Start there.

46

MOVING FROM GOAL SETTING TO GOAL GETTING

As we have said, there is no lack of resources to help you with goal setting—they are everywhere. Unfortunately, only a small percentage of those materials deals with the more important question of goal achievement.

We won't make the same mistake. We have given you hints about achievement throughout this section, and this is, as the title implies, the entire focus of this final chapter. Once you have set the goal and built the plan to achieve it, there is that little thing called doing the "work" that still needs to happen.

Knowing that it will take effort and knowing human nature, we understand why many goals are never reached—people don't put in the requisite effort.

You and your team have probably seen this tendency as well. This past experience with goal setting is also one reason that you have in the past experienced, and will continue to experience in the future, some resistance to goal-setting activities—people haven't seen success personally or organizationally. Armed with everything you have learned, and especially this chapter, you know that resistance can change. Follow these steps and, over time, it will.

Leadership Steps for Goal Achievement

As a leader, there are a number of things you can do to improve the likelihood that the goals set by and with your team are reached. This book has outlined many of these things already. The steps that follow, though, are specific and direct things you can do to improve the success of your team in achieving their goals.

Visualize

Yes, we have said it before. It's like the advice you have probably heard that you should put a picture of your goal on your mirror or your refrigerator so you see it regularly. This is a simple (and powerful) form of visualization. Your intention is to help everyone make the goal real in their minds. This helps the subconscious mind work on the goal and helps us consciously maintain focus, desire, and momentum. Visualization will help make the goal more real, and as Kevin says, "*Realizing* our goals allows us to realize our goals."

One more important point: the bigger the goal, the more important visualization becomes. As goals get bigger, it is important to make even more effort to help people visualize not only the end goal, but also the major milestone points along the way, and even to visualize success in managing the plan itself.

 Here is a repeat Bonus Byte in case you missed it earlier! For more details on how to use visualization for an individual or team goal, go to the Bonus Bytes page at BudToBossCommunity.com and click on the Visualize button.

Flex

You know you need a plan. And if the goal is of any size at all, you know that the situations and circumstances surrounding it will change. Knowing this, you need to be willing to flex your plan and your timeline to meet new realities, and maybe even flex the goal itself. Plans are important, and they will be most effective when they are flexible.

Implement Consistently

This may seem obvious, but we see evidence to the contrary in organizations all the time (and truth be known, this is an area where we are constantly trying to improve, too). We become passive, and we let work and circumstances take over (see "The Reality of Organizational Implementation"). As a leader, if you are serious about goal achievement, you must feverishly focus on implementation (we aren't exaggerating here). If you don't believe us, read the biography of any person who has accomplished significant and meaningful goals. They are masters of implementation whether working alone or with others.

THE REALITY OF ORGANIZATIONAL IMPLEMENTATION

Reality too often looks like this:

1. You set annual goals because you know they are important, and you really want the success that comes with achieving them.

2. Everyone involved is excited about the goals, and they already have plenty to do.

3. Early in the year, people are working hard to carve out time to work on the goals.

4. But the crush of work or a loss of focus slowly (or quickly) takes over.

5. People get lost in the urgent matters, and goals that are typically very important but not urgent enough to stay on the radar screen slide out of focus.

6. November comes, and people suddenly realize little has been done on the goals. A rash of activity makes some progress. But ultimately they fall far short of the goals, or they only reach the easier ones.

7. Next year's goal-setting process starts it all again, perhaps even with some of the same goals as last year. Everyone is just a little more cynical. . . .

As a leader you can break this cycle—but only if you make implementation a constant focus.

Provide Time

Google is famous for giving people one day per week to work on whatever projects they want—outside of their "regular" job. Although you may dismiss the idea out of hand as Silicon Valley silliness, the practice has led to innovations that are significant contributors to their bottom line (Google Mail is just one example). Even though it is likely that you won't or can't go that far in providing time, remember three things:

1. There will always be busywork, and people will always find a fire to fight.
2. Work expands to the time allowed.
3. The routine tasks of work are easier and likely to be better defined (even if not as motivating or exciting) than goal work. So, guess where people will generally focus?

This leaves you with an important decision. Is achieving the goals more important than completing some of the other tasks on people's work lists? If so, you must help them find the time to work on the goals. It might be through improved time management strategies or by helping them prioritize more accurately, but help them find the time.

Schedule Time

Time management strategies and prioritization are important, but not enough. If you are serious about achieving the goals you have set, and you want your team to be serious too, put goal time on the calendar. You'll know if it should be one hour a day, two hours a week, or one day a month (and it should probably be more than you initially think). Unless you schedule it in everyone's calendar (including yours), you won't achieve as many of your goals as you could.

Provide Resources

You are the leader. You may have access to dollars for training, the ability to shift workload balances, and much more. As a new leader, you may not realize all the resources you have at your disposal, but you have them. Use them abundantly in support of goal achievement.

Make It a Priority

Here is the bottom line. If the goal(s) aren't a priority for you, they certainly won't be for your team. If they are a priority for you, make sure you are showing obvious and outward proof of this fact.

Your Now Steps

Considering a current organizational or team goal:

1. Create a stronger vision for the successful completion of the goal. If it is clear in your mind, help others involved create that vision too.
2. If the vision is already clear to everyone, take immediate steps to bolster one of the other areas discussed in this chapter.

 Ultimately what matters isn't goal setting, it is goal *getting*.

A Final Thought

It seems fitting to close this book with a chapter on goal achievement. If you picked up this book and read any of it, and certainly if you have read it all, you have been engaged in goal setting. Each Now Step has been a smaller goal in the process of your bigger goal of making your transition to leadership more successful. We hope we have helped you clarify those goals and have given you significant resources for your journey.

Now it is your turn. If you want to turn those goals into reality, you have to do the things necessary to improve. It is time to show your commitment to success through your actions.

The work you have identified as you read will be richly rewarded, but only when you do it. Consider BudToBossCommunity.com as a resource to help you. There you will find all of the Bonus Bytes from the book and many more resources and connections to help you on your path. We'll "see" you there, and we and our team look forward to helping you there in any way that we can.

It's time to get to work.

REFERENCES

Cloud, H. *Integrity: The Courage to Meet the Demands of Reality*. New York: HarperCollins, 2006.

Covey, S. R. *The Seven Habits of Highly Effective People*. New York: Simon & Schuster, 1989.

Dana, D. *Conflict Resolution*. New York: McGraw-Hill, 2001.

Dana, D. *Managing Differences*. Prairie Village, Kansas: MTI Publications, 2006.

Eikenberry, K. *Remarkable Leadership: Unleashing Your Leadership Potential One Skill at a Time*. San Francisco: Jossey-Bass, 2007.

Frederickson, B. L., and Losada, M. F. "Positive Affect and the Complex Dynamics of Human Flourishing." *American Psychologist*, 2005, *60* (7), 678–686.

Glouberman, S., and Zimmerman, B. "Is the System Complicated or Complex?" Learningforsustainability.net. Accessed September 8, 2010, http://learningforsustainability.net/tools/complex.php

Heath, C., and Heath, D. *Made to Stick*. New York: Random House, 2007.

International Listening Association. Accessed June 28, 2010, www.listen.org

Lencioni, P. *The Five Dysfunctions of a Team*. San Francisco: Jossey-Bass, 2002.

Livingston, J. "Pygmalion in Management." *Harvard Business Review*, September-October 1988.

Marston, W. M. *The Emotions of Normal People*. New York: Taylor & Francis, 1999; originally published 1928.

Maslow, A. *The Psychology of Science: A Reconnaissance*. New York: Harper & Row, 1966; Chapel Hill, North Carolina: Maurice Bassett, 2002.

Maurer, R. *Beyond the Wall of Resistance*. Austin, Texas: Bard Press, 1996.

Rohm, R. A. *Positive Personality Profiles*. Marietta, Georgia: Personality Insights, 2008.

Rosenthal, R., and Jacobson, L. "Teachers' Expectancies: Determinates of Pupils' IQ Gains." *Psychological Reports*, 1966, *19*, 115–118.

Runde, C. E., and Flanagan, T. A. *Becoming a Conflict Competent Leader*. San Francisco: Jossey-Bass, 2007.

Tavris, C., and Aronson, E. *Mistakes Were Made (but not by me)*. Orlando: Houghton Mifflin Harcourt, 2007.

Tuckman, B. W. "Developmental Sequence in Small Groups." *Psychological Bulletin*, 1965, *63*(6), 384–399.

Watson, K. W., and Smeltzer, L. R. "Barriers to Listening: Comparison Between Students and Practitioners." *Communication Research Report*, 1984, 82–87.

ACKNOWLEDGMENTS

Acknowledgments for any book are important, because no one can create a useful and successful book alone. If you have enjoyed this book, we hope you will read a little more as a way to acknowledge all the important people involved in it.

We have many people and groups to thank, and though we will share some names here, they certainly aren't the only people who have had an impact on our growth as consultants, leaders, learners, authors, and people.

We both thank our families: mothers and fathers, wives and our children. No one else defines who we are more than these people.

We have learned so much from our clients. They have provided opportunities for us to observe, learn, and try out our suggestions. Whether in conversations, in coaching, or in one of the hundreds of workshops we have led, without all of these people you would not be reading these words.

A book comes not just from the experiences and thoughts collected in these ways, but also from a broader network of people. We have far too many important colleagues to mention here without risking leaving someone important out. Though unnamed, we thank all of them for their contribution to our lives as leaders and human beings.

We acknowledge and thank the entire team at Jossey-Bass for believing in this project and helping it come to life.

The Kevin Eikenberry Group team has helped create this book in many ways. They put up with us as we finished the book, provided ideas and examples, and supported both of us in countless ways up until now, and up until you read these words (and far beyond).

The team at Briefings Media Group, especially Curtis Wharton and Adrienne Knox, have helped make these ideas seen and used across North America through promotion of the Bud to Boss Workshops.

Dr. Robert Rohm and the rest of the team at Personality Insights provided valuable perspective and great experiences that contributed to and shaped the chapters describing the theory and application of the DISC model of human behavior.

There are many other people who have helped and will help with the success of this book. There are bloggers, editors, journalists, reporters, and organizational leaders who will perhaps be responsible for your reading these words. There will be people who will write kind words for the cover of this book, and there will be countless others whose efforts will help this book have an impact in the world. We thank all of these people, both those we could name and the many we'll never meet.

We must thank our children again, by name—Guy's Lydia and Alexandra and Kevin's Parker and Kelsey. They put up with us all of the time, including when we are trying to finish a manuscript and not being the best Dads. Of course, without our brides and best friends, Sandra (Guy) and Lori (Kevin), we would be far less than we are.

Finally, we thank God as the ultimate source of the blessings we have been given. We hope that we are using those blessings to make leaders (and the world) better.

ABOUT THE AUTHORS

KEVIN EIKENBERRY is a two-time best-selling author, speaker, consultant, trainer, coach, leader, learner, husband, and father (not necessarily in that order).

Kevin is the chief potential officer of The Kevin Eikenberry Group (http://KevinEikenberry.com), a learning consulting company that has been helping organizations, teams, and individuals reach their potential since 1993. Emphasizing the power of learning, Kevin's specialties include leadership, teams and teamwork, organizational culture, facilitating change, training trainers, and more.

Kevin's philosophy in business and in life is that every person and every organization has extraordinary potential. Investments of time, energy, focus, and money are required for that potential to be realized. He believes learning is an active, ongoing process, not a passive, one-time event. Learning, work, and life should be fun, and if we are doing it right, work (and learning) is play.

Kevin's students and clients consistently rave about his effectiveness, many calling him "the best trainer I've ever experienced."

He has worked with Fortune 500 companies, small firms, universities, government agencies, hospitals, and more. His client list includes the American Red Cross, A&W Canada, Chevron Phillips Chemical Company, John Deere, Nexen, OPTI Canada, Purdue University, Sears Canada, Shell, Southwest Airlines, the U.S. Marine Corps, and the U.S. Mint.

Kevin also is the creator and content developer of *The Remarkable Leadership Learning System* (http://remarkable-leadership.com), a continual leadership development process focused on developing the thirteen competencies of remarkable leaders with content virtually delivered to leaders worldwide.

He is the bestselling author of *Remarkable Leadership: Unleashing Your Leadership Potential One Skill at a Time*, a leadership primer designed to help you learn and master the thirteen competencies of remarkable leaders; and *Vantagepoints on Learning and Life*, a collection of his e-mail essays on learning from everyday experiences. He wrote *#LEADERSHIPTweet*, based on leadership thoughts from his Twitter stream (@KevinEikenberry).

He also is a contributing author in *The Handbook of Experiential Learning, Masters of Sales, 101 Great Ways to Improve Your Life*, and the best-selling *Walking with the Wise*. Kevin also has been a contributor to thirteen Training and Development Sourcebooks since 1997.

Kevin also produces two e-mail–based publications: *Unleashing Your Remarkable Potential,* a weekly publication read by more than 16,000 worldwide, to assist organizations and individuals in turning their potential into desired results; and *Powerquotes Plus,* a weekly publication read by more than 24,000 people worldwide, each one featuring a quote along with personal coaching.

As a speaker, Kevin gives keynotes for organizations and nonprofits on remarkable leadership, lifelong learning, developing human poten-tial, teams and teamwork, creativity, and more. He has presented to the National Institute of Health, the American Farm Bureau Feder-ation, the National Speaker's Association (NSA), the International Society for Performance Improvement, the National Association for Experiential Learning, the American Society for Training and Devel-opment, the International Society for Performance Improvement, and many more.

Kevin and his family live in Indianapolis, Indiana. Growing up on a Michigan farm, Kevin says he learned some of his most important leadership skills working with his father. Kevin earned a B.S. with honors from Purdue University, collects antique John Deere tractors, is an avid reader, and loves his family and his boilermakers.

If Kevin or his team can help you in any way call (317.387.1424 or 888.LEARNER—toll free in the United States) anytime.

―――――― o ――――――

GUY HARRIS draws on more than twenty-five years of combined professional and military experience when he consults, coaches, and trains in the areas of team and interaction dynamics, communication strategies and tactics, and emotional intelligence.

Guy owns Principle Driven Consulting (www.principledriven.com), a training and development company focused on helping organi-zations and individuals improve results by reducing conflict and improving communication skills. He is also a master trainer and coach with the Kevin Eikenberry Group.

Prior to becoming a trainer, coach, and author, Guy served as a nuclear engineering officer in the U.S. Navy submarine force, and he worked in leadership positions in both large and small business environments.

As a consultant, trainer, and coach, Guy has worked with large and small clients, businesses, not-for-profit organizations, and individuals from Boston to Brisbane and from Ottawa to Orlando.

Typical client concerns prior to working with Guy are forging a team from a group of individuals, moving a team past the conflict stage of team development, developing other leaders, expanding personal influence within the organization, communicating more effectively, and developing buy-in for new programs and processes.

With experience and training in technical disciplines and his further training in, and practical application of, human behavior and motivation principles, his unique skills include quickly connecting the technical and task accomplishment necessities of business operations with the human factors that often limit rapid implementation and results.

In other words, he helps people understand—and work through—the reasons that their relationships are getting in the way of getting things done.

Clients consistently comment on how quickly Guy helps them diagnose their "real" challenges and create plans for overcoming them. Workshop participants rave about the way his stories and experiences relate learning points in ways that are fun, engaging, and memorable.

Guy wrote a business parable titled *The Coach: Conversations on Leadership,* and he codeveloped a parenting system called *The Behavior Bucks System* to help parents reduce stress and frustration in their homes. He writes the Recovering Engineer Blog (recoveringengineer.com). He has also contributed to several books, including *Sell Naked on the Phone* and *Presenting with Style.*

He has both bachelor's and master's degrees in chemical engineering. He was a qualified Engineering Department head in the U.S. Navy. He is a master trainer and coach in the DISC model of human behavior and a workplace conflict resolution expert.

Guy and his family currently live in a small town near Indianapolis, Indiana. He has lived, attended school, or worked in eleven of the fifty United States in the Southeast, Northeast, and Midwest in both small towns and large cities. In his professional life, he has travelled to Europe, Asia, and Australia, and throughout North America. And he has worked with people at all organizational levels from the shop floor to the executive suite. This combined living, working, and educational experience gives him a broad view of human nature and interaction that comes through in his approach to working with and leading people.

Although the engineer in him still enjoys alone activities like woodworking, fixing things, reading, and playing with computer code, Guy loves being with his family, learning from others, and cooking for a party.

Guy and Kevin codeveloped the content for the Bud to Boss Workshops (www.BudToBossWorkshop.com), marketed by the Briefings Media Group (www.BriefingsMediaGroup.com) and held in cities across North America.

THE KEVIN EIKENBERRY GROUP

How We Can Help

If you have just finished reading any portion of this book, you will be clear about our belief in learning. The Kevin Eikenberry Group was built on the philosophy that we are at our best—and achieve our best results—when we are learning. All of our products and services support this philosophy: to help you as a continuous learner achieve success at the highest level. Read on to learn more!

Keynote Speaking

Both Kevin and Guy (and others on the team) are available to speak at your company or association event on topics related to this book, or on a broader set of leadership, communication, and teamwork topics. You can learn more at http://KevinEikenberry.com /speaking/speaking.asp.

Training

We deliver a wide variety of training services, customized to meet your needs, as well as workshops designed and ready to go, "off the shelf." For more information about these services, go to http://KevinEikenberry.com/training/training.asp. One of our premier offerings is workshops based on the skills and ideas in this book—there is more information about these public workshops in the next section.

Consulting

We regularly consult with organizations on matters of organizational change, organizational culture, and leadership development. As a reader of this book, you have a sense of who we are. If you like what you've read, we'd love to discuss helping your organization grow and succeed at higher levels. For more information, go to http://KevinEikenberry.com/consulting/consulting.asp.

Coaching

Kevin and Guy are available on a very limited basis to serve as your leadership coach. Additional coaching services are also available through our certified Remarkable Leadership Coaches. For more information and for an application, contact us at info@KevinEikenberry.com.

The Bud to Boss™ Workshop—Coming to a City Near You!

Does the book leave you hungry for more? Don't let your learning stop now! One of the biggest reasons new supervisors and leaders struggle is because they don't have the right training and support in the most important areas.

The Bud to Boss™ Workshop was created by Kevin and Guy to solve this dilemma. If you are ready to take the next step in your leadership development or if you have others in your organization that need these skills, the Bud to Boss Workshop is for you!

Bud to Boss goes beyond the nuts and bolts of your job. You already know that stuff or else you wouldn't have gotten the promotion. It takes the ideas and skills in this book and helps you learn them at a deeper level from experts and your peers in the room. You'll learn more about the ideas you've read about in this book and get answers to your specific questions and solutions for your specific challenges.

If you liked and found this book useful, you will love the Bud to Boss Workshop!

With your purchase of this book, you're entitled to the Bud to Boss Friends & Family Discount—20% off any registration! Visit http://www.budtoboss.com/book.asp and enter the promo code **B2BOOK** to receive your discount. Want to bring the workshop onsite or have Kevin and Guy customize it for you? You can contact us from the Web site to do that too. While you are there, sign up for our free Ezine.

Special Offer for Readers of *From Bud to Boss*!

This book is a step on your journey toward becoming a Remarkable Leader, but it is just one step. If you are ready to continue your journey, our *Insider* newsletter can be your monthly guide. Written with a practical, high-energy approach, you will find articles in each issue from Kevin, Guy, and others on Kevin's team, and you'll gain access to the transcript of a full one-hour interview between Kevin and an expert on a leadership skill.

Valued at over $80/month, the newsletter's standard pricing is $29/month. As a reader of this book, your investment is just $19/month—with additional first month benefits!

For all the details and to take advantage of this 100% guaranteed, *From Bud to Boss* special offer, go to http://www.remarkable-leadership.com/levels/btbinsider/.

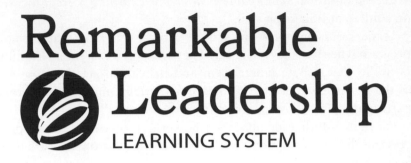

Remarkable Leadership
LEARNING SYSTEM

The Remarkable Leadership Learning System

The *Remarkable Leadership Learning System* is an ongoing process to help you take specific actions each month to build your leadership skills. It is a virtually-delivered leadership development program for you, for a small team of leaders, or for as broad a leadership development program as you would like for your organization. It is designed around the realities of work and learning, including

- **Focus**—When you can focus on one thing at a time, you will be more successful. A traditional, multiday leadership training program provides too many new things to work on at once, too often leaving people working on none of them.

- **Limited Time**—Leaders are busy people with an overflowing plate of work. They don't have the time to go to a three-day workshop on leadership skills. And if they do manage to carve out the time for the class, they can barely find time to respond to all the e-mails they have received since leaving the office; all too quickly they forget about being able to apply what they've learned.

- **Incremental Improvement**—Leaders don't become remarkable over night. They work every day to get a little bit better. By giving them a limited number of things to work on at a given time and helping them integrate those new ideas and techniques into their ongoing work, they will be more successful in making improvements.

- **How We Learn**—People learn by taking new ideas, trying them, repeating what worked, and changing what didn't. This Learning System provides new ideas, avenues to try those ideas, and a process for reflecting on their effectiveness.

Each month the *Remarkable Leadership Learning System* focuses on a different leadership skill.

Leaders can join this "one skill at a time, one month at a time" program whenever they are ready. They will receive an initial learning portfolio that will acclimate them and help them get the most out of the *Remarkable Leadership Learning System,* and they will begin participating in the live program from the month they register.

For more information about this powerful leadership learning process and the various options available to you, go to http://remarkable-leadership.com.

INDEX

Remarkable Leadership
Unleashing Your Leadership Potential
One Skill at a Time

By Kevin Eikenberry
Foreword by Jack Canfield

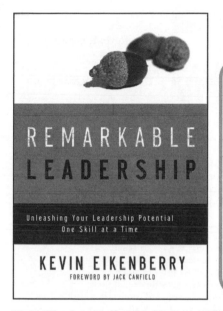

A handbook for honing the skills needed to become an effective leader

This groundbreaking book joins leadership skill development with learning principles while recognizing the realities of working life. Based on Eikenberry's Remarkable Leadership Learning System, this book provides a framework and a mechanism for both learning new things and applying current knowledge in a thoughtful and practical way. It provides a guide through 13 leadership competencies, offers a proven method for learning the skills, and shows approaches for applying skills in today's multitasking and overloaded world of work.

Kevin Eikenberry is the Chief Potential Officer of The Kevin Eikenberry Group, a learning consulting company that provides a wide range of services including training delivery and design, facilitation, performance coaching, organizational consulting, and speaking services. His extensive client list includes the American Red Cross, Chevron Phillips Chemical Company, John Deere, Purdue University, Sears Canada, Shell, Southwest Airlines, the U.S. Marine Corps, the U.S. Mint, Verizon. and more.

ISBN 978-0-7879-9619-2 • US $27.95

Available wherever books and ebooks are sold
www.josseybass.com

JB JOSSEY-BASS™
An Imprint of ⓦ**WILEY**
Now you know.

FACILITATOR'S GUIDE

12 PROGRAMS FOR CREATING REMARKABLE LEADERS

REMARKABLE
LEADERSHIP
KEVIN EIKENBERRY
author of *Remarkable Leadership*

REMARKABLE LEADERSHIP

12 Programs for Creating
Remarkable Leaders

By Kevin Eikenberry

ISBN: 978-0-470-50557-1
US $299.00 | CAN $359.00

A complete guide to the most important leadership competencies, *Remarkable Leadership: 12 Programs for Creating Remarkable Leaders* is a flexible-format learning series that combines leadership skill development with learning principles. This workshop is based on the author's Remarkable Leadership Learning System, a product designed as an ongoing process to help people at all levels become more proficient in their roles as leaders. Reflecting the realities of working life, the series guides participants through twelve leadership competencies, including:

Championing Changes • Communication • Building
Relationships • Developing Others • Focusing on
Customers • Influencing with Impact • Thinking and
Acting Innovatively • Collaboration and Teamwork •
Solving Problems and Making Decisions • Responsibility
and Accountability • Managing Projects and Processes
Successfully • Setting and Supporting Goals Achievement

The Facilitator's Guide includes everything you need to deliver high-impact training sessions across twelve modules. It also includes sample copies of the individual Participant Workbooks, as well as a flash drive with an electronic version of the Facilitator's Guide and PowerPoint slides for each of the twelve modules.

The fundamental and timeless principles and skills included make this program one that can be used as a leadership training experience across an organization. With a strong facilitator, the framework can be adapted to be of great value to a group of senior executives or first-line supervisors.

For more information, visit www.pfeiffer.com

Pfeiffer™
An Imprint of ®WILEY
Now you know.